CHICAGO PUBLIC LIBRARY
HAROLD WASHINGTON LIBRARY CENTER

R0007239252

UA
610
.C9
P47
1976
cop.1

Pérez, Louis A.

Army politics in
Cuba, 1898-1958

DATE DUE

FORM 125M

Business/Science/Technology
Division

Ref
UA
610
.C9
P47
1976
cop.1

The Chicago Public Library

DEC 13 1977

Received

PITT LATIN AMERICAN SERIES

PITT LATIN AMERICAN SERIES

Cole Blasier, Editor

Army Politics in Cuba, 1898–1958

Army Politics in Cuba, 1898-1958

Louis A. Pérez, Jr.

UNIVERSITY OF PITTSBURGH PRESS

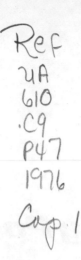

Copyright © 1976, University of Pittsburgh Press
All rights reserved
Feffer and Simons, Inc., London
Manufactured in the United States of America

Library of Congress Cataloging in Publication Data

Pérez, Louis A, birth date
   Army politics in Cuba, 1898–1958.

   (Pitt Latin American series)
   Bibliography: p. 211
   Includes index.
   1. Cuba. Ejército—History.   2. Cuba—Politics and
government.   I. Title.
   UA610.C9P47   1975   355.3'097291   75-35440
   ISBN 0–8229–3303–9

Grateful acknowledgment is made for permission to reprint material in this book:

Some of the material in chapters 1 and 2 originally appeared in the *Hispanic American Historical Review*, 52 (May 1972), 250–71. Copyright 1972 by Duke University Press, Durham, N.C.

Some of the material in chapter 3 is reprinted from *Military Affairs* (February 1973), pp. 5–8, with permission. Copyright 1973 by the American Military Institute. No additional copies may be made without the express permission of the author and of the Editor of *Military Affairs*.

Some of the material in chapter 4 originally appeared in the *Journal of Latin American Studies* (London), 6 (May 1974), 59–76. Used by permission of Cambridge University Press.

A portion of chapter 11 originally appeared in the *South Eastern Latin Americanist*.

BUSINESS/SCIENCE/TECHNOLOGY DIVISION
THE CHICAGO PUBLIC LIBRARY

DEC 13 1977

To my mother

Contents

Acknowledgments

I have drawn heavily on the knowledge, experience, and patience of many people in the course of this study, and I doubt that I can express my gratitude adequately. Several individuals in particular deserve special note for the intellectual and personal debt I have incurred in the last fifteen years. My interest in Cuba was to a large extent inspired between 1958 and 1961 by Havis Stewart, who early sensed that Cuba in revolution, abstracted from its historical context, would be little understood in the United States. Events after 1961 confirmed his fears. I owe an enormous intellectual debt to Joan Easton and John E. Flaherty, who listened patiently and responded critically to many inchoate ideas that subsequently found fruition. I am especially grateful to Jordan M. Young, who encouraged and directed my first serious inquiry into the Cuban past. Much of my understanding of Cuban developments, particularly the events of 1933, is rooted in that first undergraduate foray into Cuban history. A special debt of gratitude is owed to Mario Rodríguez, whose support and criticism enabled me to expand my understanding of the first thirty years of Cuba's twentieth century.

Many more individuals rendered direct and invaluable assistance in the initial formulation and subsequent writing of this study. Such an undertaking necessarily rests in large measure on the writing, the conversation, and the advice of others—too many, in fact, to enumerate here. To some, however, my debt is so great that I want to make specific acknowledgments. **xi**

Foremost among these is Edwin Lieuwen, who read the manuscript in its various early drafts, offered valuable criticism, and gave encouraging support. His interest in the subject contributed directly to its initial formulation. In this regard, I am also greatly indebted to Troy S. Floyd and Ronald H. Dolkart, whose critical reviews of the manuscript strengthened the organization and sharpened the analysis.

Countless friends helped crystallize my thoughts and organize my approach. Hours of conversation and exchange of ideas, during which uncertain judgments and tentative approaches were submitted to the rigors of challenge and review, contributed powerfully to this study. For their patience in listening and their interest in responding critically, I remain in their debt. Somewhere during the hours of conversation with Randy and Roma Hansis in the subterranean levels of the National Archives this manuscript started to take form. The study is in many ways the product of those "carefree" days together. In this regard, it is impossible to minimize my debt to Thomas Orum, particularly during those bleak days of halting advances into the first draft. To Francis Hammond goes special thanks for reading an early draft of the manuscript. To Nelson P. Valdés I owe a special debt stemming from years of constant collaboration. We did not see eye to eye on some fundamental issues, but conversation and correspondence forced me to reexamine some of my conclusions and focus my positions. And, lastly, I am indebted to my brother Ronald A. Pérez, who gave of his time unselfishly to test critically the logic of my approaches and the validity of my conclusions. More important, he simply listened.

Hard as friends and colleagues have worked to eliminate errors and misinterpretations, inaccuracies will no doubt be found. For these and other omissions, I am, of course, wholly responsible. Whether I have repaired all the weaknesses they discovered remains for them to judge. I have profited from their interest and learned from their insights. For this I thank them.

I received much assistance and unfailing courtesy in all the libraries and archives where I studied. A special debt of gratitude is owed, first, to the staffs of the Manuscript Collection and the Hispanic Foundation of the Library of Congress. Sandra Levinson of the Center for Cuban Studies in New York facilitated my work with the Center's recently acquired Cuban materials. I am also very grateful to the countless individuals at the National Archives, without whose assistance and interest this study would have been impossible. In particular, I wish to single out the help of John E. Taylor of Modern Military Records, whose interest in and support of my research proved to be of inestimable value. Also, Dorothy Wonsmos of the Zimmerman Library at the University of New Mexico greatly facilitated the acquisition of key research materials. No less important, the staffs at the Hoover Institution on War, Revolution and Peace, the Franklin D. Roosevelt Library, the Western Historical Manuscript Collection at the University of Missouri, the New York Public Library, and the University of Florida Library provided courteous assistance. A grant from the Ford Foundation, through the University of New Mexico, made this study possible.

Lastly, but no less important, I owe an enormous debt to my wife Susan Birrell Pérez, whose labor as an indefatigable researcher and a critical reader provided crucial margins of support at both ends of the project.

Introduction

Cuba entered nationhood without an army. United States interventions formed the crucible from which the republic's armed forces emerged. The army evolved initially as a military response to the problem of political instability within the context of Cuban treaty relations with the United States. In the course of the American occupations, the United States supervised the organization of an armed institution designed to control national disorders potentially pernicious to American strategic and economic interests on the island; the Cuban army developed as the first line of defense of American interests in Cuba. The 1898–1902 occupation endowed the republic with the Rural Guard, assigned by occupation officials to protect rural properties. And when the American provisional government (1906–1909) ended, it left behind the Ejército Permanente (Permanent Army).

The stability that Washington designed for the armed forces served to generate a political status quo underwritten by the national army. For Washington stability suggested few disorders that would endanger the lives and property of foreigners; in Havana this diplomatic imperative quickly expressed itself in the imposition of political *continuismo* spanning the first half of the twentieth century. As the independence generation found existing institutions incapable of satisfying political designs, the armed forces grew increasingly involved in the national order. Against a backdrop of institutional crisis, the army, as a result of a superior organizational cohesion and a virtual monopoly on state force, emerged as the sole national institution capable of effective political action.

From this point, it was a short and natural step for the armed forces to move directly into the vortex of the nation's political processes to appropriate national authority. Lacking national tradition, the Cuban body military could look back to but not claim organic ties with the Ejército Libertador, the Cuban Army of Liberation, which had been dissolved between 1898 and 1899. In its origins, development, and mission, the Cuban military did not respond to national needs; on the contrary, it met policy needs articulated by American officials in Havana and Washington. In this relationship to extranational authorities, the armed institution, lacking historicity, grew increasingly estranged from national traditions. The army was an anomaly in the institutional order, never quite able to identify or define a legitimate national purpose. The search for a place in the national order ended within three decades when, in 1933, in perhaps one of the most bizarre army seizures of power ever recorded, the officer corps proved incapable of withstanding a mutiny of the noncommissioned officers and enlisted men.

The sergeants in 1933 severed the officer corps from the elite sectors. The viability of the new military order—and, concomitantly, the political system leaning on the armed forces—rested precariously, again, on sources outside the national order.

The historical contradictions mounting on the Cuban armed institution over the span of the republican experience contributed powerfully to the army's collapse between 1956 and 1958. A long tradition of twentieth-century insurgency provided the setting for the armed struggle of the 1950s. The concept of a rural guerrilla *foco* from which to challenge the politico-military authority of Havana, subsequently elaborated by Ernesto Che Guevara and Régis Debray, was entirely consistent with the tradition of insurgency in Cuba. Because of the peculiar political, economic, and military relationship of Cuba to the United States, insurrection on the island placed insurmountable strains on the constituted authorities. These tensions were inevitable passed on to the national armed forces.

Almost thirty years from the seizure of power, the army commanded by the former sergeants demonstrated a singular incapacity to deal with armed rebellion. For the third time in sixty years, the Cuban armed forces were subjected to a far-reaching reorganization.

Army Politics in Cuba, 1898–1958

Genesis of the Cuban Army (I)

The United States in Cuba and the Rural Guard, 1898–1902

American intervention in the hostilities between Cuba and
Spain, converting that conflagration into the Spanish-American
War, transfigured the essential character of Cuban indepen-
dence. American armed forces appropriated conduct of a
movement conceived initially to secure national independence
and, in the process, annulled the ultimate objective of the
Cuban struggle. Within the context of the Spanish-American
War, Cuba was reduced simply to one theater of operations.

The American vision of ultimate victory over Spain included
undisputed control of Spanish insular possessions. United
States appropriation of the Cuban struggle against Spain was,
in part, designed to guarantee uncontested mastery of the
island in the postwar order. The American command limited
Cuban participation in the war effort to ancillary contributions;
Cuban troops were reduced to scouts, messengers, trench
diggers, pack carriers, and sentries.[1] The Ejército Libertador,
the Cuban Army of Liberation, was withdrawn from major
operations. These measures minimized the Cuban contribution
to ultimate victory and reduced the voice of the Ejéricito
Libertador in postwar planning. The capitulation of Santiago
de Cuba in July 1898 aptly revealed the American perception
of the war. Whereas the Cubans fought to expel the Spanish,
the terms of the capitulation permitted Spanish troops to
remain in Santiago, protected by American forces, on the   **3**

strength of a pledge not to take up arms against the United States for the duration of the war.[2]

The Santiago experience exposed the contradictions inherent in the joint United States–Cuban effort against Spain. General William R. Shafter, the American commander in Cuba, reported that General Calixto García, the Cuban army chief, declined to enter Santiago on the ground that Spanish civil officials remained in power provisionally. "It was fully explained to him," Shafter indicated, "that those officials were continued in power until it was convenient to change them for others." The "trouble with General García," Shafter concluded with some impatience, "was that he expected to be placed in command at this place; in other words, that we would turn the city over to him." The American commander reported that he had "explained fully that we were at war with Spain, and that the question of Cuban independence could not be considered by me."[3] Independence, in fact, was never more than a coincidental by-product of the Spanish-American War, subject at all times to the vagaries of American wartime policy. Cuban insurgents served functionally as circumstantial allies to the United States in the Spanish-American War rather than as agents of Cuban independence.

The Treaty of Paris, ratifying American sovereignty over Cuba, conferred on Washington responsibility for the protection of life and property for the duration of the occupation. More important, American sovereignty altered the relationship established earlier between the Ejército Libertador and the United States army during the war. The treaty, in effect, dissolved the wartime alliance, converting the erstwhile Cuban allies into subjects of an American-occupied island. The cessation of hostilities transformed the Cuban army into a body of armed nationals in a territory occupied by a foreign force; the Ejército Libertador represented a potential challenge to the American occupation of the island, threatening the life and property the United States had contracted in Paris to protect, and menacing the law and order demanded by the American provisional government. The military governor of Santiago, General Leonard Wood, found over eleven thousand Cuban soldiers in the region when he assumed command.[4] Under these circumstances, Wood foresaw "quite a period of time" before the establishment of a stable government.[5] The commander of Matanzas, General James H. Wilson, listed some three hundred fifty towns occupied by Cuban troops who refused to submit to civil authorities.[6] In the west, General Fitzhugh Lee, military governor of Havana and Pinar del Río, reported Cuban soldiers concentrated outside cities and towns, retaining their arms, and "producing more or less unrest in the public mind with the fear that many of them, unaccustomed to work for so long, would be transformed to brigands, and not become peaceful law-abiding citizens."[7]

The continued presence of an organization of armed Cubans in a postwar setting challenged American politico-military authority over the island. The legitimacy of the provisional government was further disputed when the Cuban army in October 1898 formed the Asamblea de Representantes del Ejército Cubano. Composed of forty-four generals and colonels representing different army corps, the Asamblea agitated for immediate independence, claiming sovereignty over the island.[8]

The Cuban army further possessed the capacity to contest the American occupation militarily. By preserving its organization into the period of American sovereignty, the Ejército Libertador emerged as the de facto co-occupier of the island. As long as the Ejército Libertador maintained its armed unity and promoted its political pretensions through the Asamblea, American control remained incomplete; as long as the Cubans remained armed, the specter of armed resistance to the occupation haunted officials of the provisional government.

The prospect of the Cubans' resuming the struggle for independence, renewing hostilities this time against the provisional government, produced an ominous climate during the first months of occupation. Cuban officers predicted an ultimate confrontation to resolve the fate of the island[9] In a thinly veiled admonition, one Cuban general urged the Ejército Libertador to "continue to aid in preserving order" until the Americans fulfilled the pledge of independence.[10] The Cuban army, in fact, contained the most zealous *independistas*. One traveler found the pro-Spanish sector advocating American retention of the island; merchants supported American control in anticipation of favorable business opportunities while peasants and workers "cared only for peace" and sought to "be left alone." Members of the Cuban army and the Asamblea, however, agitated for complete independence.[11]

United States occupation officials were fully sensitive to the implications of disaffection within the Ejército Libertador. General Fitzhugh Lee perceived that Cuban soldiers viewed the

Americans as intruders and sought "to rule the island, without the aid, consent, or advice of the United States, or the presence of the American soldier."[12] As early as August 1898 one American officer reported that the Cubans had "no love for the Americans" concluding that the insurgents "expected after the present war was ended a conflict between themselves and the United States; and, further, they expressed a readiness to participate in such conflict when it did come."[13]

American officials recognized very early the capacity of armed Cubans to complicate the occupation experiement on the island. In August 1898 General H. W. Lawton, commander in Santiago, appealed for definite instructions from Washington as to the policy to be observed toward the Ejército Libertador. Cuban troops still maintained their organization, Lawton explained, and were "threatening in their attitude," keeping the "inhabitants stirred up and panicky by threats and acts of violence."[14] Interference with the exercise of American authority, Lawton was instructed, could not be tolerated. Washington demanded Cuban recognition of the military occupation and the authority of the United States as outlined in the Treaty of Paris.[15] General William Shafter discerned the full dimensions of the problem confronting the United States in Cuba and expected complications until the Cuban army disbanded. Alluding to the military and political pretensions of the Ejército Libertador, Shafter stressed that a "dual government can't exist here; we have got to have full sway of the Cubans." Otherwise, Shafter predicted, there would inevitably be a war between the occupation forces and Cuban troops to resolve competing claims of mastery over the island.[16] Governor General John R. Brooke, when asked about the possibility of reducing American units in Cuba to cut costs, cautioned against any hasty withdrawals prior to the disbandment of the Cuban army.[17]

Tension in Cuba heightened considerably in February 1899, when rebellion broke out against the American provisional government in the Philippine Islands. The implications of the war in the Pacific were readily apparent in Washington. Henry Adams reported from the capital that the "President and everybody else" were as "eager to get out of Cuba as they were a year ago to get into it." The "thought of another Manila at Havana," Adams wrote, "sobers even an army contractor."[18]

Throughout the early months of the occupation American officials searched for a viable means of dismantling the Ejército

Libertador. In one effort, the provisional government sought to provide employment opportunities to lure officers and men away from army ranks. Governor General Brooke was convinced that Cuban officers without work threatened order on the island.[19] In Santiago de Cuba, General Wood exchanged jobs for arms.[20] Public works programs, designed in part to provide employment for the idle, did, in fact, pull many Cubans out of the Ejército Libertador.[21] Nonmilitary departments of the provisional government were staffed largely by veterans, care being taken to assign civil positions commensurate with the rank held in the Cuban army. Virtually every civil governor appointed held the rank of general in the Ejército Libertador; the civil government of Havana was composed largely of former Cuban senior officers.[22] By mid-1899, several thousand Cuban veterans had abandoned the army for civil employment.[23] With veterans involved in jobs, Wood predicted confidently, one "couldn't stir up an insurrection in the province with the aid of the best agitator in Cuba."[24]

Employment opportunities reduced the Cuban army but failed to produce the desired dissolution of the military organization. However reduced, the Ejército Libertador remained invested with its organization and concomitant system of allegiances. In the end, anxious to disband the Cuban army, Washington offered to fund the demobilization of the Ejército Libertador, granting each veteran a bonus upon surrendering his arms. Throughout the spring and summer of 1899, Cuban soldiers filed past specially designated sites to receive seventy-five dollars. By the end of the summer, the army had been dissolved.

The dissolution of the Ejército Libertador, and by extension the Asamblea, broke down a system of allegiance independent of American control. The assistance rendered by Cuban troops to the American occupation forces during and immediately after the war with Spain, however, suggested to United States officials a practical use for armed Cuban veterans. Whatever the dangers inherent in armed Cubans serving in the Ejército Libertador as the co-occupiers of the island, American forces, unable to occupy every village, pursue every highwayman, and arrest every law offender, detected in the island's veteran ranks an efficacious way of consolidating United States authority. An accommodation was envisioned in which armed Cubans, severed from the allegiance system of Ejército Libertador, would serve as an ideal adjunct force in the occupation. American policy planners sought to dissove the Ejército Libertador only to reconstruct from the disbanded army a new Cuban armed force, infused with a new system of allegiance more responsive to the needs of American policy objectives.[25]

In Washington the new military organization was proposed partially as a palliative designed to relieve employment pressures anticipated by the entry of some thirty thousand veterans into the labor market. The threat of violence, even after the demobilization, was underscored by President McKinley's secretary, John A. Porter, who predicted:

> Without arms it would be extremely dangerous to cast thousands of men on the mercy of the community absolutely penniless and without resources. They would have to continue to live on the country in large numbers, and some might be driven by the extremity of their wants to take food and clothing by stealth and force. With such men wandering aimlessly about, the planters would not dare buy the cattle necessary to begin the operation of their plantations, and even those disposed to work would thus not find the opportunity of doing so. Unless this element of danger is entirely removed, a large American military force will be necessary to guarantee peace, involving a great expenditure of money.[26]

Discussing the fate of the Ejército Libertador with a Cuban commission in Washington, McKinley expressed an interest in a "colonial army" composed of ten thousand veterans. The army, the president believed, would absorb countless thousands of Cubans who otherwise would encounter difficulty finding employment.[27] General Máximo Gómez shared McKinley's hope that a colonial army would spare the Cuban veterans the vicissitudes of entering a labor market not prepared to absorb a large influx of job seekers.[28]

Practical imperial considerations also underscored the need for a colonial armed force. Secretary of War Elihu Root contemplated recruiting a Cuban regiment modeled on the plan adopted by the British in Egypt, commanded by United States field officers, Cuban captains and lieutenants, and American sergeants. This colonial army would "dispose of a lot of men most likely to make trouble in Cuba," Root mused, "turn them from possible bandits, and educate them into Americans."[29] American administrators in Cuba similarly endorsed the projected military organization. General Leonard Wood saw in a colonial army a means of reducing the American military commitment in Cuba, transferring these troops to the Philippine Islands. Agreeing with Root, Wood predicted that "native regiments" would incorporate the "restless and wild spirits which have been engaged in the recent war." Reserving lieutenancies for Cubans serving under American officers would enable them through promotions to assume senior grades and eventual command of the military establishment. More important, "native regiments" offered an ideal control agency. The Cubans would "more readily and gracefully . . . submit to authority and force by their own people," Wood suggested, "than by a people of absolutely alien blood." Ultimately the Cubans would "become intensely loyal to us and our methods," Wood divined. "I do not believe you could shake Cuba loose if you wanted to."[30]

The early success of American colonial administration in Cuba, however, mitigated the need for a formal colonial military institution. The project was, in many ways, predicated on and a response to difficulties anticipated in the dissolution of the Ejército Libertador. The speedy and uneventful demobilization and the relative success of nonmilitary employment projects precluded the necessity for the projected colonial army. In addition, Governor General Brooke opposed the planned army as one generating distrust about American intentions in Cuba.[31] More important, however, the realities of American administration in Cuba had, in fact, already necessitated local paramilitary variants of the colonial army. By late 1898 and early 1899, well before senior American planners came to appreciate the efficacy of a colonial military institution, a Cuban armed force, designed by American army personnel and no less "colonial" in organization, substance, and mission than the project articulated in Washington, was at the service of the United States government of occupation.

The Rural Guard responded at once to the general objectives of the American mission on the island and the specific needs of the occupation administration. The nature of the United States mission in Cuba circumscribed the ability of American forces to exercise the full authority of the provisional government. The American task, suggested implicitly in the Teller Amendment, consisted largely of creating an institutional setting propitious for establishing a stable and viable Cuban republic. Throughout the early years the provisional government was preoccupied with establishing administrative agencies, reorganizing municipal governments, improving health and sanitation facilities, and outlining a system of constitutional government for the future republic. And however vital to the success of the occupation law and order may have been, the provisional government did not cast American troops as police agents. Indeed, upon the termination of the occupation in 1902, American forces were reported never to have engaged in active police work.[32] The U.S. army in Cuba served initially in a combat capacity; the continued presence of American troops during the occupation simply provided the military shield behind which the United States conducted the colonial experiment.

Widespread rural insecurity in postwar Cuba underscored the need for an auxiliary force to aid the occupation army. "At the end of the war," Wood reported, "many restless and disorderly spirits . . . resumed their irregular and lawless lives, and to such an extent did they carry their depredations that they became a serious menace to public order, life, and property."[33] The Cuban war of insurgency had produced a life-style in the countryside incompatible with the condition of order the American provisional government endeavored to impose.[34]

The Rural Guard served to enforce the authority of provisional government in districts remote from the locus of American power. United States military provincial commanders were simply unable to extend adequate protection to life and property in the interior.[35] For example, the military governor of Puerto Príncipe, Colonel L. H. Carpenter, reported that "people were afraid to go into the country and make any start with cattle or in other directions without being assured protection"; these conditions, Carpenter indicated, necessitated creating a Rural Guard force for regions where it was reasonable to expect incidents of lawlessness.[36]

The Rural Guard was of inestimable service in fulfilling needs peculiar to the setting of the occupation. The substitution of American troops by Cubans reduced the health hazard inherent in the susceptibility of the occupation forces to tropical disease.[37] Cuban veterans in the Rural Guard, acclimated to and familiar with the districts in which they served, were particularly effective in minimizing rural insecurity. In addition, Cuban forces reduced the misunderstandings otherwise inevitable as a result of the language and cultural differences between the armed agencies of the provisional government and the island's population.[38]

Political considerations, requiring American prudence in dealing with the population, further necessitated the use of Cubans in paramilitary law enforcement. The provisional government cast the Cubans as the primary executors of law under the occupation, thereby sparing American troops from acting directly, in the process of law enforcement, against the people. Sensitive to developments in the Philippine Islands, American military commanders sought to avoid any situation potentially capable of precipitating hostilities on the island. The military and political repercussions of a clash between the Cubans and American soldiers were immediately apparent to military administrators on the island. General Wood feared that the use of American troops against the Cubans was courting a disaster of the magnitude of the struggle in the Pacific.[39] General Fitzhugh Lee suggested to a Washington lawmaker that "if by accident or bad management an exchange of shots took place anywhere between the Cubans and the American soldiers, resulting in many of the former falling into ranks again, the country might have a guerrilla war on its hands and our troubles [would] multiply."[40] One of the objectives of the colonial army was, in fact, to substitute Cubans for Americans. "The Cubans," Wood wrote, "are perfectly willing to accept the acts of their own civil officers, which, if performed by soldiers of the United States, would give rise to a great deal of bad feeling and friction."[41]

A new system of allegiance was built into the Rural Guard. Recruitment enforced institutional loyalty and assured American control. United States officials carefully selected officers and men from the "best material" in the Ejército Libertador.[42] The Rural Guard came to consist largely of Cubans sympathetic to the occupation effort; loyalty to American commanders was underscored. The Cubans were required to be, in Wood's terms, "obedient and faithful" to the provisional government.[43]

Dependence upon the American military presence was grafted onto the Rural Guard. Cuban officers were selected by and responsible to American commanders; the authority exercised by the Rural Guard was determined by the provisional government. Captain H. J. Slocum, the American advisor to the Cuban armed force, reported that members of the Rural Guard had "gradually stiffened up to their work, protecting life and property, as they came to realize that they were backed by a powerful Government." The Cubans were made to understand from the outset, Slocum wrote, "that the strong arm of the Government of the Intervention was supporting them." Cuban forces accompanied American troops on maneuvers, in part, to "let the people see that, if necessary, they would work together in harmony to preserve peace."[44]

Because of the very setting in which the Cuban armed force emerged and the mission to which it was assigned, the Rural Guard exercised effective authority only in the presence of American forces. This symbiotic relationship, underscoring the weakness inherent in the Rural Guard, became a source of concern to American officials as Washington prepared the evacuation of the occupation forces. The Rural Guard did not preserve order; rather, as Secretary Root suggested in 1899, the maintenance of order was substantially the product of the "restraining influence" of the American military occupation.[45] General Wood, military governor of the island, was not entirely optimistic in his assessment of the efficacy of the Rural Guard in unoccupied Cuba. Haunting doubts undermined Wood's confidence in the ability of the Rural Guard to provide stability after the departure of American troops. The military governor betrayed his fears in his insistence that the Cuban force would be "ample to maintain public order in the rural districts of Cuba even after the withdrawal of the army of occupation."[46] The use of the word *even* implies that Wood appreciated the qualitative difference produced by an American military withdrawal. In the end, the military governor gave full expression to his uncertainties, requesting in 1901 that an American force consisting of two cavalry regiments and one regiment of artillery remain on the island after the departure of the occupation forces. This small force, Wood indicated, was to remain as a guarantee of order after the establishment of the Cuban government; the military governor sought a "moral force to hold these people up to their work until the decent element assumes its normal position in the government of the island."[47]

Preparation for Cuban independence further extended the supporting American military presence on the island. The Platt Amendment established an organic link between Cuba and the United States in which American authority was grafted onto the Cuban national consciousness by appending the amendment to the Cuban Constitution and ultimately drafting the statute into the Permanent Treaty. By authorizing United States intervention "for the preservation of Cuban independence, the maintenance of a government adequate for the protection of life, property, and individual liberty,"[48] the Platt Amendment guaranteed military assistance to bolster the Havana government if the Cuban armed force proved inadequate.

The Guantánamo Naval Base added still another dimension to the American armed support of Havana. In many ways, Guantánamo served to enforce the Platt Amendment. "When we turn the government of Cuba over to Cuban hands," Secretary Root suggested, "some one will have to decide what means the United States shall retain to require that government to fulfill all the obligations for protection of life and property." And to maintain a strategic disembarkment point for American forces, Root was very desirous of securing the Guantánamo naval station.[49]

In anticipation of the American withdrawal, the provisional government prepared the Rural Guard for Cuban independence. The force was trained, equipped, and garrisoned to assume responsibility for guaranteeing life, property, and order; in addition, it was reorganized. In February 1900 the haphazardly organized force yielded to the establishment of a national Rural Guard, distributed into companies with a unified command.[50] Throughout 1901 the provisional government instituted new reforms. In January the military governor invited provincial Rural Guard chiefs to Havana to study a new reorganization proposal; after several months of deliberations, in April 1901, the provisional government issued the Organic Law of the Rural Guard. Four provincial chiefs exercised authority over the island's six provinces; the distribution of the Rural Guard was determined by incidents of lawlessness, the relative proportion of the rural and urban population, the efficiency of communications, and the extent of private property. The provisional government, in addition, created an artillery corps to command the island's coastal fortifications. In April 1902 General Alejandro Rodríguez, a veteran officer of the independence struggle, assumed command of the Rural Guard.[51]

By 1902 the Rural Guard had acquired a character peculiar to the occupation experience. It did not perform in a regular military capacity. The milieu in which it emerged, the nature of its mission in occupied Cuba, and, particularly, the relationship of the Cubans to the American army of occupation reduced the Rural Guard to an elaborate police organization. Whatever military features the Rural Guard might have acquired in the republic was vitiated by the presence of the very devices the United States had instituted to sustain it. The military dimensions of protecting the island's international integrity, for example, was appropriated by the United States. The Platt Amendment committed American military power to underwrite the viability of national authorities in Havana.

The mission assigned to the Rural Guard during the occupation was not altered substantially by the imminence of independence. Rather, the responses fashioned during the provisional government developed into a *modus operandi*. The preeminent responsibility assumed by the Rural Guard consisted of protecting properties in the interior. Under the provisional government, the Cuban armed force served, almost exclusively, the needs.of the rural economic sectors. During the occupation property holders frequently offered part of their own land or property adjoining it rent free in the effort to secure a Rural Guard post to protect their estates. Landowners often included in the offer sufficient space to permit maneuvers and drills, grazing land for livestock, free building materials, access to drinking water, free construction of roads serving the detachment, and the establishment, free of charge, of a communications network to connect the smaller posts with provincial headquarters.[52] In the district of Cienfuegos, for example, planters and land proprietors supplied free telephone communications connecting all Rural Guard posts and sugar mills with the provincial capital headquarters. All this was done, the regional commander reported with some satisfaction, "without entailing any disbursement to the present or future government of the Island."[53] The Rural Guard was assigned most frequently, as one Cuban official urged it should be, to "the country-properties situated at strategic places, in order that it may be enabled to attend with more efficiency and activity to that which constitutes its main duty, which is no other than that of giving to agriculture, to cattle-raising, and to all other branches of wealth ... defense and assistance."[54] By 1905 the overwhelming majority of Rural Guard outposts were on property privately owned. Of 288 *edificios,* a mere 28 were owned by the state; the remainder were either privately rented or donated rent-free by municipalities and business concerns, including the Chaparra Sugar Company, the Juraguá Iron Company and the United Fruit Company.[55]

The link between the rural economic sectors and the Rural Guard was further strengthened by the recruitment system. Enlistment qualifications included the possession of good character and an excellent standing the community. Moreover, applicants were required to submit letters of recommendation from at least two well-known citizens, "preferably property owners."[56] Planters frequently interceded directly with government officials to secure appointment or reappointment of particular officers who had been uncommonly cooperative.[57]

The American occupation left a far-reaching imprint on the Cuban armed force. The exclusion of nonwhite officers, for example, was particularly apparent. Literacy requirements, the necessity of having to pay for uniforms and mounts upon enlistment, and the need for landowners' recommendation excluded the vast majority of Afro-Cubans from commissioned rank.[58] In police departments, for example, one traveler reported that most patrolmen seemed to be "members of the best Cuban families. Some them had been wealthy, some looked like former business men."[59] The social mobility possible for soldiers who had won field commissions during the independence struggle was annulled when the military context in which those ranks had meaning was dissolved. Those avenues of mobility in the reconstructed armed force, where not excluded by literacy requirements, expenses, and personal contacts, were choked by official policy. In the artillery corps, for example, American military advisors insisted that "all officers will be white."[60]

The provisional government endowed the republic with an armed force molded by a foreign occupation. The Rural Guard, in many ways, served a foreign government; its authority did not rest on a national mandate or the legitimacy inherent in serving a national government, but rather found sanction in the American military occupation. The circumstances under which the Rural Guard emerged made a "national" relationship—national in the sense of a common nation-building relationship—between the Cuban armed force and its countrymen impossible. The Rural Guard was, from its inception, alienated from a national setting and denied a sense of national mission. The occupation experience, in fact, bestowed upon the Rural Guard a mission and a set of loyalties not necessarily consistent with the national needs of the republic. Armed Cubans in the service of the provisional government and subordinate to American commanders acquired a mission vastly distinct from that inherent in the Ejército Libertador. Indeed, the institutional expression of Cuban nationalism had been dissolved. The controls devised to define the relationship between an independent Cuba and the United States further institutionalized the mission for which the Rural Guard was intended at its inception. Within this peculiar relationship, the Cuban armed force—continuing to serve the country in precisely the same patterns established during the American occupation—seemed to assume the role of child to parent.

The Republican Interlude, 1902–1906

A civilian schoolmaster, Tomás Estrada Palma, who had spent the war years in exile, assumed the presidency upon the departure of the American occupation forces. Under Estrada Palma, who had made the theme of his campaign "more teachers than soldiers," the Cuban armed forces increased markedly. The continued presence of American armed forces garrisoning the island's fortresses rankled member of the first national Congress. Cuban legislators, dismayed by the apparent compromise of national sovereignty, asked the president to increase the Cuban artillery corps in order to hasten the complete evacuation of foreign troops.[61] In August 1902, arguing that "national defense should only be entrusted to the valor of Cubans," the Cuban House of Representatives authorized the creation of four artillery companies to replace American troops.[62]

The evacuation of United States occupation troops also produced a general apprehension among the economic sectors of the island. Property owners doubted the ability of the Cuban government to provide adequate protection in the absence of the American forces. Increasing pressure, consequently, was applied on the Cuban executive to enlarge the 1,250-man Rural Guard force. According to Herbert G. Squiers, the American minister in Havana, the armed institution was simply too small to cover the entire country effectively; the need for an augmented force was particularly heightened during the "*tiempo muerto*," when cyclical unemployment reached seasonal peaks and idleness threatened order.[63]

The withdrawal of U.S. military forces thus necessitated an increase in the island's armed force to meet the needs of property owners. This expansion was designed to enhance the efficacy of the Rural Guard in the interior and to inspire confidence among the economic sectors, whose complaints to American diplomatic officials often resulted in United States pressure in Havana. The American minister, Squiers, appealed to Estrada Palma to enlarge the Rural Guard. Estrada's increase of the artillery corps, for example, evoked the anger of the American minister, who argued that government spending to enable the corps to guarantee national defense—a commitment already assumed by the United States—reduced funds available for the Rural Guard. Rural Guard Chief Rodríguez complained to Squiers that while Congress proposed to fund an increase in the artillery corps, Rural Guard appropriations, "so small and inadequate," produced difficulties in meeting the authorized strength of the force.[64] The American minister urged the president to abolish the artillery force, "for which Cuba had no use," and to apply the funds thus saved to improve the efficiency of the Rural Guard, "a body of men on whom the country must rely for peace and good order."[65]

United States strategic interests further tended to encourage the development of an effective Cuban armed force so as to permit the integration of the Cubans into the greater American circum-Caribbean defense network. American military planners assigned specific tasks to the Cuban armed force. In addition to protecting American economic interests on the island, Washington expected Cuba to aid the United States in the defense of the island against foreign aggression. Cast as the "southernmost" American frontier, Cuba constituted "one of the weakest points in our line of defense," a weakness "that should not be permitted to continue."[66] It was, therefore, in the national interest to promote the efficiency and size of the Cuban armed forces, "the logical and proper substitute for United States forces," to avoid the necessity of deploying American troops in an emergency.[67]

By the end of the Estrada Palma administration, the Cuban armed forces had doubled in size. In 1903, the Rural Guard numbered some fifteen hundred officers and men, about three hundred each province.[68] By 1905, the Rural Guard had passed three thousand and the artillery corps had reached seven hundred; moreover, the government contemplated adding another thousand men to the Rural Guard, bringing the total to nearly five thousand.[69]

The armed forces molded during the United States occupation and augmented during the Estrada Palma administration proved incapable of sustaining the new political order against armed resistance. A Liberal party uprising in 1906, led by presidential candidate José Miguel Gómez, protesting frauds in the reelection of President Estrada, successfully challenged the armed institution of the state. On August 16, 1906, the Liberal congressman from Pinar del Río, Faustino "Pino" Guerra, launched an armed protest in the west; within days, provincial Liberal leaders throughout the island joined the revolution.

The Liberal "Constitutionalist Army" made a successful drive against the government. Apparent administration weakness encouraged the growth of insurgent forces; within a week, rebel groups operated throughout the island.[70] By the end of August, an estimated fifteen thousand insurgent troops were in the field against Havana.[71] Rebel tactics consisted largely of destroying the island's communication and transportation network, further isolating the already scattered Rural Guard outposts.[72]

Insurgent successes forced the government into a defensive posture. On August 20 the president authorized a two-thousand-man increase in the Rural Guard; five days later Estrada established a national militia under the command of General Alejandro Rodríguez. The government also created the Foreign Legion of Artillery, commanded by Americans, Germans, and Englishmen.[73]

Havana's position grew increasingly tenuous. Insurgent bands continued to reach menacing proportions; desertions and betrayals impaired the capacity of the government to withstand the rebel offensives. On September 8, presiding over the collapse of his government and unable to protect foreign life and property, Estrada Palma called upon Washington for military assistance.[74] President Roosevelt, less than anxious to intervene in a situation capable of involving American forces in a guerrilla war, dispatched Secretary of War William H. Taft and Assistant Secretary of State Robert Bacon as peace commissioners to seek a conciliation between the contending factions. After days of fruitless negotiations and in the face of the utter collapse of government in Havana, the American peace commissioners established a provisional administration on the island.[75] The Cuban government, Taft concluded ruefully, had "proven to be nothing but a house of cards."[76]

The Rural Guard and the Republic

The success of the armed protest revealed the artificiality of the armed institution with which the republic had been endowed. If the Cuban government had indeed been a "house of cards," it was one stacked by the first American occupation. The very mission of the Rural Guard nullified military efficacy. The armed force was entrusted with the preservation of order, a task substantially preventive—not recuperative—in nature. To achieve this, the Cubans relied on a network of far-flung detachments that dispersed patrols into the surrounding countryside. The effectiveness of the Rural Guard rested on political stability, which, in the absence of a regular military institution, consisted almost entirely of a voluntary consensus in allegiance to constituted authority. The withdrawal of the United States army in 1902 shifted the military underpinnings of political stability to the American military assistance implicit in the Platt Amendment. The amendment, Senator Orville Platt wrote, removed the need for a Cuban army or navy. The Connecticut lawmaker introduced legislation to guarantee an independent ... stable republican government which the United States will assist in maintaining against foreign aggression or domestic disorder."[77] Secretary of State Elihu Root similarly suggested in 1904 that the Platt Amendment counteracted "such revolutions as have afflicted Central and South America", for it was "known to all men that an attempt to overturn the foundations of that government will be confronted by the overwhelming power of the United States."[78] The Rural Guard, then, continued in auxiliary service to the United States armed forces. It was the Cuban "utter military incapacity," Roosevelt later wrote, that necessitated intervention.[79] In the final analysis, however, the Rural Guard was never designed to possess a military capacity; the intervention that Roosevelt had sought to avoid was inevitable within the context of American treaty obligations for, in fact, the United States had assumed the military defense of the Cuban government.

The Liberal protest exposed the impotence of the island's armed organization. The Cuban government was unprepared for internal war. The revolution, Estrada Palma lamented, had "surprised" the administration without sufficient arms, ammunition, and troops.[80] The absence of a standing army further undermined the government's ability to respond to the rebellion. At the moment vital for counteroffensive measures,

Havana was preoccupied with raising an adequate armed force. Commander William F. Fullam, commanding a warship dispatched to Cienfuegos, learned from local political and Rural Guard authorities that it would have required "at least a year to raise the troops and prepare for an active campaign," by which time the country would have been "devasted by the rebels."[81] The time consumed preparing government forces for battle enabled the insurgency to spread quickly throughout the island. The American intervention simply delivered the *coup de grâce* to a doomed government. Upon their arrival the peace commissioners reported some eight to ten thousand insurgent troops preparing to converge upon Havana.[82] The commander of a naval force dispatched to Havana similarly indicated that the "immediate effect" of his arrival "was to prevent the occupation of Havana that night by the rebels."[83]

Genesis of the Cuban Army (II), 1906–1909

American inquiry into the fall of Estrada Palma brought Rural Guard deficiencies into bold relief. As Provisional Governor Charles Magoon suggested, the civil properties of the Cuban armed force precluded military efficacy; the Rural Guard was, first and foremost, designed to patrol the interior, arrest law offenders, and perform other police duties.[1] The distribution of the 5,300 officers and men into some 250 scattered and isolated outposts had further weakened the Rural Guard. Captain C. F. Crain, appointed to advise the Guard, discovered far too many outposts, particularly in the sugar districts of Oriente. "Every person of property," Crain complained, "desires to have a post of the Rural Guard near his possession." The distribution of the Cuban force, consequently, responded "to the influence certain persons have been able to exert." The government's policy of accepting land, equipment, and building rent free, Crain emphasized, placed the Rural Guard "under the obligation to the owners—which obligation undoubtedly at times conflicts with their duty.[2]

The provisional government found the Rural Guard demoralized. Political activity on behalf of the Estrada government in the 1905 election had discredited the armed institution in Liberal party circles; the summary abrogation of political liberties had shattered the moral authority of the Rural Guard nationally.[3] The armed force, Governor Magoon reported, was in general disfavor owing to its political involvement.[4]

The provisional government found the Rural Guard professionally bankrupt. The far-flung outposts had discouraged direct administration and surveillance; relative freedom from direct supervision and infrequent inspection had produced laxness in remote detachments. Post discipline reflected an inverse relationship with Havana—the further from the capital, the poorer the professional standards.[5]

The provisional government quickly devoted itself to the task of correcting the most apparent deficiencies of the Rural Guard. Officers of the American Army of Pacification were detached for advisory duty; the provisional administration in Havana established a panel of United States officers to study changes and recommend improvements. The larger American mission in Cuba consisted primarily of breathing life into the moribund republic and providing the resuscitated political order with the institutions necessary to resume self-government.[6] Seeking to underwrite the revived political system, Washington turned its attention to designing an armed force of sufficient size and efficiency to guarantee the integrity and stability of the Cuban national order.

American administrators planned first to augment the size of the Rural Guard. As early as October 1906 Secretary of war Taft, doubting the effectiveness of a mere five thousand Rural Guards, advised Magoon to increase the force. "If it is necessary to make an additional appropriation," Taft instructed the provisional governor, "I would make it because the truth is that Palma had not a large enough force, and the appropriation was not sufficient."[7] The provisional government planned to increase the armed institution to some ten thousand officers and men, confident that such a force would be sufficient to guarantee stability. Within weeks, Secretary Taft outlined plans to create a force to sustain the Cuban government. The main problem, the provisional governor suggested, was first to determine an adequate size, and "then make it an agent of the Government and not of a political party."[8] In January 1907 the secretary of war ordered Magoon to "go ahead and recruit the Rural Guard up to 10,000" so that "when we leave the government there we shall leave it something with which to preserve itself."[9]

American army advisors assigned to the Rural Guard attempted to correct the worst features of the outpost system. Major H. J. Slocum, recognizing the weakness inherent in the detachment network of the force, resisted demands of property owners for the distribution of the Rural Guard posts of a few men and proposed, instead, to concentrate Cuban troops. Fewer outposts, Slocum reasoned, would necessitate a wider range of patrol, enabling the Rural Guard to acquire greater familiarity with the surrounding countryside.[10] Concentrating troops in larger numbers, moreover, would facilitate closer supervision, increase the frequency of inspections, and encourage a general improvement of post discipline.[11]

The provisional government also turned its attention to the improvement of training, discipline, and morale of the Rural Guard. By late 1907, army schools were operating in Havana, Matanzas, Camagüey, and Santiago de Cuba; Cuban officers received additional courses and training in specially designed programs.[12] New recruits were selected carefully; enlistments, Magoon cautioned, could not be made hastily. The provisional governor purged the Rural Guard of "objectionable" men, particularly those "who were taken without due care under the stress of insurrection."[13] The government encouraged the Rural Guard to mingle freely with American forces on duty, on maneuvers, in the barracks, and off duty. In this fashion, the governor reported, "the native troops have acquired much knowledge of benefit to them."[14]

American military advisors designed reforms to raise the professional quality of the Cuban force. Governor Magoon labored to remove politics from the armed organization, banning all partisan activity. The Rural Guard was denied police authority in municipalities without having proper local authorization.[15] The provisional government pledged that promotions would not be secured by political activity or influence;[16] instead, Rural Guard Chief Rodríguez assured new recruits, merits, ability, and study would some future day earn promotions.[17]

The Rural Guard never recovered fully from the 1906 uprising. The Liberal party, victim of the government's application of state force in 1905–1906, remained opposed to the Rural Guard, however much reformed by the provisional government. Liberal leaders remained unconvinced that the Rural Guard had been divested of the political loyalties pernicious to the party cause. "The present officers of the Armed Forces," suggested Juan Gualberto Gómez, a leading Liberal spokesman, "became prominent in all the irregularities of the regime which has been overthrown. The wickedness and abuse committed have caused them to lose for-ever the confidence of the majority of the people, and it is not possible that we enjoy tranquility with the delivery of the public power into hands, a great many of which are suspicious, and others which we deem even criminal."[18]

Leading Liberal military and political leaders comprising the Liberal directorate advocated the creation of a regular military force to replace the Rural Guard. As early as November 1906, Liberal Generals Faustino Guerra, Carlos García Velez, and José de Jesús Monteagudo, in a meeting with the provisional governor, outlined their opposition to any increase in the Rural Guard. García reminded Magoon that a mere one thousand Rural Guards had sufficed during the first occupation and insisted that an increase in the armed force would not fill any real need.[19] Liberal leaders submitted a counterproposal to the provisional governor advocating the creation of a permanent army. Further, they urged the governor to retain the Rural Guard in its police capacity while creating a distinct army organization to assume the military task for which the Americans were attempting to mold the Rural Guard.[20]

Liberal leaders also invoked the public economy to support their army proposal. Senator Tomás Recio predicted that a ten-thousand-man Rural Guard would cost an additional eight to nine million dollars. The budgetary problems created by an augmented Rural Guard, Recio feared, would force the subsequent Cuban government to "increase taxes, making living more expensive," ultimately requiring the reduction of the very armed force enlarged, and "abandon other government services," including public works and education. Increased taxation, the Liberal senator warned, would align the "tax-paying classes against us, of whom we must be considerate."[21] Juan Gualberto Gómez insisted that an enlarged Rural Guard, composed of cavalry, would cost a great deal more than infantry. The Liberals were confident that a regular army consisting of infantry and artillery, that is, without horses, would reduce state expenditures considerably.[22]

American advisors to the Rural Guard unanimously opposed the organization of a regular army. United States officers, suspicious of the motives behind the Liberal project, were not convinced of the need for or the efficacy of a regular army organization. Major H. J. Slocum described the proposed army, composed "as it probably would be, from those who recently took part in the insurrection," as a grave political error. Slocum believed that the Liberals intended that "this army will be a machine of their makings and workings."[23] In the view of Captain E. Wittenmyer, the addition of a separate armed organization could not "fail to breed jealousy and discord and with politics creeping in, as it is sure to do under native administration, these two bodies will only be a cause for inciting rebellion and revolution." There would be "twice as many opportunities to be disloyal in two organizations as there are in one."[24] "Is the future of Cuba," Captain J. A. Ryan asked incredulously, "to be trusted to an army created by the direction of one political party? Is it difficult to see the use to which this army would be put?" It was only a small band of political aspirants, bidding for popularity, who hoped to "win adherents to their banners by holding out to them positions in the new army that is to be created." Ryan further doubted the ability of a regular army to protect the "vast money interests," including plantations, crops, and the expensive machinery "that make possible the wealth of Cuba." "Would an army," Ryan asked, "be of any protection to these wealth producing elements, with its stations far away, at points selected for convenience of supply and distribution?"

> The parts of Cuba that need protection and without which all Cuba will suffer are the country districts, the large tracts of land devoted to agricultural pursuits and which on account of the scarcity of population cannot afford a municipal police force. The roads must still be patrolled to make the life of the highwayman still undesirable, to assist travellers who may become injured by accident along the less frequented ways, to preserve from fire when possible the houses and crops of the people, to discover and extinguish forest fires on the public lands, to arrest and detain suspicious persons whose presence might be dangerous, to examine and report cases of crime committed, to report danger from inundation, to prevent roberry [sic] of fruits and vegetables, from farms as well, as horses and cattle . . . ; in short to do all things necessary for the safety of life and the protection of property that is necessary in a well regulated civilized country. Would an army do any of these necessary acts? Will soldiers kept in barracks serve the state to as good a purpose as the Rural Guard on his rounds in the country? Which kind of force does Cuba need? IS IT AN ARMY? NO.[25]

However convincing the opposition to the creation of a permanent army may have seemed, larger policy considerations were governed preeminently by the need to establish political stability on the island. Liberal statements appealed directly to the American search for order. General Faustino Guerra shared the provisional governor's view of the need for a large armed force, but he insisted on a regular army to replace the Rural Guard. Guerra recommended reducing the Rural Guard to some thirty six hundred officers and men, restricting its function to purely civil duties during peacetime, and using it as a cavalry division in the military during national emergencies. He concluded by sharing with Magoon an insight into the source of the Laberal party's success in 1906:

> The secret of revolutions is the fact that there has not been an effective army. A small band would to out, say in Santiago for instance, strike a few effective blows, and as the Government had no efficient force to turn against it, the people began to believe that the victory was on the side of the insurgents, whose number gradually increased until there was a large revolutionary army, when, if, in the beginning, a sufficient force could have been turned against it the revolution would not have lasted 48 hours. I say that if the Government has well organized troops, and if a revolution is immediately opposed by them, it will not receive converts, but if it is permitted to grow, it will soon have thousands of adherents.[26]

The force of the general's argument lay precisely in its authorship, for it was Guerra who had inaugurated the successful 1906 rebellion. A regular army, he concluded confidently, would make it a "difficult task to bring about a revolution."[27]

The necessity for the establishment of an armed force, precisely to make it a "difficult task to bring about a revolution," struck a responsive chord in American administrators. Support for the proposed army spread as the American provisional government and policy planners in Washington detected in the Liberal proposal an instrument for promoting United States policy objectives. The Platt Amendment had elevated Cuban politics above a purely national setting. Unsettled politics in Cuba reverberated in Washington; instability produced conditions capable of compelling the United Sates, however unwilling, to intervene in the fulfillment of treaty obligations. During the early months of the provisional government, military and civilian administrators labored to fashion an effective military fulcrum for Cuban stability and, at the same time, prevent the rise of conditions necessitating future intervention. American administers sought to give Havana an armed agency that would preserve stability, protect life and property, and defend successfully its integrity against internal challenge without foreign assistance. "A military force pure and simple," Magoon concluded, "is a reasonable and necessary agency for the stability of the Government. The necessity of such a force was demonstrated by the insurrection of 1906."[28]

The initial impulse to mold the Rural Guard into the armed foundation of the republic yielded to Cuban political needs and American policy objectives. "My idea," Secretary Taft wrote, "was after we got the Government fairly elected it was our duty to possess that Government with the means of maintaining itself, and naturally we turned to the Rural Guard as the body which might do it."[29] The effectiveness of the Rural Guard in preserving order in the interior was largely undisputed but policy makers were seeking a force capable of preserving political stability and national order. In the end, American officials, swayed partly by the strength of the Liberal arguments and partly by United States needs, arrived at an accommodation between the economic requirements of the rural districts—"the vast money interests"—and the political needs of Havana. In 1906, Estrada Palma found it necessary to guard Havana and provincial capitals and maintain, at the same time, a force of sufficient size and strength to defend the interior. The Cuban president ultimately chose to concentrate government forces in the cities, leaving the countryside to uncontested insurgent control. "This would not have been the case," Magoon speculated, "if a small military force had been available in each of the Provincial Capitals."[30] The provisional governor sought to create a dual armed force that could preserve the integrity of a regime, thus enabling the government to protect the island's source of wealth. The projected function of the military institution was entirely consistent with the mandate of the Platt Amendment. The new army would simply guarantee "the maintenance of a government adequate for the protection of life, property, and individual liberty."

The Rural Guard, in the end, simply could not meet the long-range stability objectives of Washington and the provisional government in Havana. Magoon ultimately rejected the effort to transform the Rural Guard into the military support of the restored Cuban republic. "In reorganizing the armed forces of the Republic," he reported, "the advisory commission found that the rural guard was, under the provision of the law creating it, rather a body of surveillance and safety than a real military force."[31]

In April 1908 the provisional government approved the necessary statutes organizing the Permanent Army. The Rural Guard was preserved intact, consisting of some 5,180 officers and men distributed in 380 detachments.[32] The new Permanent Army consisted of an infantry brigade, to be enlarged by the transfer of men from the Rural Guard. Separate command of the army was designed to reduce the danger of militarism and discourage any combined use of the armed forces against the central government.[33] As the American provisional government prepared to return the island to Cuban administration. U.S. officials shared Magoon's confidence that the new government would "start off well equipped with the ordinary means and agencies of stability."[34]

National Politics and the Cuban Army, 1909–1924

Politicizing the Army: The Liberal Order, 1909–1912

Elections in 1908 swept the Liberals into national office. The recently formed army, the nature of which remained to be determined by the José Miguel Gómez–Alfredo Zayas administration, gave the new government an ideal organization with which to reward the party loyals of 1906. Thousands had flocked to the Liberal banner in the August revolution only to have imminent victory aborted by the American intervention. Appreciation of the party leadership for rank-and-file support in 1906, delayed by the hiatus of Cuban government, reached fulfillment in the Gómez government.

The new Cuban army received at its inception a highly political orientation. Partisan loyalties determined the army's composition; political objectives shaped its national mission. The Gómez administration cast the new army in a Liberal mold to fit the needs of the incumbent executive, distributing commissions and appointments to Liberal chieftains prominent in the 1906 rebellion. Faustino Guerra, the insurgent leader in Pinar del Río, assumed command of the new Permanent Army; Gerardo Machado, the Liberal leader in Santa Clara, was appointed inspector general; José de Jesús Monteagudo, arrested for conspiracy in 1906, secured command of the Rural Guard. Commanders in the Rural Guard who had served the *miguelista* effort in 1906 were promoted to senior grades; officers loyal to Estrada Palma, on the other hand, including the Rural Guard chief Alejandro Rodríguez and two of the three regimental commanders, were dismissed summarily. Civilians, whose professional qualifications were confined exclusively to party loyalty, secured commissions in the new army. The case of one Higinio Esquera was illustrative. A civilian at the outbreak of the 1906 uprising, Esquera, in exchange for ten thousand dollars, offered to recruit a cavalry force to defend the Estrada Palma government; upon receiving the money, he defected and joined the Liberal protest. In February 1909 Esquera was commissioned colonel in the Permanent Army.[1]

The armed forces were factionalized further by internal divisions in the Liberal party. Differences between Gómez and Vice-President Zayas polarized factions in the Liberal party, finding expression in the military establishment. *Miguelista* and *zayista* groups emerged within the ranks of the armed forces. The chief of the army, Faustino Guerra, was a *zayista*; the commander of the Rural Guard, Monteagudo, supported Gómez. Interservice suspicion and hostility undermined the president's confidence in the army.[2] As early as April 1909 Gómez contemplated removing Guerra. The *miguelista* wing of the party, fearing that the army chief would use his authority to influence elections or, more disconcerting, lead the army against the president, applied increasing pressure to Gómez to retire Guerra.[3] Gómez chose to manipulate the institutional controls available to the chief executive to reduce Guerra to a figurehead commander, stripping the army chief of effective power. Officers known to be friendly to the Liberal general were detached from army headquarters; *miguelistas* secured staff appointments. Guerra was surrounded by officers hostile to the army commander.[4] The power of the army chief over posts and subposts was broken by appointing the commanding officers of the Infantry Brigade to assume charge of these detachments.[5] Efforts to remove Guerra included an offer of a post abroad and culminated in 1910 in an assassination attempt. Although the assassination was abortive, the administration did achieve its objectives, for in December 1910 Guerra resigned his command. The removal of the army chief enabled Gómez to construct the armed forces along a tighter partisan line, appointing *miguelistas* to virtually every important military position.[6] In early 1911, the government united the Permanent Army and the Rural Guard under the command of *miguelista* José de Jesús Monteagudo.

Military discipline was subject to political expediency. Punishment for serious breach of discipline was often vitiated by political intervention. The president frequently reversed court-martial decisions, undermining efforts by senior commanders to infuse discipline into the armed services.[7]

The armed forces expanded considerably under the Gómez administration. Within a year of his inauguration, the president reported army strength at 3,372 officers and men;[8] by 1912 the total approached 12,500 officers and men.[9] Much of this increase, one observer suggested, was for "the purpose of furnishing many lucrative places for the followers of the President and still more lucrative opportunities for corrupt personal profit."[10]

Under Cuban administration the distribution of the Rural Guard continued to respond to pressure from private interests. As late as 1910, the government continued to receive petitions from landowners demanding an increase of Rural Guard detachments in specific districts.[11] The Rural Guard occupied 329 *edificios*, of which the government rented 208; the remaining 121 were owned by the state or provided rent-free by landowners, foreign companies, and municipalities.[12] The distribution of the Permanent Army responded to the political needs of Havana. Army detachments were established in Havana and other provincial capitals, including Pinar del Río, Matanzas, and Santiago de Cuba.[13] By mid-1910, the American minister reported confidently that the Cuban government appeared "to be in a position to control any uprising which might break forth."[14]

Recasting Army Politics: The Conservative Order, 1913–1920

The political mold in which the Gómez administration organized the armed forces immediately pulled the military institution into a partisan orbit. With the circulation of national offices among rival political parties, the army command's loyalty to the outgoing administration was often inimical to the interests of a new government. The politics of a new administration and the lingering devotion of army leaders to past governments repeatedly threatened to undermine the incumbent order. In the 1912 election, the *miguelista* armed forces, following instructions from Havana, supported the Conservative candidate Mario Menocal over Gómez's rival Alfredo Zayas.[15] Four years later, the Conservative incumbent Menocal, seeking reelection against a reunited Liberal ticket, received a serious challenge from Liberal partisans in the armed forces devoted to the antiadministration candidates.

The Liberal military threat to the Conservative government assumed two dimensions. First, Liberal officers used their influence and the authority of their command during the 1916 election to promote Liberal candidates. Officers in Las Villas, for example, campaigned actively against the administration ticket.[16] The political activity of Liberal factions within the armed forces compelled Menocal to recast the army command to suit his own political needs. Thus, the military command of Las Villas was entrusted to a loyal *menocalista*, Colonel W. I. Consuegra.[17] Second, Menocal's purge of Liberals within the armed forces and his determination to secure another term of office encouraged *miguelista* partisans to enter into an antigovernment conspiracy with civilian counterparts. Planners of the 1917 revolution hoped to receive sufficient military support to execute a swift coup d'état through collaboration with the large number of Liberals within the army. The Liberals anticipated a quick, institutionally based movement whose major objectives were the seizure of both Camp Columbia and La Cabaña military fortress in Havana. Former President Gómez and Faustino Guerra established contacts in Camp Columbia and La Cabaña. The conspirators won the additional support of military commanders in the provinces. Gerardo Machado recruited army support in Santa Clara; the three ranking officers in Camagüey, including the chief of the military district, pledged to support the Liberal uprising. In Santiago de Cuba, one of the more popular military chieftains, Comandante Rigoberto Fernández, promised to lead the First Military District into the Liberal fold.[18] Liberal leaders anticipated widespread military endorsement, with Zayas expecting as much as 75 percent of the army to join the Liberal uprising.[19]

Betrayals, miscalculations, and precipitant action aborted the conspiracy in Havana. Liberal officers were arrested *en masse*; others fled eastward into the interior to join successful provincial uprisings. A smaller group, undiscovered, remained on active duty. Failure in Havana, however, had a general demoralizing effect in military districts nearest the capital. In the end, adherence to the government was largely determined in direct proportion to nearness to Havana; the closer to the capital, the greater was the reluctance to join the Liberals in the east after the failure of the conspiracy in the west. In Santa Clara, only the persuasiveness of the *menocalista* commander, arguing that the movement had collapsed completely when it failed in Havana, saved the province, an important link between the capital and the rebellious provinces, for the government.[20]

Liberals managed to win over a sufficiently large contingent of defectors to form the Constitutionalist Army. Where defections occurred they were complete; pro-Liberal officers secured control of the garrisons in Camagüey and Santiago de Cuba. Military endorsement of the revolution was virtually unanimous in the east; army and Rural Guard outposts passed quickly to Liberal control at the outbreak of the movement. Equally important, municipalities and cities served by the mutinous garrisons also came under insurgent authority. Santiago de Cuba, for example, the second largest city on the island, became the seat of the Liberal government in arms.

The threat of the Liberal challenge ended within a month. The Menocal government's successful domination of the 1917 revolution and the concomitant military defections produced by the abortive Liberal conspiracy permitted the Conservative administration to restructure the orientation of the armed institution. An estimated one thousand officers and men had joined the ill-fated Liberal cause.[21] These defections allowed Menocal to advance Conservative politics and gain support of his administration in the armed forces; he used all the instruments available to the commander in chief, including promotions, transfers, new commissions, retirements, and posts abroad, to promote a Conservative consensus in the armed forces. Loyal *menocalistas* were placed in key positions; civilian partisans who had received emergency commissions in the national militia secured ratification of these grades in the regular army. By mid-1918, disloyal elements were reported thoroughly eliminated from the military establishment.[22] Within a year of his reelection, the Conservative president had converted the hitherto predominantly Liberal institution into a *menocalista* organization. Liberal sympathizers were not ousted entirely, but sufficient numbers had defected to permit the administration to alter the political allegiance of the army command. By the last part of 1917, one trained observer reported that the army had been so thoroughly "re-arranged as to be pro-government."[23] Rural Guard detachments suspected of antigovernment activity were reorganized and converted into "thoroughly trusted" units.[24]

In addition, Havana strengthened the rural defense of the political order. Military troops in the interior provinces, traditionally the first to defect during an insurgency, were reorganized and reinforced; the government created another military district in Holguín, Oriente. Municipalities hitherto ungarrisoned by national armed forces were subject to army supervision, and a total of ten new towns were garrisoned by government troops.[25]

The Army and Electoral Politics: The Cuban Election of 1920

The Cuban army had very early acquired the character of an armed adjunct of the incumbent political party. Even during the government of Estrada Palma, Havana had applied the armed forces to political chores, drawing the military into the vortex of the political process. Political leaders elected to national office discovered in the armed forces a valuable instrument with which to promote partisan objectives. The willingness of military commanders to serve partisan ends, moreover, reflected the political character infused initially into the armed forces. The political culture grafted onto the new army converted the military institution into the agent of the incumbent party; and the practice of restructuring military commands to meet the needs of the ruling administration further heightened the political sensitivities of the armed forces. The success of military careers fused with the fortunes of a political party. Precisely because a political criterion was employed to appoint army commanders, the military establishment was compelled to underwrite the continuity of the prevailing political order. A vast, complex network of vested interests, fostered and sustained through continued political appointments, engendered pervasive partisan loyalties in the army. Sensitive to the political underpinnings of their careers, military commanders attached professional aspirations to the fortune of the incumbent president. Within this context, successful execution of duties, however political, carried promotions, salary increments, and transfers to coveted posts.

By the same partisan yardstick, the army was the wary onlooker of political tensions, coming increasingly to monitor national political processes. Opposition candidates, by the very act of seeking to modify the prevailing partisan order, raised a challenge potentially harmful to the established structure of the armed forces; a new administration, hostile to the defeated incumbent government, would, of necessity, reorganize the armed forces. The entire military command, from the army chief of staff to the commander of a remote Rural Guard outpost, acquired a vested stake in the outcome of elections.

Underwriting political continuity assumed an institutional character as insurrections heightened partisan passions and made political antagonisms acute. Political disorders in which Havana used the armed forces in defense of the constituted authorities tightened the bonds between the military command and the incumbent administration to the detriment of the opposition party. The armed forces defended the incumbent political party rather than the abstract integrity of national government.

The passions of the 1917 revolution had not subsided when national elections in 1920 rekindled political rivalries and personal feuds. Competition between José Miguel Gómez and Alfredo Zayas for the Liberal party nomination ended when Gómez secured the party's appointment and expelled his rival. Zayas subsequently organized the Partido Popular Cubano and, casting about for allies among the anti-*miguelista* ranks, joined forces with the Conservative party to form the Liga Nacional. The union, orchestrated by President Menocal, offered the Conservative leader the opportunity to frustrate the political ambitions of his long-time Liberal adversary; in turn, Zayas pledged to support Menocal for the presidency in 1924.[26]

Military leaders shared the Conservative president's hostility toward the Liberal presidential candidate. The army command had substantial reason to fear the *miguelista* candidacy. In the aftermath of two successive Menocal administrations and an abortive Liberal insurrection, a successful *miguelista* campaign in 1920 threatened to shatter the military order resulting from eight years of Conservative rule. Officers who had staked their careers on the ability of the Menocal administration to survive the *miguelista* armed challenge in 1917, commanders who had benefited directly—through promotions and assignments— from the defections of Liberal officers in the February revolution, and, in general, all officers and men who had profited professionally and personally during the second Menocal administration and who had beaten down the Liberals in 1917 shrank from the specter of a Gómez government. The reorganization awaiting the preponderantly Conservative command in a turnover of administrations compelled army leaders to support the government candidate to prevent an abrupt change in political continuity, the military repercussions of which were apparent to virtually every officer.

Administration leaders exploited military suspicion of the Gómez candidacy, hoping to harmonize military acitivity with the administration objectives. Liga partisans encouraged apprehension within the armed forces against the Liberal ticket, warning that a *miguelista* victory would see Liberal officers who had defected in 1917 return to positions of command.[27] The Conservative newspaper *El Día* asked in an editorial how Gómez, who attempted to destroy the fabric of the armed institution in 1917, could be permitted to become commander in chief. Gómez's candidacy, the editorial concluded, was a "grave offense to the Army."[28] *Zayistas* predicted that the election of the Liberal standard bearer would disrupt and disorganize the military services; *menocalista* commanders would be retired, Conservatives suggested, to permit Liberals to return to the armed forces with the rank they would have held had they remained on active duty.[29] Whatever reservations military leaders may have held toward Zayas the ex-Liberal were allayed when the Liga candidate pledged early in the campaign to respect the command structure of the armed forces.[30]

Administration propaganda portrayed the 1920 campaign as a contest of vital importance to the future integrity of the armed forces. The *zayista* campagin heightened the army's fear of political change, convincing many officers that a Gómez victory was inimical to the best interests of the service. Once military leaders came to believe a *miguelista* triumph pernicious, they willingly intervened, for the good of the service, in the electoral process. Many officers began to see the viability and stability of the armed institution as the key underlying issue of the 1920 election. The army as a whole was reported hostile to the Liberal candidate.[31] In Oriente Province, for example, the military district commander was determined to defeat the Liberals to keep the army intact.[32] The provincial commander of Camagüey announced publicly his intention to use "intimidation, fraud or . . . any other means available" to block the election of Gómez.[33]

Many commanders acted entirely out of personal fears and motives. Officers and men whose careers depended on the prevailing Conservative order feared the reprisals that were expected to follow the installation of Gómez in the Presidential Palace.[34] In Oriente some officers worked "conscientiously, in order to save their commissions."[35] Rural Guard commanders, "pretty badly compromised" by past political activity, feared that a Liberal government would retire scores of officers.[36] One American official reported that he "would not be surprised to see some of the principal officers of the army attempt to start trouble as they are fearful of what will happen to them if the Liberals get into power."[37] *Menocalista* officers were, in fact, prepared to lead the army in revolt to prevent the inauguration of José Miguel Gómez.[38]

In the final months of the campaign, Havana prepared to assure the election of the administration candidate. In September 1920 Secretary of Gobernación Charles Hernández, the alleged architect of electoral frauds in 1916, assumed the portfolio of war and navy. Merging the two most powerful cabinet officers under Menocal's most trusted political advisor allowed Havana to centralize government control of virtually every phase of the electoral contest, including the election machinery, authority over municipal governments and police forces, assignment of the armed forces, and licensing of firearms.[39]

The tense preelection atmosphere, traditional during campaign months, provided the administration with the pretext of introducing the armed forces into the electoral contest. Liberal warnings against election frauds permitted Havana to couch military activity in the guise of precautionary measures. Adinistration officials themselves evoked the specter of revolution and stimulated fears of political violence to facilitate centralizing electoral controls and intimidate and discourage the Liberal campaign.[40] The Conservative government chose to interpret Liberal allusions to postelection rebellion in the event of fraud into intimidations of political disorders prior to the November 1 election, thus justifying an extraordinary military presence in the closing weeks of the campaign. With much publicity the administration announced the discovery of a Liberal plot to overthrow the government.[41] The alleged conspiracy, scheduled for October 17, 1920, permitted the government to detach large numbers of troops to frustrate any future antigovernment schemes, arrest provincial Liberal leaders, and step up a campaign of harassment against the opposition.

The administration appointed military supervisors throughout the island in response to an announced military necessity. The Menocal government, Secretary Hernández explained, would "not be caught unprepared by another rebellion."[42] The appointment of supervisors, sanctioned by the Constitution, the Organic Law of Executive Power, and the Organic Law of Municipalities, was a device through which the central government, superceding provincial and municipal officials who were alleged incapable of maintaining order and stability, enforced its will on any part of the island. The almost exclusive use of army personnel for supervisory detail suggested the magnitude of military involvement in the election. Havana detached officers and men from the authority of the Department of War and placed them under the jurisdiction of Gobernación; in 1920, Hernández possessed the authority of detaching select officers to serve under Gobernación in any given district. The selection of Conservative officers as military supervisors further underscored the political mission entrusted to the commanders appointed by Havana. Hernández defended the appointment of Conservatives as provincial inspectors on the ground that the administration could not "be expected to send out Liberals in such capacity."[43]

The administration's professed concern for order concealed the political objectives assigned to the armed forces during the 1920 campaign. Menocal early summoned commanders of provincial military districts to Havana, encouraging them to use their influence and authority to promote the candidacy of Alfredo Zayas;[44] prominent army officers were seen daily about the Conservative party headquarters in Havana.[45] Military supervisors were expected to win for the administration candidate the municipality or province to which they were assigned, with the promise of promotion if successful.[46] Such political involvement, in fact, was frequently responsible for rapid promotion. The personnel selected for supervisory duty included officers and men most vulnerable to promotion incentives; young and inexperienced officers, as well as sergeants and corporals, received appointments.[47] Moreover, Havana employed officers most hostile to the Liberal candidate in supervisory chores, thereby exploiting the fears of individual officers to promote the government candidate.[48]

Officers with a distaste for political service were transferred to Havana and placed under the supervision of the army headquarters. Commanders with fewer inhibitions replaced the transferred personnel.[49] Still other officers, reluctant to serve the administration politically but unwilling to jeopardize their careers by defying instructions from Havana, chose to take furloughs for the duration of the electoral period.[50] Transfers, leaves of absence, and missions abroad displaced still more officers unsympathetic to the government effort. The administration completed the process inaugurated after the February revolution by purging all of the officers suspected of Liberal sympathies and replacing them with Conservative commanders.[51]

The provinces and municipalities placed under military supervisors conformed to the political needs of Havana. Army interventors were most commonly appointed to districts in which the apparatus of provincial and municipal administrative control, including the *ayuntamiento* (municipal government), judicial authority, and regional law enforcement agencies, was under the jurisdiction of local Liberal authorities. In regions where Conservative voters found themselves numerically inferior to registered Liberals or thwarted by local Liberal government, a simple complaint by local Conservatives to Havana accusing officials of abuse and irregularities sufficed to warrant the appointment of a military supervisor.[52] In Santa Clara, a traditional Liberal stronghold, 20 of the province's 30 municipalities were under the authority of military supervisors; districts safely in the Conservative-Liga fold were spared military intervention. By election day, military interventors occupied 73 of the island's 116 municipalities; the remaining 43 districts were judged by Havana to be safely in the government column.[53]

The occupation of a majority of the island's municipalities, however, belied the full dimensions of Havana-directed military intervention. In the 1917 revolution many Liberal mayors-elect had abandoned their elected offices to join the party leadership against Menocal; the resulting municipal vacancies were filled by presidential fiat, allowing Havana to appoint *menocalistas* to replace the insurgent Liberal officials. Regions with predominantly Liberal constituencies found themselves under Conservative administration as a result of the failure of the Liberal uprising. By 1920, then, Havana saw no need to appoint military interventors in Camagüey Province, for municipalities under the control of progovernment officials appointed in the wake of the 1917 revolution possessed sufficient local power to deliver the district to the Liga candidate.[54]

The political activity of local military detachments further reduced the need for the formal appointment of military supervisors. In Pinar del Río regular provincial commanders were sufficiently pro-Liga as to obviate the necessity of army interventors.[55] Similarly, a key appointment or transfer often sufficed to enlist the political support of a local military post; officers and men of tactical units distributed in the provinces and municipalities sympathetic toward the government candidate were assigned to Rural Guard posts and military subdistricts.[56] In Oriente the army was reported "converted into a political machine," with the province's Rural Guard used exclusively for political purposes.[57] Santa Clara was described as "militarised province."[58] It was thus possible for the administration to control a province or municipality without formally appointing a military interventor, relying instead of the assistance of a cooperative army post. This practice was most commonly employed in the remote municipalities of the interior, where formal vote-getting by the Liga generally relied on the coercion and intimidation of the rural population.

The military supervisor operated against a backdrop of martial law, wielding extraordinary power over the district to which he was appointed. He represented the intervention of Havana into municipal affairs, usurping municipal immunities and prerogatives for national political ends. Upon appointment, the military supervisor appropriated executive authority, including direction of the municipal police force, supervision of the *ayuntamiento,* and the administration of the local treasury; further, he wielded authority over the local Rural Guard detachment, thereby adding the rural constabulary to his command.[59] The military supervisor was responsible only to the secretary of *Gobernación.*

The power invested in the military supervisor encouraged Havana to usurp municipal authority. From this position it was a short and natural step for the supervisor to distort his statutory authority for political ends. His political mission consisted largely in neutralizing the campaign of the opposition. Appointed ostensibly to preserve order, he acted in an inordinately highhanded political fashion to discharge his trust. Liberal campaign rallies were banned as pernicious to public order; Liberal political speeches, judged inflammatory and provocative, were prohibited.[60] Supervisors frequently expelled local Liberal officials, forcing *miguelistas* to flee in fear of their lives. Arrests, intimidation, threats of violence, shootings, and occasionally a mysterious murder undermined the Liberal campaign in virtually every municipality and province to which a military supervisor had been appointed.[61]

In the interior, remote from the reclamations of organized opposition and isolated by poor communications and transportation, the armed forces practiced less restraint in imposing a Conservative consensus. In provincial cities and larger municipalities, the government effort was confined to undermining the Liberal party infrastructure, intimidating Liberal candidates and officials, and generally harassing the Liberal electoral campaign. Whatever restraints circumscribed army activity in an urban setting were abandoned in the isolation of rural communities. In the interior, the armed forces, largely Rural Guard detachments, were applied against the individual Liberal voter in the attempt to coerce registered Liberals into staying away from the polls on election day.[62] In Camagüey, government officials collaborated with provincial military leaders in preelection surveys to determine districts where local commanders of posts could be counted upon and others designated as "doubtful." To "doubtful" regions, the administration dispatched soldiers to visit the homes of Liberal voters; wives of registered Liberals were told not to let their husbands out of the house on November 1 "because if they did, something will happen to them."[63] In Oriente province the armed forces appropriated *cédulas* (voting credentials). Soldiers entering a household seeking a fictitious individual would threaten at arrest the head of the house. Protesting he was not the individual sought, the householder was required to present his *cédula* as proof of identification; upon presentation, the arresting officer, claiming to be personally satisfied, indicated the necessity of taking the *cédula* to his commanding officer as proof of the holder's true identity. The *cédula* was never returned. "The thing is done in such a way," reported the American consul in Santiago de Cuba, "that the man is actually grateful to the soldier for not taking him to prove his identity before the judge after a night in jail, and if he afterwards realizes that a trick had been played on him, he is afraid to complain about it."[64] Moreover, formal complaints to local magistrates were futile, for regional army officials were active in intimidating district judicial authorities.[65]

The armed forces subjected the Liberal constituency in the interior to methodical intimidation and harassment. Midnight raids by Rural Guard units to the homes of known Liberals warned the household of the dangers attending voting.[66] Army officials often attired as civilians took wider liberties in assaulting Liberal voters.[67] Mass Liberal abstentions, particularly in districts where registered Conservatives were numerically weaker, proved particularly effective in determining the outcome of local returns. One American military observer predicted that if immediately before the election the Rural Guard went about in the interior warning Liberals "not to vote, or threatening violence, reprisals, expulsion or other penalties," causing many to remain away from the polls, "a municipality may be lost, or even a Province."[68]

On election day the military continued to promote the government candidate. Troops were assigned to polling places, a measure predicated on the prior intimidation of Liberals by the armed forces and designed to frighten Liberal voters into staying away from the polls.[69] The legal sanction against the public presence of the armed forces on election day was largely ignored; on November 1, troops paraded in the streets and villages, conducting "maneuvers" in the interior provinces. These last government measures succeeded in preventing a considerable number of Liberals from voting.[70]

Alfredo Zayas won five provinces, losing only Havana. The new president had received inestimable assistance from the island's military institution. By 1920 the army had emerged into a powerful political force whose favor and support were to be cultivated by whatever group aspired to national office. Conversely, the army acquired a direct and vital interest in the conduct of national politics. Operating through the Presidential Palace, it developed the capacity and the collective disposition to affect the outcome of elections; military intervention in the electoral process institutionalized the role of the armed forces as power brokers in the political system. The absence of viable political parties or alternate agencies endowed with the ability to aggregate consent conferred on the army primary responsibility for delivering the necessary support to political aspirants. In 1920 candidates for national office solicited for the first time the support of the military institution as a separate and distinct constituency. By the early 1920s the Cuban army was deeply enmeshed in the fabric of the national political order.

The United States and
the Cuban Army, 1909–1924

4 Treaty arrangements between Havana and Washington added another dimension to the political orientation of the Cuban armed forces. At its inception, the Permanent Army, like the Rural Guard before it, represented an accommodation between Cuban political needs and American policy requirements. American support of the Cuban army underscored a growing perception in Washington of the burden imposed by the Platt Amendment. United States interventions were at once costly and unpopular, always carrying the inherent risk of involving American troops in a prolonged insurgency in Cuba. The new army, designed to guarantee the integrity of constituted authority, responded specifically to American hopes of avoiding future interventions. The Permanent Army substituted Cubans for Americans, relieving the United States of the military responsibility of maintaining a government "adequate for the protection of life, property, and individual liberty." As the Liberals had proclaimed earlier, a revolution challenging the government required the "intervention of soldiers," not Rural Guards.[1] Soldiers intervening to underwrite the order and stability mandated by the Platt Amendment, however, did not necessarily have to be American. Behind the general demand for order in Cuba lay specific American concerns; in promoting the development of the Cuban armed forces, Washington created a front-line defense of American strategic and **44** economic interests on the island. The United States bilateralized the enforcement of the Platt Amendment, for in assigning the responsibility of stability to Cuban authorities, American policy planners revised the Platt and Root pledge of American military protection against internal warfare.

United States military policy rested on shifting the responsibility for upholding the stability requirements of the Platt Amendment onto the Cuban army. According to a General Staff study in 1922, under the provisions of the Permanent Treaty the United States had a moral and legal obligation to intervene whenever and wherever the instability of the Cuban government was such that it was unable or unwilling to accord the necessary protection to life, property, and individual liberty.[2] It was precisely this moral and legal obligation that Washington wished the Cuban army to share. The thrust of American policy henceforth was designed to enhance the ability of the Cubans to provide order and protect the political integrity of national government in the hope, as General Enoch H. Crowder indicated, of saving "the United States from a costly military intervention and the loss of prestige incident to failure of the experiment of Republican government in Cuba."[3] Consequently, it was vital for the Cubans to possess a military institution of sufficient size, strength, and efficiency "so as to have them attend to their revolutions without the need of our intervention."[4] The responsibilities imposed on Havana under the Permanent Treaty raised the army's ability to preserve order into an international issue; for both Washington and Havana, internal security against revolt or public disorders was the primary mission of the Cuban army.[5] By guaranteeing the international integrity of the island, and thereby permitting the Cuban army to concentrate its energies and resources internally, the United States hoped that the island's military institution would "maintain peace, law and order throughout the Republic at all times at the smallest cost and without the assistance of any foreign government."[6] The Cuban army, United States military advisors counseled, had to be placed in a position from which it could, with dispatch and efficiency, "maintain order . . . and restore normal conditions." Otherwise, during the "considerable time required for the arrival of an expedition from the United States, insurrectionists would have an opportunity to inflict tremendous damages on very valuable properties." It was incumbent upon the American goals of stability and order, and consistent with the "policy of the United States to avoid intervention," to have Cuba in a position "to honestly and efficiently handle her own problem."[7]

The Cuban army developed the organizational substance consistent with the mission for which it was designed. The theory of combat responded essentially to the suppression of revolutions, rural uprisings, and riots, and the maintenance of internal public order;[8] the strength and composition of the army conformed to the national requirement for maintaining public order and prompt suppression of civil disturbances.[9]

The distribution of the Cuban military was a further response to the army's mission. The strategic distribution of the Cuban armed forces, the American military attaché reported, was "made with a view to immediately crush rebellion, revolution or other public disorder."[10] The armed forces were distributed into eight military districts, two of which were located in the capital, the remaining six conforming to provincial boundaries. The Rural Guard consisted of forty-two squadrons invested with first-line duty; the squadrons were assigned throughout the interior to protect rural estates and assist municipal police departments in the suppression of local disorders. Six regular cavalry squadrons formed the local reserve and were designed to reinforce the Rural Guard when disorders proved beyond the law-enforcement capacity of local units. The general reserve, confined in Havana, included six infantry battalions, three coast artillery battalions, two mountain artillery batteries, one light artillery battery, one engineer's battalion, and one signal corps battalion. The general reserve reinforced provincial commands and garrisoned strategic sites, including major cities and the transportation and communication networks. During national emergencies, finally, the president possessed the authority to organize a national militia for the duration of the crisis.[11]

The development of the Cuban armed forces was consistent with the nature of anticipated disorders. The traditional rural base of armed protests dictated the necessity for mounted troops. American advisors, influenced to a considerable extent by traditional forms of warfare on the island, supported converting the armed forces into cavalry units, for "infantry would be lost in the jungle in Cuba in case of the pusuit of anybody." The lack of cavalry, the American chief of staff suggested, had contributed powerfully to Spain's inability to suppress the Cuban independence movement.[12] Mounted units, consequently, were proportionally stronger than the infantry, and the infantry stronger than artillery. The specter of mounted rural insurgents compelled Cuban military leaders to develop an efficient cavalry. The infantry served as an auxiliary force; it operated in terrain prohibiting the use of horses, including swamps and heavy bush, and garrisoned communication and transportation centers, rural property, and urban centers.[13]

In a Cuban context, fashioning the military to enforce stability and the requirements demanded by the Platt Amendment further contributed to institutionalizing a political status quo. Entrusted to uphold constituted authority and supervise order and stability, the Cuban army sustained whatever incumbent happened to constitute authority. American military advisors, attempting to infuse professionalism into the new armed institution, stressed to the Cubans "the necessity of loyalty to their government, supporting it at all times and not questioning whether it might be right or wrong."[14] In a Cuban partisan setting, this counsel contributed to converting the military institution into the armed agency of a closed political order; the Cuban army became the means of promoting *continuismo* under the aegis of stability.

Enforcing stability through the support of the partisan order acquired nationalist overtones within ruling political groups. Defending constituted authority successfully against an internal challenge spared the island from the compromise of national sovereignty attending foreign intervention. Defense of national sovereignty was thus expressed by imposing the will of the incumbent administration on the competing sectors of the body politic; the political involvement of the armed forces and their role as deterrents against a resort to arms as a method of political change contributed to narrowing meaningful political competition. Unable and unwilling to repel an American armed intervention, the Cuban army contracted inward, constrained to support constitued authority—however unpopular—in defense of the island and the preservation of national sovereignty. Armed stability produce the conditions auspicious for a government, relying on the military institution and complying fully with the Platt Amendment, to impose a political dictatorship supported entirely by the United States.

The international repercussions of Cuban instability further underscored the necessity of an efficient army. In giving support to the island's international integrity, the United States assumed responsibility for acts committed by Cubans against the life and property of foreigners; Washington emerged as the buffer between Havana and foreign powers. Political disorders endangering the life and property of non-American foreigners on the island were capable of precipitating a confrontation between the United States and a European power. "By virtue of the Platt Amendment," one United States military official reminded Washington, "internal political conditions have an important bearing on international relations."[15] Frequent disorders, endangering foreign interests, taxed the patience of major powers committed to the protection of their nationals in Cuba. During the 1906 revolution, the French and British contemplated action to protect their citizens in Cuba.[16] In 1912, an insurrection against the Gómez administration caused the British government to ask Washington to guarantee the lives and property of British nationals on the island.[17] During the same rebellion, moreover, French, British, and Spanish representatives in Cuba made reclamations to the American government for protection.[18] During the Liberal revolution in 1917 consular agents representing England, France, Belgium, Spain, Germany, Austria, Dominican Republic, Venezuela, Colombia, Italy, Chile, Haiti, Mexico, Costa Rica, and Canada asked the United Sates to protect the lives and property of their nationals in Cuba.[19] "A country which has many and serious disturbances of public peace," one writer warned, "and also has a large foreign element in its population, with large business interests controlled by foreign capital, is sure, sooner or later, to become a source of international peril on account of incompetent administration."[20]

The newly completed Isthmian canal represented still another dimension to stability vis-à-vis the foreign population on the island. Cuban politics were woven into the fabric of American defense considerations. Cuba possessed the "key to the locks of the Panama Canal"; and the nation controlling Cuba, it was suggested, "can inevitably maintain control over the Atlantic exit of the canal."[21] As late as 1921, American military planners reiterated that control of Cuba insured command of the Gulf of Mexico.[22] Consequently, American national interests required in Cuba "such stability . . . and such a system of administration of Cuban laws, that Cuba shall never become a source of international peril on account of incompetent government."[23]

The ability of the Cuban government to provide stability and enforce order was invariably measured within the context of the Platt Amendment—Havana's ability to protect foreign lives and property. It thus behooved the Cuban government to provide maximum protection to foreign lives and property during political disorders. Insurrection presented a set of problems, the contradictions of which Cuban governments throughout the first half of the twentieth century were never quite able to resolve. Havana was required, on the one hand, to suppress the political challenge inherent in a revolutionary threat, and on the other hand, to minimize the loss of foreign lives and property. In the final analysis, the only measure employed to test the efficacy with which the Cubans fulfilled stability requirements was the protection of foreigners and their property. However successful Havana may have been in suppressing the politico-military threat attending revolution, the integrity of national administration remained jeopardized by American intervention as long as a handful of insurgents possessed the capacity to destroy property. In 1912, for example, President Gómez, confident that his government could suppress the revolution, nevertheless felt compelled to advise Washington that he anticipated some difficulty in controlling the destruction of property. The government was unable with the troops at its command, Gómez informed the American minister, to "station on all foreign properties sufficient forces to guarantee absolute protection."[24] And when American pressure for protection continued to build, the Cuban president declared that such service would, of necessity, preoccupy at least 1,250 of his "best troops for the protection of one group of foreign properties in one part of the disaffected district"; at this rate, Gómez declared impatiently, his "entire army of regular and volunteers would not suffice for police work alone without considering the prosecution of a campaign against the insurrectionists."[25]

The American minister in Havana informed the State Department that "the greatest burden now resting on the Cuban government is the protection of foreign property. There is in the disaffected district a huge amount of valuable property belonging to American, British, French, German and Spanish citizens and companies." All these interests, the American agent reported, were most insistent in their complaints that the Cuban government meet "to the letter of their demands the request for military protection."[26] Similarly, during the 1917 revolution the United States insisted upon adequate protection of foreign property. Repeatedly, the American minister was instructed to "demand, in a very insistent way," that the Cuban authorities provide adequate protection of the sugar estates.[27]

Insurgents invariably discerned the added military handicap under which Havana labored when confronted with the destruction of foreign property. Developing ultimately into a weapon forged by a tradition of insurgency precisely because of its inherent tactical value, the destruction of foreign property became an institutionalized approach to internal war. The responsibility of having to protect property weakened the government's ability to mobilize and apply the full force of its military strength in a given revolutionary situation. The American consul in Santiago de Cuba in 1912 described the insurgents as "incendiaries" who could "destroy in an hour property representing millions of dollars in value and that has taken years to construct." Rebel tactics, the consul noted, were designed essentially to "compel the Government to detach soldiers for the protection of foreign property, thereby impairing the effectiveness of the military forces, enabling them to continue indefinitely the movement."[28]

An inability to prevent the destruction of property revealed Havana to be incapable of meeting the treaty obligations imposed by the Platt Amendment. The security of foreign interests served as the final measure of stability and order under the aegis of the Platt Amendment, subjecting the incumbent administration to American intermeddling and, ultimately, raising the fear of American armed intervention. In 1917 the insurgent leadership, annoyed in learning that "the Menocal Government tells Washington that he guarantees the *zafra* [sugar harvest] and property," ordered all sugar-grinding to a halt in rebel-held regions simply to demonstrate the government's inability to provide adequate safeguards to foreign property.[29] The rebels in 1917 hoped to redeem their moribund movement by precipitating an American intervention through the destruction of foreign property; they pledged to destroy systematically all American property and, if failing to draw United States intervention, alluded to a campaign of terror against American citizens.[30]

The responsibilities that Havana found necessary to discharge under the Platt Amendment passed onto the armed forces, casting the military into an alien mold. Any measure of Cuba's fulfillment of the Permanent Treaty rested almost exclusively upon its ability to protect the lives and property of foreigners. Invariably, the government detached a large number of Cuban troops for garrison duty on foreign properties. The susceptibility of the Cuban government to American pressure vis-à-vis the arrangements of the Platt Amendment gave the Cuban armed forces a mercenary quality; the lives and property of foreigners assumed priority in the effort to convince Washington that the constituted authority in Havana was, in fact, a viable administration capable of discharging its responsibilities under the Permanent Treaty. The lives and property of nationals were subordinated to the greater diplomatic exigencies of revolution. In 1912 the American minister reported that "Cuban interests in Oriente are receiving practically no protection because of the fact so much pressure is being brought to bear on behalf of foreigners."[31] If, in fact, the viability of the Cuban government depended upon its ability to satisfy the needs and demands of foreigners, it behooved the government to place the armed forces of the state at the service of the distant locus of power. As early as 1910, a year after the withdrawal of the military forces of the second occupation, the United States minister defined American intervention policy, suggesting that the "American Government does not propose to intervene unless it is clearly shown that the legally constituted government of Cuba is incapable and cannot maintain its authority."[32] The dislodging of Cuban authorities resulting from the inability of Estrada Palma to protect property in 1906 cast a long shadow on the national consciousness of *plattista* Cuba. It was incumbent on constituted authority, therefore, to possess an armed institution sufficiently competent to "maintain its authority" and avoid the fate of the first president. In 1912 the American secretary of state reminded the beleaguered Gómez administration that a "continued failure on the part of his [Gómez's] government adequately to protect life and property will inevitably compel this Government to intervene in Cuba under and in response to its treaty rights and obligations."[33]

In addition, foreign property demanded the attention of Cuban authorities during periods of political quiescence. The armed forces continued to be distributed in conformity with the needs of rural landowners. During the *zafra*, cavalry units patrolled the sugar districts. "To take their place," one American military observer speculated, "would require a large number of American cavalry," and even this would not be effective.[34] During the *zafra* of 1918, some thirteen thousand Cuban officers and men were assigned to the sugar regions.[35] The army, furthermore, suppressed labor agitation during the harvest, assuring a tranquil *zafra* and uninterrupted grinding. One trained observer reported in 1918 that local military authorities in Santa Clara were determined to "suppress severely any labor troubles" during the harvest.[36]

Moral and material support was the American commitment inherent in the *a parenti* arrangement with the Cuban army. If American interests on the island required the Cuban government to be in an independent position to maintain order and stability, it followed that United States support was vital to maintain "a loyal force sufficient in size, so organized, so trained, so equipped and so supplied that it would be able to put down large bodies of insurrectionists in any part of the Island."[37] In pursuit of this objective, the United States assumed responsibility for meeting the technical and professional needs of the Cuban armed institution. As early as 1910, Army Chief of Staff General J. Franklin Bell justified the detachment of American army advisors as being entirely consistent with the Platt Amendment. In passing the statute, Bell suggested, Congress "tacitly gave its consent to such interventions as the United States, through its proper authorities, might deem it necessary to exercise to discharge the Treaty of Paris." The objective of American military assistance was to aid Havana in maintaining a government adequate for the protection of life, property, and individual liberty. "This could not possibly be done," the chief of staff insisted, "without an army. Assisting the Cuban government in organizing and training an army which would enable the Cuban government itself to discharge this obligation is in accordance with the provision of Article III of the Platt Amendment."[38]

Supplies and training were designed to enhance the effectiveness of the Cuban army in discharging its government's obligations under the Permanent Treaty. Presupposing the importance of Cuban sugar, American military planners perceived three viable options: to forgo all protection, to employ American forces to guard the sugar fields, and to use Cubans for protection. The withdrawal of all protective troops was dismissed immediately; the use of United States forces, on the other hand, would have inevitably necessitated further expense and additional effort, and would have created great friction. The use of Cuban armed forces remained the most practical alternative. Within this context, consequently, it was incumbent upon the United States to provide the Cubans with adequate training and supplies. The Cuban army if properly supplied," one military advisor maintained, "is capable of protecting the sugar crop." Indeed, the "cheapest, safest, and most efficient way" to guard foreign property was for the Department of War "to make it its business to see that the Cuban army receives the proper amount of supplies."[39]

Providing supplies and instruction in their use was designed to assist the Cuban military institution enforce order. One American advisor recommended training the Cuban army in the use of machine guns and automatic rifles, for these were "most effective in putting down mobs, insurrections, etc."[40] Colonel Frank Parker, long involved with the Cuban armed forces, suggested that "we should have, at all times, with the Cuban army a well equipped American instructor, of our highest type, capable of instructing and assisting generally (particularly by his personal example), the Cuban forces, and of keeping them in touch with our most recent methods, practices and general standards." Parker recommended that the United States assist the Cubans in maintaining their armed forces "so as to have them attend to their revolutions without need of our intervention."[41]

Cuban officers received further instruction and training in American service institutions. American advisors repeatedly urged the expansion of programs designed to train Cuban officers in the United States.[42] By 1925, officers from virtually every branch of the Cuban armed forces, including the medical corps, the infantry, the coast and field artillery, the aviation corps, the signal corps, the cavalry, and the corps of engineers, had attended various military academies in the United States.[43] By 1928 it was reported difficult to "find a regular officer of any rank who has not studied abroad."[44]

The circumstances and ceremony surrounding the delivery of supplies often carried distinct political and moral endorsements. A speedy delivery of arms, ammunition, and supplies during emergencies meant nothing less than unequivocal support of the incumbent administration. In 1917, days after the outbreak of disorders, the War Department quickly publicized its intention to ship some ten thousand rifles and five million rounds of ammunition to the Cuban government;[45] days later, Havana announced the purchase of eight machine guns.[46] Moreover, the Cuban armed forces secured a number of airplanes to aid the government in reconnaissance and bombing missions against the insurgents.[47] The speedy and well-publicized response to Cuban military needs, Menocal later acknowledged, had exerted a "tremendous moral effect" on his administration.[48] Indeed, the unqualified expression of American support was a decisive factor in preserving the loyalty of most of the armed forces.[49]

Under the dual stresses of American policy planners in Washington and Cuban political leaders in Havana, the army developed into something of an anomaly in a skewed institutional order. Pressured into making political processes conform to the requirements of the Platt Amendment, political leaders lost a national purpose; the accommodation of the political system to the Permanent Treaty established sources of legitimacy outside the national order. By the late 1910s and early 1920s, a mercenary political culture had reached full fruition. The military was only one institution whose integrity was constantly subject to the vagaries of Cuba's treaty relations with the United States. Serving foreign politico-economic interests insured the solvency of national administration against foreign enemies of Cuban independence; support of the prevailing political order against internal adversaries appeared to be the most effective manner in which to preserve intact the army establishment.

Sources of Army Preeminence: The *Machadato*, 1925–1933

Gerardo Machado and the Army, 1925–1928

Gerardo Machado inherited in 1925 an army conditioned by past experience to conform to the political predilections of a new administration. The new president quickly perceived, however vaguely at first, the potential importance of the army in the political order. An experienced veteran of almost three decades of *miguelista* politics and himself once the inspector general of the army, Machado discerned that the sources of national power at some point inevitably interlaced around the armed institution. The political party structure, a constellation of personality clusters orbiting about a dominant figure, offered only an ephemeral, at best tenuous, instrument for aggregating support. American diplomatic endorsement, together with the support of the island's foreign and domestic economic community, remained contingent precisely on the stability underwritten by the armed institution.

Machado quickly fashioned an army command compatible with the politics of the new Liberal order. Officers of dubious partisan sentiments, particularly remaining *menocalistas*, retired. Trusted *machadistas* filled senior grades; old *miguelistas* returned to active service. Appointments, promotions, and transfers placed key army commands under the authority of officers politically loyal to the new administration.[1] Politically inspired promotions, in fact, violated the Organic Law of the Armed Forces. Promotion to lieutenant colonel, for example, was regulated by a ratio of three executive appointments to one **55** advancement based on seniority; between 1926 and 1932, of the six officers promoted to lieutenant colonel, Machado appointed five. Promotion to comandante was governed by a one-to-one ratio; of the eleven comandantes commissioned between 1926 and 1932, ten were presidential designations.[2]

The Machado administration made a conscious effort to win army support. By the end of 1925, Machado had lifted the ceiling restricting the size of the army;[3] through the Military Reorganization Act of 1926, which permitted the president to reorganize the armed forces at will, Machado authorized a new peacetime strength for the army at 11,772 officers and men.[4] Living conditions for military personnel improved markedly; the government established new housing units throughout the island's military garrisons. Training facilities, including the construction of the *Escuela de Aplicación*, improved.[5] A government decree in September 1926, moreover, expanded army jurisdiction to secondary schools, authorizing officers to supervise gymnastic drills and marching exercises and to teach elementary military science.[6] The Liberal administration also established an aviation corps, adding air power to the armed forces. At the end of his first year in office, the president proclaimed with some pride that the army had attained, through instruction and training, the level of perfection nations "most advanced in the art of war" had invested in their military establishments.[7] By 1928, the armed forces were reported "solidly behind" the president.[8]

Impressed with the administrative efficiency of the armed forces, Machado increasingly introduced into his government the rigors of a military regimen. Martial values were offered to the body politic as qualities deserving emulation and worthy of application in national administration. By the late 1920s, in fact, Machado had recruited the services of a considerable number of military chieftains in a variety of administration positions. The army, Machado exhorted;

> has been a school of discipline and must deserve in the future all my attention, as it has deserved it in the past. This national institution must be considered and appreciated in its true and just value by all Cubans. I have placed many chiefs and officers of the army in civil positions as supeivsors. I have not done this with the purpose of militarizing the officers of State, but to give to the civil offices the standards of order,

duty and rectitude that exist in the army. These supervisions do not represent a government rule, but only passing needs of the moment. It could be well said that far from militarizing the administrative organization, the matter has resulted in an evident demonstration of the excellent civil qualities of our army officers.[9]

Machado devoted the last years of his first term to preparing for reelection. By 1927, he had forged a coalition among national political organizations, binding the Liberal, Conservative, and Popular parties to his candidacy for a second term. Through the appropriate application of coercion and favors, he imposed a political consensus dissolving party independence, traditionally the source of opposition to reelection. *Cooperativismo*, as the arrangement became known, conferred on parties outside the circumference of power the prerogatives, perquisites, and patronage available in the past only during national incumbency; opposition leaders, hitherto in competition with the incumbent administration, received vested interests in a political status quo.

The Cuban president also solicited support for his reelection abroad. In early 1927, seeking an endorsement from Washington, Machado explored with the State Department his plans for another term of office. The American ambassador in Havana urged the secretary of state to reassure the Cuban president informally that the "Department would not be hostile to his reelection" in the impending national contest.[10] A visit to Washington later that year gave Machado the opportunity to discuss the future of Cuban politics with the American president. President Coolidge tacitly approved Machado's plans for a second term, adding that the United States "only desired that the people of Cuba should have whatever Government and Constitution they themselves wanted."[11]

By the end of his first term, the Cuban chief executive had orchestrated a progovernment bloc consisting of all major parties, neutralizing internally and abroad all agencies capable of opposing his reelection. All political parties nominated Machado in common for a second term. The political quiescence and stability that he seemed capable of providing for another term, moreover, won him the endorsement of economic and diplomatic authorities. Uncontested in 1928, Machado was reelected for a new and extended six-year term.

Opposition and Resistance, 1928–1933:
The Independence Generation

Machado inaugurated his second term in a political order institutionally disjointed. For thirty years, the veterans of the independence struggle against Spain had dominated the island's political processes, bargaining among themselves for political accommodations to insure their preeminence; by 1928, this political bargaining had found its logical conclusion in the *cooperativista* experiment. The economic sectors, foreign and domestic, and American diplomacy, underwriting in many ways the Libertador political concordance, found comfort in the *machadista* consensus as an arrangement promising to stabilize intra-elite competition for power. Machado organized tradi- tional sources of power into his second administration; by up- setting the order of institutional competition, he undermined prescribed conventions of traditional political activity, destroy- ing all sources of legitimate opposition independent of executive control. In 1928, the administration had escaped the armed protest characteristic of past reelections by appropriating the political organizations capable of inaugurating anti-reelectionist violence.

The leaders of parties absorbed in the *cooperativista* consensus who opposed collaboration with Machado fled into exile or were imprisoned. Prominent exiled spokesmen of the Conser- vative and Popular parties, including Carlos Mendieta, Roberto Méndez Peñate, and Mario Menocal, plotted abroad, building opposition organizations, collecting funds, purchasing arms, and coordinating plans with agents on the island. In August 1931 the scattered Libertador opposition leaders in exile, under Mendieta, Méndez, and Menocal, launched an invasion of the island. Hoping to secure a beachhead long enough to inspire a national uprising, the invaders landed armed ex- peditionaries simultaneously in the westernmost province of Pinar del Río and Oriente in the east. Former President Mario Menocal, moreover, hoped to exploit whatever influence he still possessed within the military institution to rally army support of the invasion.[12]

The 1931 uprising failed completely. In Oriente, the ex- peditionaries managed to hold Gibara, the point of disembar- kation, only briefly before a massive government effort, com- bining air, naval, and ground units, recaptured the town.[13] In the west, Mendieta and Menocal were captured almost immediately upon landing, signaling the collapse of the invasion in Pinar del Río.[14]

The stillborn rebellion heralded a hiatus of a style of armed protest in which the protagonists established a rural base from which to launch war against Havana. The training, drill, and distribution of the armed forces, long inspired by precisely this type of combat, had prepared the army to meet, without United States armed assistance, the rural insurrection peculiar to Cuban revolutionary tradition; by 1931, military efficacy and technology had surpassed the insurgent capacity to wage rural war. Air power, used for reconnaissance and bombing, naval forces, and army units dispatched by the government on the newly constructed Central Highway, using rapid motor transport, overwhelmed the Libertador rebels in 1931.[15] The Cuban army had seemingly mastered the technique of suppressing rural revolution.

The 1931 uprising augured the final collapse of the generation of 1895 as a viable national force. The *cooperativista* experiment had discredited participating Libertador political organizations; the economic depression found the old politicos unable to respond to the economic crisis. By 1931, the Libertador incumbents and the Libertador opposition alike had revealed a singular incapacity to resolve the contradictions and tensions within the Cuban political system. The usurpation of institutional channels of political competition drove the veterans to employ a style of armed protest they themselves had devised almost forty years earlier. This was the lesson of 1931: the *cooperativista* consensus and military efficiency had preempted institutional competition for power while successfully neutralizing the traditional form of armed protest.

Opposition and Resistance, 1928–1933: The Republican Generation

As early as the mid-1920s, forces beyond the restraints of existing institutions—hence free of *machadista* controls—emerged to challenge the *cooperativista* order. Precisely because these forces operated outside institutional legitimacy, they developed initially as marginal agents of change. Any challenge to the *machadista* order was, in fact, "illegal," for incumbent authorities, in appropriating the "legal" vehicles of political change, had outlawed opposition; antigovernment violence in response to a closed institutional order emerged as the sole possible expression of opposition to Machado. Once institutional controls faltered in the support of the *machadista* consensus, counterviolence emerged as the prime agent of maintaining a political status quo. As the application of extrainstitutional opposition pressure intensified, the government grew increasingly dependent on the armed forces to enforce the consensus. The failure of political institutions to contain opposition activity compelled the body military to widen the scope of its involvement in national processes; the army, in turn, pre-empted institutions exposed as incapable of supporting continued stability.

Labor launched one of the earliest extrainstitutional challenges to the Libertador political order. During the early republican years, workers' organizations developed in direct proportion to the vast influx of foreign capital, presenting their most formidable sustained challenge during Menocal's second administration.[16] Between 1917 and 1919, the industries most heavily capitalized by foreign investment, including utilities, transportation, and sugar, were affected by labor agitation.[17]

Almost from the outset, labor possessed extraordinary power not subject to the constraints of institutional controls. Workers' organizations formed one of the earliest sources of "illegitimate" power against which the government applied the armed forces. The disorders frequently accompanying labor agitation often lacked political content and only tangentially threatened the constituted order. Rather, the government felt compelled to adopt strong antilabor measures precisely because labor assailed most directly the locus of power on the island—the foreign economic and diplomatic sectors. The political demands imposed on Havana by the Platt Amendment placed workers' protests in an international context; labor's challenge to capital through prolonged and recurrent protests, in short, had the potential for toppling the incumbent administration by precipitating an armed intervention justified within the context of the Permanent Treaty. Strikes had to be suppressed, Machado explained in 1928, because "foreign firms had appealed to the government of Washington and of other nations soliciting protection, which signified the threat of a new intervention."[18]

Lacking the institutional control mechanism to restrain or direct the course of workers' associations, the government applied the armed forces directly against labor in an effort to regulate proletarian activity. Previously the army provided an equilibrium among competing sectors of the Libertador ruling elite; governments applied the military institution objectively to an internecine contest for partisan objectives. Labor challenged the entire Libertador order, however, and represented a threat foreign and external to the political caste accustomed to presiding over the national processes unmolested. Havana applied the military against a sector of the population possessing the pressure capacity of toppling the political order and yet beyond the reach of institutional manipulation. The government reacted to strikes by the imposition of martial law, the appointment of military supervisors, and the armed occupation of cities, towns, and municipalities.[19] Army labor frequently maintained services disrupted by strikes. A strike of the Havana street cleaners in 1921 forced army units to clean the streets of the capital;[20] railroad strikes necessitated the use of military detachments to prevent the interruption of service and guard rolling stock and rail stations.[21] In 1927, the War Department organized a program to instruct officers and men in the skills necessary to operate rail transportation; the government contemplated, in addition, the creation of a permanent railroad corps to assume direction of the rail system during strikes.[22] The public force guarded property and industries affected by labor walkouts. Strike-breaking techniques included intimidation, violence, deportation of foreign workers, and the arrest of strikers and union leaders.[23] The government measured strikes, however peaceful and controlled, in direct proportion to the ability of the affected economic sector to mount a diplomatic offensive capable of provoking an armed intervention. Indeed, peaceful strikes often presented the greatest difficulty. "The fact that these strikes are carried out peacefully," one rail manager complained, "only make[s] them more dangerous because it is difficult for the Government to find grounds in which to employ the public forces."[24]

Machado's ascendancy did not alter labor-state relations. On the contrary, the government applied state violence with increasing urgency. Strikes were repressed brutally; the administration deported foreign-born union leaders and arrested, exiled, and assassinated national organizers. In addition, it raided and closed labor offices, destroyed union records, and ordered organizations to dissolve.[25] According to one officer, the armed institution fulfilled its duty when it acted against those who took advantage of social perturbation to make common cause with the proletariat.[26]

Labor organizations continued to grow and consolidate throughout the first Machado administration. By 1925, the first national central labor organization, the Confederación Nacional Obrera Cubana, was established, claiming four years later some seventy-one thousand members; in 1930, the first national sugar workers union, the Federación del Trabajo de Cuba, was organized.[27] Unenfranchised politically, labor activity moved further onto the fringes of illegality. The growth of national labor associations raised the apparition of a general strike of national proportions threatening the political and economic order on the island. And however brutally repressed, labor defied government action and continued to pose a threat to the *machadista* consensus.

Students represented a second national force functioning beyond the limits of sanctioned political activity. Violence and counterviolence announced the political involvement of the first republican-born generation. By 1927, Havana students had endowed their association, the Directorio Estudiantil Universitario (DEU), with a political—anti–Machado—orientation.[28] Antigovernment activity frequently provoked violent confrontations between students and the armed forces throughout the island. In September 1930, during a mass demonstration in Havana, Rafael Trejo became the first student martyr;[29] a month later, street fighting between students and police in Santiago de Cuba ended only when troops from the provincial regiment arrived to assist municipal law enforcement agencies.[30] By the end of the year, Machado had suspended classes in the university and in high schools, detaching army units to occupy the restive centers of education throughout the island.

The failure of Libertador politics, revealed bankrupt after the abortive 1931 revolution, summoned into existence new political groups to challenge the *machadista* order. The new extrainstitutional opponents, reaching maturity in the republic, consisted largely of urban professionals frustrated politically by the monopoly of power exercised by members of the Libertador ruling elite. The young political activists competing for control of the state repudiated the political culture of the veterans, of whom Machado, they insisted, was only the most recent manifestation, and demanded a complete restructuring of the national order.[31]

The ABC revolutionary society represented the largest opposition faction to emerge in the aftermath of 1931. Organized into clandestine action cells, the ABC systematically applied political violence against the Machado government; by 1932, it had matched government terror and assassination with organized counterterror and reprisals.[32] The Organización Celular Radical Revolucionaria (OCRR) developed as another post-1931 response to the *machadato*. Also composed of young professionals and students, the OCRR predicated its antigovernment tactics on the conviction that only violence was capable of toppling the incumbent administration. After 1931, in addition, a host of antigovernment factions, including the Communist party, women's resistance groups, university professors, and normal school teachers and students joined the underground opposition. By early 1933, the leading opposition factions had united in a revolutionary junta in New York and were calling for a revolution to remove Machado.[33]

The rise of antigovernment factions unresponsive to institutional regulation, operating on the periphery of the political system and employing force to promote political change, short-circuited the *machadista* consensus. It was now possible for labor, institutionally unassimilated, to produce through a general strike, for instance, conditions capable of causing the collapse of the constituted order. Moreover, the new political opposition, rejecting rural insurgency, fashioned a form of armed protest unprecedented in the tradition of Cuban revolutionary warfare—urban resistance. The anti-Machado struggle was essentially an urban phenomenon, characterized by work stoppages in the cities, running gun battles on Havana streets, bombings, and political assassinations. As early as 1931, rural Cuba remained relatively quiescent while violence wracked Havana and the provincial capitals; resistance was largely the product of unrest and dissatisfaction in all the cities.[34]

Opposition, Resistance, and the Army, 1928–1933

By the early 1930s, the institutional order underwriting the *machadista* consensus revealed signs of strain. Traditional means of consolidating and aggregating power, including patronage, political pressure, and fixed elections, grew increasingly inadequate and irrelevant to post-1931 developments precisely because the new opposition lay entirely beyond the realm of the institutional order. The moment the government outlawed competition and appropriated the instrumentality capable of containing and expressing discontent within the political system, it drove the opposition, however ill-matched, to use force. Opposition violence, in turn, necessitated a qualitative modification in the means employed by the government to retain power. Sophisticated and relatively uncoercive restraints yielded to institutional force; where state violence had early been irregular and selective, after 1931 it grew increasingly systematic and indiscriminate.

Army functions expanded in direct proportion to the apparent inability of national agencies to preserve the *cooperativista* consensus. The prostration of the institutional order compelled the national leadership to introduce the armed forces into areas confined traditionally to civil authorities. The frequent and prolonged suspension of constitutional guarantees, abrogating civil rights, facilitated government use of the armed institution. Military supervisors displaced civilian political administrators; army personnel replaced provincial governors and municipal *alcaldes* (mayors) throughout the island. Civilians accused of antigovernment activity were tried before military tribunals. In February 1932 the administration amended the military penal code to grant the army judicial authority over cases involving explosives, crimes against the military, destruction of sugar or cane machinery, and disruption of transportation and communication facilities. A retroactive clause of the revised penal code, moreover, required civil courts to surrender all such cases pending to army tribunals.[35] The creation of a national militia in 1932 subjected the island's national, judicial, and secret police agencies to army jurisdiction; and the government militarized municipal law enforcement agencies by appointing army officers as police chiefs.[36] Virtually every government agency passed under some form of military jurisdiction or review. In early 1933, army lieutenants and captains replaced civilian censors;[37] all members of the armed forces received the authority to investigate and arrest individuals suspected of antigovernment activity. Military authorization was required to permit an assembly of three or more persons. By mid-1933, the armed institution had emerged as the single most importnat underpinning of the beleaguered Machado government.

Growing government reliance on the armed forces enabled the body military to secure a variety of privileges and immunities from the administration. In January 1932 all military personnel obtained exemption from civil prosecution, being subject from then on only to military justice. The institutional integrity of the armed forces remained intact while the government, struggling to remain solvent during the worst months of the depression, slashed national expenditures. In July 1933 the army consisted of some twelve thousand officers and men—more than the strength authorized during Machado's first year in office.[38] War Department appropriations continued to account for nearly 20 percent of the national budget; the actual cost of the armed institution, in fact, was suspected to be several million dollars in excess of published budgetary figures.[39] While the government reduced salaries, released thousands of civil servants, and permitted pay schedules to fall hopelessly into arrears, and while hundreds of thousands suffered the full impact of the depression, soldiers were reported "enjoying unheard-of luxury."[40] Administration leaders privately admitted fears that army reductions would encourage retired officers—and commanders facing a similar likelihood of forced retirement—to join the opposition.[41]

The application of the armed institution against the opponents of the government produced among the opposition sectors a doctrinal antimilitarism. The army had stepped into a buffer position between the administration and its opponents, emerging at once as the defender of a discredited government and the visible agent of repression. Moreover, the extraordinary expenditures devoted to "national defense," particularly objectionable during the economic crisis, evoked among opposition groups a general reexamination of the proper relationship of the armed institution to Cuban national life.

Most immediately, opposition sectors demanded that the armed forces be restructured. The military institution, protested the ABC, had developed into a political instrument designed to underwrite "presidential imposition," perpetuating crimes against the population to defend an unpopular government. The ABC demanded the "de-militarization" of the Rural Guard, the suppression of privileges which placed the army above the law, and the adoption of obligatory military service to eliminate politics from the army.[42]

Old-line politicians also attacked the privileged position of the military. One Liberal legislator complained that the government had "enthroned" militarism on the island, protesting the misdirected priorities in which a hospital patient received fifteen cents a day while an army mule was allocated fifty cents.[43] Cosme de la Torriente, one of the most prestigious Libertadores, attacked military expenditures and expressed dismay over the use of the national armed forces against the civilian opposition factions.[44]

Hostility against the armed forces found expression in the private social lives of officers. Army commanders were reported shunned "on every possible occasion" by civilian acquaintances, and the social ostracism reached sufficient magnitude to lead some officers to contemplate retiring rather than remain with a government that had "no friends outside its own official group."[45] Several officers complained of the loss of social prestige as a result of their association with the administration; some army leaders resigned or failed to attend the meetings of various social clubs in Havana.[46]

Defense of the political order earned the armed institution the enmity of the opposition groups arrayed against the government. Reduced simply to the armed extension of a discredited administration, the military was henceforth subject to the political vagaries produced by Machado's refusal to step down. Indeed, a tactical imperative elevated the armed forces into the primary targets of the opposition. Rural Guard posts made excellent targets of antigovernment attacks, and larger military installations were frequently bombed. Senior officers became the objects of assassination; police patrols and army sentries, the front-line defense of the government, were attacked principally to acquire arms.[47]

Army duties during the last years of the *machadato*, discharged with considerable efficiency behind the defunct constitution, placed the armed forces in a privileged relationship to Cuban society. The armed institution served a government expanding military authority and privileges while combating a body politic determined to reduce army influence in national life. By 1933, the body military perforce opposed any political movement potentially harmful to the corporate integrity of the armed forces, a requirement transcending in many ways any commitment to the incumbent political authority. From then on any change in the political order vitally concerned the armed forces; the military had secured its newly augmented influence and authority under a government whose legitimacy was contested by a host of politically ambitious opposition factions during a period in which the Constitution lay in suspension most of the time. Military preeminence extended well beyond legal limitations and institutional sanctions and found legitimacy only in the *machadista* order; any threat to the constituted authorities involved inextricably the very fate of the armed institution.

The Politics of Army
Intervention, 1933

6

The Fall of Machado

Cuban instability necessarily involved the United States. As
early as 1932, the inability of Machado to restore order on the
island had prompted a reexamination of U.S. Cuban policy.[1] In
Washington, the Cuban ambassador warned the new Democratic administration in 1933 that the beleaguered Machado government required immediate support, "otherwise chaos would
result, the sort of chaos that might easily require the United
States to intervene in a military way."[2] In May 1933 the
Roosevelt administration outlined a tentative policy approach
to help relax political tensions on the island. The administration instructed the new ambassador to Cuba, Sumner Welles, to
offer the "friendly mediation" of the United Sates government.
Secretary of State Cordell Hull hoped negotiations would lead
to a "definite, detailed, and binding understanding" between
the government and leaders of the opposition.[3]

The arrival of the new ambassador in Havana had an
immediate salutary impact. The government pledged constitutional reforms, lifted censorship, and released a host of political
prisoners. By the end of June, the Cuban government and a
large portion of the opposition sectors, including the ABC, the
OCRR, the Unión Nacionalista led by Carlos Mendieta, the
marianistas headed by Miguel Mariano Gómez, women's opposition sectors represented by Hortensia Lamar, and normal-
school instructors had agreed to participate in the projected

negotiations. Several opposition factions, among them the DEU, the Communist party, and the *menocalistas*, declined to participate. The ABC split over the mediations; those who refused to join formed a dissident organization, the ABC Radical.[4]

The mediation sessions opened auspiciously on July 1, 1933. Within several days, the government released additional political prisoners; on July 6, Machado guaranteed the safety of participating factions during the course of the mediations, extending protection to a thirty-day grace period should the mediations end unsuccessfully.[5] The participating opposition groups, in turn, pledged to suspend antigovernment activity for the duration of the negotiations.

The American ambassador organized the mediations with very specific ends. Welles sought to arrive at a conciliation permitting "absolutely fair and uncontrolled" elections in the autumn of 1934, an arrangement predicated on Machado's willingness to shorten his term by one year.[6] Before leaving Washington for Havana, the ambassador expressed his desire to replace Machado before the completion of his term, or at least during the electoral period, with someone in whom all the political factions had confidence.[7] By mid-July, Welles predicted confidently that the Cuban chief executive would accept his proposal.[8]

The public disclosure of Welles's objectives in the course of the talks shattered the mediations. The negotiation recommendations, articulated by the American ambassador, immediately produced a realignment of political forces on the island. Sensitive to the political repercussions of Welles's proposal, the Cuban president quickly repudiated the propositions asking him to reduce his term, declaring that he was under no obligation to accept the proposals of a mediator lacking an official position in the negotiations. Machado attempted to demonstrate to the Cuban body politic that Welles acted as a disinterested individual, not the official representative of the United States government. Within several days, Machado's position became untenable when the Department of State announced that the American ambassador had, in fact, acted with the full approval and support of the United States government.[9]

In the days that followed, Welles worked to undermine the president's domestic position, hoping in this fashion to force

Machado to accept the mediation proposals. The American ambassador first assailed the political foundations of the *machadista* order. *Cooperativista* parties foresaw accurately the inevitable climax of a confrontation between Machado and Washington. It was incumbent upon the leaders of the Conservative, Liberal, and Popular parties, seeking to guarantee their positions and the integrity of their respective organizations in post-Machado Cuba, to be involved in the final solution. If Machado fell solely through American pressure, old-line political parties, already discredited by their long *cooperativista* collaboration, faced the prospect of drastic reorganizations at best, or complete suppression—as many opposition factions demanded. The success of a revolution against the *cooperativista* order similarly threatened the old party structure, subjecting *machadista* collaborators to the political reprisals of the new political organizations. Joining the American ambassador in support of his recommendations, however, carried implicit assurances that the parties would survive the *machadato*. In early August, Welles reported with some satisfaction that the Liberal party, "for the first time" since Machado's election, had "summoned up sufficient courage to dictate to the President" and was "not being dictated [to] by him."[10] Several days later, the leaders of the Liberal, Conservative, and Popular parties accepted the mediator's proposals, preparing to act in Congress to expedite Machado's departure.[11] The Popular party, Welles reported, endorsed the suggestion so as "to reestablish moral peace among the Cubans."[12] At the same time, the Conservative party called upon the president to retire as an "act of the highest nobility."[13]

Welles also threatened the diplomatic foundations of the *machadista* structure. Unsettled internal conditions gave him the pretext with which to forewarn the withdrawal of American support; within the context of the Permanent Treaty, Machado had simply failed to maintain a government "adequate for the protection of life, property and individual liberty." The Cuban government proved incapable of restoring stability and order.[14] In early August 1933 political discontent, fusing with economic grievances, culminated in a general strike paralyzing the island. On August 9, the ambassador concluded:

1. There is absolutely no hope of a return to normal conditions in Cuba as long as President Machado remains in office. No one other

than the small clique of office-holders surrounding him has any trust or confidence in him and he represent in his person to every other Cuban the cause of economic distress and personal suffering which has existed during the past 3 years.

2. So long as this condition continues here there is no possible chance of improving economic conditions in Cuba, and there will be immense loss to the Cuban people themselves and as a natural corollary to all the American interests doing business in or with Cuba.[15]

Welles proposed to Washington the withdrawal of American recognition if, at the end of a resonable period, Machado continued to reject the mediator's proposal; he assured the State Department that this would obviate an armed intervention, making it impossible for Machado to survive in power for more than a very short period.[16] In addition, Welles threatened Havana with punitive measures, alluding to the obligations of the United States under the Permanent Treaty and indicating that the specific purpose of his mission in Cuba was to avoid the necessity of an armed intervention.[17]

Machado seized this thinly veiled threat of intervention as the banner around which to mobilize national support for his government. President Machado would not, the Cuban ambassador in Washington informed the State Department, be "pushed out" by the United States.[18] In Havana, Machado denounced American intermeddling in Cuban internal affairs. Recalling his service to the republic during the war for independence, he announced bluntly that he preferred armed intervention rather than collaborating with the mediator's compromise of Cuban sovereignty.[19] The preservation of Cuban independence, Machado exhorted his countrymen, required the service of all patriots to defend the homeland against the North American invaders.[20] As a last resort, Havana appealed to the court of Latin American public opinion, asking the Western Hemisphere republics to condemn United States intervention in Cuba.[21]

Welles and Machado struggled against a backdrop of national tensions growing increasingly acute. The general strike continued to deepen the crisis, raising for many, including the American ambassador, the specter of a radical social and political resolution to the impasse in Havana. A clash between strikers and government forces further crystallized the political content of the workers' protest. By August 7, Havana was paralyzed.[22]

Almost two weeks after Welles had submitted his original proposal, he devised a "new solution." On August 11, he reported having had a "confidential talk" with Secretary of War General Alberto Herrera, the government representative in the mediations, in which the former army chief of staff pledged to support the ambassador's new proposition. Welles's newest project allowed the president to present a counterproposal, thereby saving face by ostensibly accepting a plan of his own making. Machado's counterproposal embodied the substance of Welles's earlier suggestion: the president was to request a leave of absence, accepting the resignation of all cabinet members except General Herrera, who thereupon became acting president.[23]

By offering General Herrera the presidency, Welles apparently deliberately invited the armed forces to impose the political settlement continuing the elude his best efforts. He no doubt realized that the former army chief's only contribution to the "new solution"—certainly a contribution of sufficient magnitude to warrant naming him president—lay entirely in the armed forces. The participation of the secretary of war, Welles predicted confidently, insured "the loyal support of the Cuban Army," which was "unanimously devoted" to Herrera.[24] Thus Arthur Krock of the *New York Times* could write several weeks later that Welles reported "before Machado himself knew it, that the army was about to desert the Cuban president."[25]

On August 12, the armed forces turned against the Cuban president. The major military installations in Havana, including Camp Columbia and La Cabaña, and the aviation corps informed Machado that they could not longer support his administration.

Direct military intervention responded in many ways to the position of apparent powerlessness—and the concomitant vulnerability of that position—in which the body military perceived itself. As the balance of power tipped against the administration, the armed forces, marginal observers of the midsummer's events, found the imminent alternate solutions unacceptable. In each instance, the fate of the military establishment rested on a political settlement that the army lacked the effective power to influence: the threat of an American intervention, the likelihood that the mediator would attempt to impose a political settlement pernicious to the armed forces, and the prospect of a social and political upheaval resulting from the general strike represented unsatisfactory solutions to the crisis produced by Machado's unwillingness to accept Welles's recommendations.

The August 12 military action, moreover, was a reaction to the apparent imminence of U.S. intervention. The armed forces shrank in horror at the spectacle of Machado's defying American military and political pressure, haranguing the population to defend the island against the anticipated intervention and appealing to Latin American public opinion to condemn Wshington. The "sole purpose" of the army movement, one military spokesman announced, "was the avoidance of American intervention."[26] An intervention to displace Machado would have inextricably involved the army, undoubtedly leading to reduction, if not the suppression, of the military institution.[27] As early as July 25, Welles informed Herrera that he had obtained the authority from President Roosevelt to land marines.[28] To have disclosed the fact of this far-reaching authority to the former chief of staff was, in effect, intimating the inevitability of an armed intervention unless the Cubans arrived at a solution consistent the the ambassador's proposals. The armed forces acted to eliminate the potential catalyst of intervention—in this instance, the Cuban president himself. Military leaders, in fact, invested the August 12 *golpe* with the noblest objectives, suggesting that army noninvolvement was tantamount to treason, for it would have permitted American troops to compromise national sovereignty.[29]

Army commitment to the constituted government was effective only as long as that administration retained a means of preserving the military institution. This necessarily meant government mastery over the process regulating political change and succession. The support that the Platt Amendment had invested in the constituted order, guaranteeing political continuity, exerted a powerful counterpoise assuring army loyalty. Within this context, the American ambassador undermined Machado's domestic position vis-à-vis the armed forces when he recommended that the president shorten his term by one year. Indeed, this announcement must be viewed as nothing less than a calculated maneuver to force Machado to accept the mediator's recommendations. Welles possessed sufficient insight into the subtleties of Cuban politics to appreciate the

repercussions that public disclosure of this proposition would
have in Havana. In June 1933 Welles the ambassador, committed to personal diplomacy in order to persuade Machado to
retire early, guarded his proposal carefully, fearing that a
premature disclosure would "weaken" the president's control
over Congress and the armed forces.[30] Frustrated by his
inability to convince Machado to step down, Welles the
mediator, by revealing the withdrawal of American support of
the president, precipitated a realignment of alliances, releasing
Machado's supporters to seek the most effective means of
protecting their interests long vested in the now faltering
machadista order.

The tenor of the mediations, in addition, had failed to inspire
the confidence of the military command in the factions competing to substitute for Machado. Opposition sectors seized the
negotiations as a forum to articulate programs designed to
reform the army. The ABC, for example, advocated reducing
the size of the military establishment, restricting army authority, and abrogating the military law of 1932.[31] Rumors during
the negotiations had a disquieting effect on army leaders. One
report circulating throughout Havana suggested that the opposition planned to reduce the army from twelve thousand to
three thousand officers and men; business and professional
groups, much agitated by the excessive taxation necessitated in
part by the large military appropriations, similarly endorsed
the reduction of the army.[32] One *machadista* official later
speculated that the armed forces would have been at the
"mercy of the triumphant revolution made by the Ambassador"
had the mediations been successful in ousting Machado.[33]

The opposition's antimilitary projects, menacing the corporate integrity of the armed forces, provoked an army intervention to prevent a political settlement potentially pernicious to
the military institution. Participation in the mediations had
conferred legitimacy on the formerly outlawed opposition
organizations, thereby virtually guaranteeing the sectors which
the army had harried in the preceding years positions of
authority and responsibility in the post-Machado political order. The armed forces had a powerful vested interest in the
course of the mediations but lacked the direct influence to
affect the outcome of the negotiations. It behooved the army
command to intersect somewhere the trajectory of the rising
power of the opposition in order to retain sufficient authority

to preserve itself. For the army to have remained distant from the mediation solution and on the fringes of national decisions would have inevitably placed it at the mercy of a subsequent government likely to be composed of former army foes. Machado himself later attributed the military defection to fear of seeing enemies of the administration triumph and thus intervening to offset the anticipated reprisals against the armed institution.[34] By participating directly in the transfer of power, the army protected its own corporate self-interest by supervising a political continuity compatible with that interest.

The army intervention of August 12 was not, in fact, unconditional. Military commanders acted only after having secured from opposition leaders assurances, to which the American ambassador subscribed, that the subsequent government would respect the integrity of the armed forces. A "strictly confidential" memorandum, couched in Machado's counterproposal, pledged that the armed forces of the republic would be maintained without any alteration until May 20, 1935, the scheduled expiration of Machado's second term. The proviso further stipulated that "members of the said armed forces . . . cannot be removed from their positions nor punished" in any way inconsistent with the existing laws.[35] The military institution, before accepting the projected political solution, had thus guaranteed in advance its own preservation in the subsequent order.

The August 12 military intervention responded also to the fear of social upheaval produced by the general strike. Welles later indicated that the "ominous signs provided by a paralyzing strike" necessitated a "radical solution" of the Cuban problem to "forestall the cataclysm which otherwise was inevitable."[36] At least one leader of the military movement preceived the August general strike as "revolutionary" in intent.[37] By the first week of August, one correspondent in Havana described the situation as "a race between mediation by the United States Ambassador and open revolution."[38] Such considerations undoubtedly motivated Welles to contact General Herrera to implement the "radical solution"; however anxious Welles may have been to depose Machado, his means remained consistently constitutional, orderly, and, above all, always under control. The strike represented a development beyond the control of the ambassador, raising the specter of an "open revolution." The military institution commanded by the generation of '95 had thus acted in an effort to preserve the Libertador order; by disposing of the civilian politicos whose continued presence in power jeopardized the old order, the army prolonged the life of Libertador politics.

On August 12, Machado duly requested his leave of absence. The dramatis personae, observing the best constitutional forms in accordance with Welles's plan, acted out the change of government. In the early hours of August 12, army leaders rejected Herrera's appointment as acting president, necessitating a modification in the plan.[39] Otherwise, the new administration assumed power uneventfully. All *machadista* cabinet members, except Herrera, resigned; the secretary of war was inaugurated provisional president and served long enough to appoint Carlos Manuel de Céspedes secretary of state. Herrera then resigned as president, permitting Céspedes to assume office. The architects of the Machado-Herrera-Céspedes turnover planned an orderly constitutional transfer of power. So smooth, in fact, was this transition, that Secretary of State Hull could later write that it was not necessary to grant the Céspedes administration "formal recognition since that government had been achieved by constitutional processes."[40]

The Céspedes Interlude

The new Céspedes government brought into sharp focus all the contradictions generated during the struggle against Machado. Participation in the mediations had legitimized the anti-Machado political associations, guaranteeing, in addition, their inclusion in the post-Machado governmental order. The decisive démarche of the *cooperativista* parties in the final days of the government, moreover, had assured their institutional integrity in the post-Machado administration. The mediations had provided the mechanism by which diverse—often ideologically and generationally irreconcilable—forces worked jointly to win political legitimacy in the ensuing national order. In the end, these very factions, largely due to their participation in the negotiations, formed the haphazard association of political groups in the Céspedes government. The new administration distributing the portfolios of government to diverse groups created an anomalous arrangement in which political groups, including the ABC, the Liberal party, the OCRR, the Unión Nacionalista, the Conservative party, University Professors, *marianistas*, and the Popular party, earlier implacable enemies, came together to constitute the new government. Whatever effectiveness and unanimity the Céspedes government might have had was sacrificed to propitiate the factions contributing to the post-Machado political settlement; the government, forced to steer a course between the visions of the ABC and the OCRR and the memories of the Liberals and Conservatives, lacked the decisiveness, cohesion, and the single-mindedness vital for national government in post-Machado Cuba.

Furthermore, the mediations had conferred on the American ambassador an authority in the new government commensurate with his contribution to the Cuban solution. Welles's powerful influence in the inner councils of the new administration sharpened the contradictions weakening the Céspedes government. Largely the product of the mediator's efforts, the new regime was overshadowed by the omnipresence of the American ambassador. Anxious to preserve embassy support, the Céspedes government—composed largely of political novices—all too willingly abdicated decision-making to the ambassador. Within a week of Machado's flight, Welles reported his extraordinary relationship to the new administration:

> My personal situation is becoming increasingly difficult. Owing to my intimate personal friendship with President Céspedes and the very close relationship which I have formed during these past months with all the members of this Cabinet I am now daily being requested for decisions on all matters affecting the Government of Cuba. These decisions range from questions of domestic policy and matters affecting the discipline of the Army to questions involving appointments in all branches of Government.[41]

Former anti-Machado opposition groups that had either boycotted the mediations or been denied participation further weakened the ability of the precariously constituted administration to govern. As early as June 1933, former President Menocal had rejected Welles's projected negotiations, pledging that he would not feel compelled to honor whatever arrangement emerged therefrom.[42] The DEU and the ABC Radical, denouncing the organic link between the *machadato* and the Céspedes government, demanded a truly revolutionary response to the island's problems. Labor organizations besieged the new administration, demanding minimum wages and maximum hours and using strikes as well as demonstrations to dramatize their grievances.

Plagued by inner contradictions and relentless opposition from without, the authority of the harried Céspedes government gradually deteriorated. By late August, many former opposition groups in exile had returned to Havana, demanding a voice in the new government. The old-line political parties labored to recover their lost prestige and authority; the new political organizations struggled to consolidate their positions and expand their influence in the government. *Machadista* officials were reported returning to high government positions, further weakening the moral authority of the Céspedes administration.[43] Meanwhile the cathartic rioting and looting produced by Machado's flight continued to keep the government in a defensive position; mob rule dispensed revolutionary justice to suspected *machadista* officials. The "inability of the Government as yet to enforce the maintenance of public order," Welles reported in mid-August, had created "an almost anarchic condition."[44] As late as August 24, he predicted "a general state of chaos" as a result of the administration's inability to restore order.[45]

National tensions found further expression in the armed forces. The military was reluctant to enforce order, afraid that applying state force against the population might revive antiarmy sentiment among the former opposition organizations. In Santiago de Cuba, for example, during mass demonstrations produced by the news of Machado's departure, army officers attempting to reverse the hostility against the military remained oblivious to disorders.[46] Army authority was further weakened by civilian retributions, particularly against junior officers, sanctioned by the weak government. Demands for the prosecution and punishment of officers suspected of crimes during the *machadato* and the general clamor for a purge of all *machadista* officers intimidated army commanders from adopting decisive action to stop disorders. An anonymous accusation of complicity in a *machadista* crime usually sufficed to order an accused officer to report to general headquarters for an investigation; upon arrival, the officer would be detained for the duration of the inquiry.[47]

The armed forces grew increasingly restive under the Céspedes government. The long-awaited general army reorganization anticipated by many junior and middle grade officers seeking promotions was delayed by procedural tangles. Hopes for promotions were further undermined when the few vacancies created by resignations were filled by officers called out of retirement.[48] Céspedes appointed retired *menocalistas*, many of whom, in fact, had resigned during Machado's first administration to key positions in the armed forces.[49]

The military policy of the new government demoralized many junior officers who saw the opportunities for promotion choked by the return of old-line commanders. Discontent spread throughout the ranks of the younger officers.[50] Officers unhappy with government policy demonstrated against the administration; young commanders held meetings, issued manifestos making their grievances public, denounced the continued presence of *machadista* officers in the army, and demanded the immediate reorganization of the armed forces.[51] Some officers requested the summary dismissal of commanders above the rank of captain accused of complicity in a *machadista* crime; in addition, lieutenants and captains asked authority to participate in the requested army reorganization. Junior commanders also attempted to expand their ranks at the expense of noncommissioned officers. Lieutenants asked Secretary of War Horacio Ferrer to annul a 1921 statute permitting sergeants with eight years of active service and twenty years in the enlisted service to fill vacancies in second lieutenancies; the petitioners requested that these positions be reserved exclusively for cadet graduates of the military academy.[52] In late August, the army staff complied and abrogated the decree that had permitted sergeants successfully completing officers' training programs to secure commissions on an equal basis with graduates of the military service institutions; henceforth, priority was assigned to cadet graduates.

Unrest in the armed forces inevitably reached noncommissioned and enlisted ranks. The demands of the junior officers, much to the dismay of the sergeants and corporals, had reduced considerably the rather fluid promotion opportunities long characteristic of the Cuban army. By late August, moreover, rumors intimating a drastic troop reduction and a cut in sergeants' pay produced widespread perturbation within the armed forces.[53] Noncommissioned officers and enlisted men, in direct imitation of their superiors, organized to protect their interests; the Enlisted Men's Club in Camp Columbia provided the arena in which sergeants and corporals aired their grievances and planned their future course of action.

Widespread disaffection with the Céspedes government produced a variety of antigovernment conspiracies. Civilian antigovernment factions, vaguely perceiving the army as the only institutional leverage capable of imposing a new political settlement, found the military establishment particularly receptive to conspiratorial intrigue. Divisions within the armed forces corresponded strikingly to civilian political alignments. Menocal proselytized among senior commanders, seeking support for an antigovernment coup.[54] Young professionals and students conspired with junior officers; radical students were in contact with the noncommissioned officers and enlisted men.[55]

Widespread civil-military conspiratorial liaisons developed out of the August 12 military intervention. The euphoria produced by the fall of Machado encouraged wide-scale fraternization. In the days and weeks following Machado's departure, one journalist reported, soldiers enjoying the gratitude of the jubilant populace often took leave without permission to deliver speeches from street corners and balconies, describing to cheering crowds exactly how the army had "won the war."[56] In Havana, the morale and discipline of troops were badly shattered when soldiers on post and patrol duty throughout the city fraternized with the population.[57] Similarly, in Santiago de Cuba officers and soldiers were mingling freely with the celebrating population.[58] Secretary of State Hull learned that members of the army, while apparently still loyal to the new government, were "drinking considerably and fraternizing with rioters."[59]

Fraternization in the days and weeks immediately after the fall of Machado contributed powerfully to the general deterioration of order and stability. The armed forces, now converted into the "idols of the populace,"[60] simply refused to jeopardize their newly won popularity and prestige by enforcing order. More important, fraternization between the armed forces and sectors of the opposition, placing officers and men in direct contact with antigovernment factions, juxtaposed military grievances with political discontent.[61]

By late August and early September, the armed forces lay demoralized, compartmentalized into three antagonistic factions. Deep divisions polarized the officers corps. Junior officers accused their superiors of complicity in the crimes and corruption of the *machadato*.[62] Remote from but affected by the officers' quarrel, the noncommissioned officers and enlisted men contemplated their course of action. By early September, the military foundations upon which the Céspedes government rested were no longer capable of sustaining the administration.

September 4, 1933: The Sergeants' Revolt

On the evening of September 3, 1933, sergeants, corporals, and enlisted men secured permission to meet in Camp Columbia to discuss their grievances—the rumored pay cuts and the reduction of promotion opportunities for the noncommissioned officers.[63] After impassioned pleas for official redress, the sergeants drew up a list of demands to be submitted to the commanding officers. Officers on duty, however, refused to accept the demands of the aroused soldiery and departed. Leaders of the noncommissioned officers' protest, organized into the Unión Militar de Columbia, which included Sergeants Fulgencio Batista, Pablo Rodríguez, Manuel López Migoya, Corporal Angel Echeverría, and enlisted men Ramón Cruz Vidal and Mario Alfonso Hernández, exhorted the troops to assume command of Camp Columbia until the General Staff met their demands. Upon securing control of Camp Columbia, the sergeant leaders dispatched delegates to solicit the support of other military installations in the capital.

Army detachments throughout Havana quickly endorsed the mutiny in Camp Columbia. Troops of the aviation corps and the First Artillery Battalion in La Cabaña detained officers present and proclaimed their solidarity with the men of Columbia. By the early hours of September 4, noncommissioned officers and enlisted men had gained control of the important military installations in Havana. Officers refused to negotiate troops' demands as long as the noncommissioned officers controlled military posts; the seditious troops refused to relinquish command of occupied army installations without a promise of negotiations.

Sergeants, corporals, and enlisted men protested unsatisfactory conditions prevailing in the armed forces, particularly the rumored pay cut and troop reduction. Rumors had grown to sufficient proportions, in fact, to warrant Secretary of War

Ferrer, on September 3, to disclaim officially all allegations of a pay cut.[64] Batista indicated on the morning of September 4 that the protest was simply a reaction against the proposed pay cuts.[65] The mutiny also protested restrictions on commission opportunities for sergeants. At the time of Machado's fall, a considerable number of sergeants awaited commissions; the abrogation of the law regulating sergeants' promotions struck at the aspirations of scores of noncommissioned officers.[66] The sergeants' protest also responded to generally poor conditions in the armed services. Noncommissioned officers agitated for better housing facilities, improved quality of food, improvement of the condition of uniforms, and permission to wear leather puttees and officer-styled kepis.[67] "The personal treatment the soldier received," Batista recalled at a later time, "was crude, to say the least, and he was inadequately housed, fed, and clothed."[68]

The noncommissioned officers' protest of September 3–4 developed into a mutiny when army officials summarily rejected troop demands. The seizure of Camp Columbia and the detention of officers present were measures designed to enhance the negotiating position of the protesting noncommissioned officers.[69] The sergeant leaders initially intended to hold the military post for several hours, during which they were confident that a satisfactory settlement would enable them to relinquish command of the installation to the officers.[70] Officers refused to take any action against the seditious troops and withdrew instead, fully confident that the mutiny could not sustain itself and expecting military justice ultimately to exact full toll for breach of discipline when the act of insubordination ended.[71] Physical control of Camp Columbia was accomplished with relative facility; limited housing on the post had made it necessary for large numbers of officers to live outside the post.[72] The rebellious troops easily overpowered the few officers on duty.

The noncommissioned officers' protest responded entirely to military issues. At its inception it lacked political substance. The sergeants did not plot the overthrow of the Céspedes government or the removal of the officers corps. Noncommissioned officers' objectives were limited to service grievances and, in fact, only the pusillanimity of the officers corps permitted a moment of insubordination to expand into a full mutiny. Batista later stated that the sergeants "began a conspiracy which had for its object more of protection to ourselves than anything else."[73] And two co-conspirators of the army protest, Manuel López Migoya and Pablo Rodríguez, later disclosed that the movement did not plan the removal of the officer corps but rather expressed simply a collective dissatisfaction within the ranks.[74]

The first civilians arriving at Camp Columbia corroborated the purely military objectives of the mutiny. One member of the DEU recalled that Batista showed the civilians present a list of demands that the noncommissioned officers and enlisted men had prepared to submit to President Céspedes.[75] Another civilian participant wrote that until the early hours of the morning, that is, until the arrival of members of the DEU, nothing had been accomplished to create a government to replace the Céspedes administration.[76]

The intervention of civilian antigovernment factions on the morning of Septmeber 4 altered the purely internecine character of the army mutiny. The involvement of the DEU invested the sergeants' mutiny with a political dimension transcending the limited objectives inherent initially in the protest.[77] Civilian revolutionary sectors, seeking to breathe an ideological life into the noncommissioned officers' movement, offered to legitimize the mutiny by converting it into a political act; by agreeing to support the political, economic, and social objectives of the DEU and other antigovernment factions present, the mutineers had engineered a political coup. The sergeants, corporals, and enlisted men had secured a civilian base of support to promote their interests. They perceived that their demands stood a better opportunity of being fulfilled under a new government, one they had assisted in creating, than under the Céspedes administration.[78]

On the morning of September 4, the new government within Camp Columbia, basing its authority on a simple categorical affirmation proclaiming national authority, displaced the Céspedes administration. The Pentarquía, as the new government became known, consisted of a five-man executive commission composed of Ramón Grau San Martín, Portifio Franca, Guillermo Portela, José Irizarri, and Sergio Carbó. From Camp Columbia, the Pentarquía moved into the Presidential Palace, a feat facilitated by the president's absence from the capital.[79]

The Pentarquía quickly consolidated the military bases of the de facto government. Havana dispatched army agents to the interior to inform provincial commands of the political and military events transpiring in the capital. Throughout the island, noncommissioned officers and enlisted men relieved their superiors of command in accord with the directives issued by the new government in Havana.[80]

In the days following the installation of the new government, the military base of the sergeants' movement broadened. Whatever hopes many junior officers entertained for promotion after Machado's departure had been quickly crushed in the early days of the Céspedes government. These junior commanders, many of them technically trained and the products of domestic military academies and foreign service institutions, had long suffered professionally. It was not uncommon for an enlisted man, commissioned second lieutenant at the same time as a graduate of the service academy, to reach the grade of major while his cadet counterpart remained a lieutenant.[81] The majority of the officers in the Cuban army had not, in fact, emerged from the island's service academies; on the contrary, an estimated 56 percent of the officers under Machado—417 out of 757—had risen through the ranks.[82] The graduates of the cadet classes of 1913, 1914, and 1915, with few exceptions, were all lieutenants on September 4, 1933; no member of the graduating class of 1912, the first class produced by the military academy, had reached the rank of major.[83]

The September 4 movement offered to junior officers the long-awaited promotion opportunity. Nearly 20 percent of the junior officer corps, some 112 lieutenants and captains, joined the sergeants' movement.[84] Many officers who remained in the army under the sergeants' leadership had earlier languished through five administrations—some fifteen to twenty years—in the grade with which they joined the revolt.[85] Many lieutenants and captains had received their last promotions during Menocal's first term in 1916. Francisco Tabernilla, for example, a first lieutenant in 1920, was still a lieutenant on Septmeber 4, 1933. When Manuel Larrubia, promoted to first lieutenant in 1919, joined the September 4 movement, he still held the rank of first lieutenant.

The sergeants' movement further revealed the social tensions and frustrations extant within the armed forces. The practice of limiting nonwhites from commissioned status, instituted during the American occupations, continued through the three decades of republican government on the island. In the final analysis, a white officer corps, tied to the island's political elite through consanguinity and position, was deposed by a largely nonwhite noncommissioned officer corps. The sergeants' mutiny precipitated a social upheaval within the armed services, shatterning the corporate racism of the military and enabling large numbers of nonwhite sergeants and corporals to secure senior grades in the army in the months that followed. The last several years of the Machado government had witnessed a large increase of black recruits,[86] providing the racial constituency to support the noncommissioned officers who had become commanders. After September 4, an increased number of Afro-Cubans moved into positions of army command. In Matanzas, for example, of eleven new officers, six were black.[87] In Santa Clara, many white troops were reported hostile "to the influx of negro officers" in command positions.[88] By the end of 1933, nonwhite enlistment had risen to an estimated 35 percent.[89] This estimate was corroborated by the American military attaché who speculated that "pure blacks" made up 30 percent of the army, with "mulattos, quadroons and octoroons" composing another 35 percent.[90] One reason Batista enjoyed widespread popularity among the enlisted men was the social mobility he early infused into the hitherto predominantly all-white officer corps.[91]

Finally the sergeants' movement shattered the association between the political-social elite and the armed services. The new officers, one observed remarked, were former cooks, harness makers, and blacksmiths.[92] Formerly the patrimony of the veterans of '95, the political oligarchs, and the upper social sectors, the officer corps after September 4 lacked roots in the traditional sources of power and influence in Cuban society. The new army commanders, *lumpenproletariat* in uniform, as Andrés Suárez has noted,[93] lacked the authority traditionally inherent in the military expression of national elites. Without roots in traditional sources of power, the new officers were compelled to join whatever group promised to guarantee the integrity of the new *septembrista* military order. The students and professors of the DEU and Pentarquía were the first to ratify the sergeants' sedition, protecting the mutineers from government reprisal by converting an act of insubordination into the midwife of the new government.

Diplomacy, Army Politics, and the Collapse of the Cuban Officer Corps

7 ## Welles and the Pentarquía

From the outset, Ambassador Welles vigorously opposed the new government, characterizing the de facto administration in terms calculated to evoke opposition and suspicion in Washington.[1] He described Commissioner Irizarri as a "radical of the extreme type" and referred to Grau and Portela as "extreme radicals." Welles conceded that Franca was a "conservative businessman of good reputation" but hastened to add that he was being used as a "window dressing."[2] The army had fallen under "ultra-radical control"[3] and the new government, Welles concluded bluntly, was "frankly communistic."[4]

For the remainder of his stay in Havana Welles sought to mobilize all the resources at his command in an effort to topple the new government. He immediately assumed leadership of the antigovernment factions on the island. With the old political parties divested of influence in government councils and army officers deprived of command, the ambassador attempted to secure the support of official American agencies to overthrow the new administration. Immediately after the Pentarquía claimed national authority, Welles summoned the dispossessed political and military factions to collaborate in plotting the restoration of the Céspedes government. On September 5, he asked Washington to land "a certain number of troops" to guard the American Embassy and protect American nationals. More to the point, Welles feared that the Cuban army officers could not restore the overthrown political order without the "aid of an American guard."[5] The ambassador apparently shared the opinion of the ousted "political leaders" that the enlisted men would submit to the authority of the officers "if they could be freed from the control of the non-commissioned officers." The only way to underwrite the resuscitated order "until a new Army could be organized under Cuban Army officers," Welles suggested, was "for the maintenance of order in Habana and Santiago de Cuba and perhaps one or two other points in the island by American Marines."[6] Several days later, he proposed his most ambitious project, recommending a "strictly limited intervention" involving the "landing of a considerable force at Habana and lesser forces in certain of the more important ports of the Republic." The ambassador hoped that the "limited intervention" would lend a "police force to the legitimate Government of Cuba for a comparatively brief period" to enable the Céspedes government to function as it had prior to its overthrow. Welles reminded his superiors in the State Department:

> It is obvious, of course, that with a great portion of the Army in mutiny it [the Céspedes government] could not maintain itself in power in any satisfactory manner unless the United States Government were willing should it so request, to lend its assistance in the maintenance of public order until the Cuban Government had been afforded the time sufficient, through utilizing the services of the loyal officers of the Cuban Army, to form a new Army for which it would possess a nucleus in the troops which are still loyal and detachments of the rural guard, most of whom have not come out in support of the present regime.[7]

American military representatives in Cuba also plotted antigovernment interventions to return Céspedes to power. Major P. A. del Valle, a U.S. Marine officer attached to the special naval squadron dispatched to Havana, contacted representatives of the deposed officers, offering American support against the de facto government. Once the Cubans reconstituted the overthrown government, however tenuously organized, a request of United States assistance to aid in maintaining order would be issued to Washington. Del Valle informed his Cuban co-conspirators that "if a responsible Cuban Government requested us to land for the purpose of assisting them to maintain order there was good reason to believe that the

United States would consent." The presence of American forces ashore, assigned to strategic positions, would provide a shield of moral support enabling the government to reconstruct itself; Céspedes was to be recognized immediately, older officers of the army retired, and Batista arrested.[8]

Officials in Washington received intervention entreaties with some dismay. The administration, which only months earlier had proclaimed the "era of good neighborliness," was loath to inaugurate its hemisphere diplomacy on the debacle of a Cuban policy. President Roosevelt immediately prohibited the landing of American armed forces to protect property alone.[9] Secretary of State Hull also shrank from intervention. "Despite the legal right we possessed," Hull later wrote, "such an act would further embitter our relations with all Latin America." An intervention in Cuba, Hull feared, would have undone "all our protestations of nonintervention and noninterference."[10]

Trained American observers on the island also counseled against precipitate action. The American military attaché reported that the Cuban army, under the influence of "over-radical elements which control the Government," could be expected "to be hostile" toward American troops.[11] One naval observer predicted that the Cubans would resist American armed intervention. "Almost the entire male population," noted the commander of a battleship assigned to the special squadron, had "some form of fire arms," a situation lending itself to resistance not of an "organized nature."[12] The commander of the Atlantic Fleet, C. S. Freeman, discovered a "growing spirit of hostility toward Americans," warning that an intervention would greatly endanger Americans on the island.[13]

Failure to obtain the projected intervention proposals compelled the American Embassy to resort to alternative agencies of political and diplomatic pressure against the de facto government. As early as September 5, Welles counseled against recognizing "any government of this character"; Secretary of State Hull, anxious to end the Cuban problem, qualified the ambassador's insistence, suggesting instead that the regime's ability "to preserve law and order" would suffice for recognition.[14] The State Department's position on recognition, in fact, ideally suited the objectives of the American ambassador, for the determination of the Cubans' ability to fulfill the minimum requisites for recognition lay almost entirely within the purview of the American Embassy in Havana. In the subsequent weeks and months, Welles consistently denied that the de facto government had met any of the attributes necessary to justify American recognition. The Cuban government, Welles early reported, had "neither popular support nor any means at its disposal with which it can maintain order";[15] a month later, he continued to insist that there was "neither protection for life nor property."[16] When political disorders occurred, Welles was quick to predict the "complete collapse of government throughout the island";[17] when quiet prevailed, the ambassador, unimpressed, reported that it was the "quiet of panic."[18]

The Pentarquía and the Army

The posture adopted by the American Embassy converted a difficult situation into virtually an impossible one for the new administration. Nonrecognition worked powerfully against the de facto government. As long as the United States denied recognition to Havana, opposition factions were inspired with the belief that they were invested with the authority to seek a solution consistent with American policy objectives on the island. Those who otherwise might have supported the administration demurred, fearing future reprisals; those who disapproved of the government were animated into active conspiracy and armed resistance. Nonrecognition, in addition, crippled the government economically. The diplomatic rupture undermined commercial relations between Cuba and the United States, depriving Havana of badly needed customs duties and revenue. Tax collection suffered precisely because the de facto quality of the government raised the possibility that another administration at some later date, would attempt to collect the same revenue.[19]

The armed forces posed the most critical problem for the Pentarquía. The mutiny had separated officers from their commands, producing a deterioration of morale and discipline. The dispossessed commanders, moreover, served as the axis of conspiracy and antigovernment intrigue. Throughout early September, the government labored to reintegrate the armed forces. The return of the officers promised to reinvest the military with the technical and professional skills necessary to preserve the armed institution. Moreover, the officers' resumption of command would implicitly relieve the noncommissioned personnel and enlisted men of the odium of mutiny while strengthening the government internally and abroad, validating the September 4 movement in much the same fashion as the officers' participation on August 12 had lent support to the Céspedes government.

On September 7, the Pentarquía summoned an officers' delegation to the Presidential Palace to meet with Commissioner of War Sergio Carbó and Sergeant Batista. The government pleaded for the reintegration of the armed institution, inviting the officers to form a military junta of five officers and Sergeant Batista to supervise a full-scale reorganization of the armed forces. The officers' representatives, after consulting with their colleagues, rejected the government's proposition, refusing to recognize in any fashion the legitimacy of the sergeants' mutiny.[20]

The unwillingness of the officers to rejoin the armed forces, not an unintentional by-product of the policy pursued by the American Embassy in Havana and sustained by the State Department in Washington, was entirely consistent with Welles's objectives. As long as the officers withheld endorsement of the government, the Pentarquía was forced to function weaker morally and politically, both within the island and outside it. Against the background of nonrecognition and the threat of American intervention, the officers, for their part, failed to formulate a policy independent of the objectives of the American Embassy. Opposition to the Pentarquía may or may not have been in the best interests of the officer corps; by adopting Welles's ultimate objectives as their own, however, the army leaders committed themselves to nothing less than the overthrow of the de facto government, the realization of which, powerless to accomplish it on their own, they delegated the American ambassador.

Throughout September, the separated officers plotted their course of action entirely within the diplomatic construct outlined by the American Embassy. Placing their hopes on the ultimate success of Welles's policy maneuvers, and at all times organizing their plans to conform to the needs of the embassy, officers kept appraised at all times of the policy Washington planned to pursue. As early as September 11, former Secretary of War Horacio Ferrer conferred with Welles, learning that the de facto government would "continue unrecognized by the United States."[21] Nonrecognition exerted a powerful restraining influence on the officers, encouraging army leaders to remain away from their commands in the belief that the new government could not survive for long deprived of United States diplomatic support. On September 9, Welles reported that the officers had entered into a "definite compact" not to support any administration except the "legitimate government."[22] Several days later, Ferrer pledged that the officers would never serve under any chief executive not recognized in Washington.[23] Some officers, in fact, were ready to pledge allegiance to any government recognized by the United States.[24] As long as Washington refused to confer on the de facto administration the endorsement inherent in recognition, army commanders would refuse to rejoin the armed institution. Had the United States accepted the regime and allowed it to constitute itself into a de jure government, it would have been highly unlikely for the officers to prolong their boycott. Such a turn of events, in fact, would have made their position untenable, paradoxically casting them in a state of mutiny against the duly constituted and recognized authority. As long as the administration remained unrecognized, and hence censured, however, the officers could claim to uphold the legitimate authority invested earlier in the overthrown Céspedes government.

Planned intervention projects to restore the former regime to power further encouraged the officers to remain away from their commands. In early September, hours after the sergeants' mutiny, intervention seemed imminent.[25] An estimated one thousand marines were mobilized in Quantico, Virginia, and prepared for deployment to Cuba;[26] the Atlantic Fleet, a flotilla of some thirty warships, formed a cordon around the island.[27] The intervention projects proposed by official American representatives in Cuba contributed to creating a general belief that the United States would intervene to restore the status quo. Under these circumstances, the deposed army officers chose to await expectantly the arrival of American armed forces to return their dignity and commands.[28] One officer later recalled that Welles had dissuaded the commissioned personnel "from returning to their commands, which would have strengthened the position of the student government and might have tipped the scales in their favor both with the Cuban public and the American government." The American military attaché likewise advised the officers "under no circumstances to return to their commands, stating that the American government would never tolerate a revolt of the enlisted men, such as had taken place, nor a change of government by them, and that American intervention was undoubtedly the next step."[29]

A week after the mutiny the ousted army commanders retired to the Hotel Nacional to plot their course of action. The hotel selected by the officers enhanced their position, for it happened to serve as the temporary residence of the American ambassador and the refuge of the American colony.[30] The ousted officers apparently chose the Hotel Nacional in the knowledge that the building had been selected to shelter American nationals, confident that if it were attacked, American military forces would disembark.[31]

The urgent need to restore stability and discipline to the officerless army compelled Commissioner Carbó, on September 8, to promote Sergeant Batista to colonel, appointing the former sergeant-stenographer chief of the army and charging him to commission the officers required to maintain the stability of the armed institution. Carbó's unilateral action produced government dissension and, ultimately, the dissolution of the Pentarquía.[32] In the act of disbanding, however, the commissioners created an executive government headed by Ramón Grau San Martín.

Throughout the first weeks of the new government, Grau worked to reintegrate the armed forces. By mid-September, the Hotel Nacional had emerged as a major center of antigovernment activity; some four hundred officers were in a continuous state of conspiracy with civilian antigovernment factions, plotting the overthrow of the administration and inspiring continued resistance throughout the island. One plot, for example, planned to smuggle the former president into the hotel, proclaiming the overthrown administration reconstituted and asking for recognition as the legitimate authority on the island.[33]

By late September, the government had abandoned all hopes of a settlement with the officers. After weeks of fruitless negotiations, it declared the officers deserters. American citizens were evacuated and government forces threw an armed cordon around the hotel, prohibiting traffic across the established military lines. After several days of tense quiescence, the long-expected hostilities erupted on October 2. The officers, isolated for weeks, poorly armed, and lacking sufficient ammunition, capitulated in the first days of the conflagration.[34]

In general, the victory over the officers strengthened the position of the new government. More specifically, the military triumph immeasurably enhanced the authority and influence of the new army chief. The elimination of the deposed officer corps as a military consideration, moreover, permitted the new army command to fashion, virtually *in toto,* a new body of officers. By the end of 1933, some 363 sergeants, 26 corporals, 32 privates, 28 warrant officers, and 63 civilians had received commissions in the Cuban army.[35]

The sergeants' revolt did not topple the Cuban officer corps. Rather it produced a government to which the officers refused to pledge allegiance. Reliance upon assistance from the United States to overthrow that government and the subsequent failure of the American intervention to materialize left the officers without viable options of their own. The failure of nonrecognition to topple the government left the officers congregated in the Hotel Nacional declared deserters, at the mercy of a government they pledged never to support.

The Diplomatic Imperative and
the Rise of Fulgencio Batista

8 The civilian political opposition to the administration, sustained by continued nonrecognition, continued throughout the fall of 1933 to withhold support from the Grau government. The new political organizations emerging from the anti-Machado struggle, including the ABC and the OCRR, and the old-line political associations, such as the Liberal and Conservative parties, and prominent Libertador politicians, including Mario Menocal and Carlos Mendieta, actively opposed the provisional government. *Grauísta* social and economic legislation, including minimum wages for cane cutters, compulsory labor arbitration, an eight-hour day, a 45 percent reduction of utility rates, and workers' compensation drove economic sectors on the island into antigovernment alliances with the political opposition. Domestically, commercial and financial interests were reported "unanimously opposed to the regime."[1] Powerful foreign business groups, in addition, plotted the overthrow of the de facto government abroad. The Continental Bank and Trust of New York sought to learn from Charles W. Taussig, a member of President Roosevelt's "Brain Trust," the administration's attitude toward the lending of five hundred thousand dollars to the ABC to finance antigovernment activity. Taussig reported with some distress that this was only one of many projects being developed in the United States in which our bankers are to finance the over-throw of the Grau Government."[2]

The ousted civilian political organizations also opposed the
94 new *septembrista* military order. The ABC, for example, ran

relief missions through army lines around the Hotel Nacional to aid the beleaguered officers. The upper classes looked upon the new officer corps with contempt and disdain, lending moral and financial assistance to opposition groups. Members of the Rotary Club of Havana and the Yacht Club actively participatedin antigovernment conspiracies.[3]

Throughout the fall of 1933, the government's shrinking political base created a crisis in civil authority. A political crisis increasingly evolved into an army problem, transforming the political situation into a military concern. As long as civilian political factions continued to withhold their support, and indeed, conspired against the administration, the government grew increasingly dependent on the armed forces; the almost unanimous refusal of the political opposition to endorse the regime, refusing to confer on the government civil properties, opened a breach in national administration between the civilian politicos and the army leaders. The moment civilian factions refused to support the administration voluntarily, the stability of the government became a military concern; throughout the island, the balance of power passed on to the body military. In Matanzas, one official reported that the army stood "between the present situation and chaos."[4] The armed forces, Commander C. S. Freeman reported, appeared "very anxious to do all within their power to contribute toward the establishment of a stable government."[5] As early as September 21, Welles reported that Batista's influence was "very powerful";[6] several weeks later, the American military attaché concurred, suggesting that the army chief was the power behind the government.[7] By the end of October Batista was considered the "strongest factor in the government."[8]

The inability of the government to develop a civilian counterpoise tipped the scales of power in favor of the military institution. By early October, this changing civil-military relationship offered the American ambassador the opportunity to consummate the antigovernment policy adopted on the morning of September 4. Welles very early discerned the contradictions inherent in the provisional government, differentiating between the military and the civilian loci of power in Havana. On October 5, Secretary of State Hull informed Welles that Roosevelt was satisfied that the capture of the officers had consolidated the government sufficiently to justify recognition.[9] The ambassador, attempting to dissuade Washington from undermining his policy in Cuba through recognition, quickly sought to "make it very plain" that the surrender of the officers did not "indicate consolidation of the position of the government but solely a decidedly increased prestige for the Army as distinguished from the government." Admitting the "difficulty of realizing that such a distinction can exist in view of the apparent identification of the Army with the Grau San Martín government," Welles reminded Washington that the army mutiny did "not take place in order to place Grau San Martín in power." The "divergence between the Army and civilian elements in the government," Welles reported, "is fast becoming daily more marked." He noted in conclusion that as Batista's influence grew, "the power of the students and Grau San Martín diminishes."[10]

Welles discerned in the precarious civil-military foundation of the de facto government a means of ending the *grauísta* experiment. Each locus of power had particular interests to protect and promote. The interdependence between the armed forces and the civilian factions constituting the government was the result of a politico-military expedience necessitated by the peculiar origins of the regime and the *septembrista* commanders. The armed forces supported the Grau government because the administration had extended legitimacy to the mutiny and had validated some four hundred new commissions. Only another source of power, capable of constituting itself into a viable government and willing to underwrite the *septembrista* military order, or evidence that the Grau administration no longer seemed able or willing to sustain the pretensions of the former noncommissioned officers, could persuade Batista to abandon the government which had originally infused political life into a military sedition. Throughout the late fall of 1933, the American ambassador labored to put together a counterbase of authority, attempting to provide an alternate source of power outside the Grau government to give the army chief the option of deserting the provisional administration.

Using nonrecognition to prolong the political, diplomatic, and economic isolation of Havana, Welles cultivated the military leadership within the government, appealing directly to the army leaders to impose a political solution consistent with the visions of the American Embassy. On October 4, days after the *batistiano* army had defeated the officers, Welles reported having had a "protracted and very frank discussion" with the

Cuban chief of staff. Welles had informed Batista that as chief of the army he was the "only individual in Cuba... who represented authority." Batista's actions in the preceding weeks had won the army leader the support of "the very great majority of the commercial and financial interests in Cuba who are looking for protection and who could only find such protection" in the army chief. In addition, Batista's earlier refusal to permit students to control the nation's newspapers had won him the support of the press. Political factions which had only weeks earlier scorned the new army chieftain were now "in accord that his control of the Army as Chief of Staff should be continued as the only possible solution and were willing to support him in that capacity." Welles had reminded Batista that the regime, lacking popular support, had failed to implement one constructive measure during its first four weeks in office. The only obstacle to an equitable arrangement and presumably recognition, the ambassador suggested, "was the unpatriotic and futile obstinacy of a small group of young men who should be studying in the university instead of playing politics and of a few individuals who had joined with them for selfish motives." In a thinly veiled warning, Welles had reminded Batista of his peculiar position vis-à-vis the government; "should the present government go down in disaster," Welles indicated, "that disaster would necessarily inextricably involve not only himself but the safety of the Republic, which he had publicly pledged himself to maintain."[11]

Three days later, Batista again met with the ambassador, noting that he was "deeply impressed by the fact that delegates of all the important business and financial groups in Cuba" had visited him "to insist upon the creation of a government in which the public could have confidence." The army chief now realized "fully" that the Grau government "was a complete failure and that a concentration government in which the political groups and the commercial interests of the country could have confidence was an absolute necessity." Batista had also come to appreciate the necessity of United States recognition "before any improvement in conditions" on the island could be expected.[12]

Welles's early conversations with the army chief could not have been interpreted by Batista in any other fashion than an invitation to create a "concentration government." The American Embassy had put together a loose coalition consisting of the new political factions coming out of the *machadato*, old-line parties, business and financial sectors, the press, and tacit American diplomatic support, creating an alternative base of power to which Batista could turn.

Batista's conversations with Welles suggested the uncertainty of the army chief's position. Nonrecognition, continuing to encourage opposition and inspire antigovernment agitation and conspiracy, kept alive the likelihood of an ultimately successful antigovernment plot that would be capable of nullifying the *septembrista* army order and deposing the newly commissioned officers. The specter of intervention, moreover, had not entirely passed, further raising the possibility of an American intervention to restore the former officers to their commands. Batista's authority in the armed forces continued to suffer from his association with a government apparently diplomatically insolvent abroad and politically bankrupt at home; indeed, his position grew increasingly tenuous in direct proportion to the inability of the Grau administration to aggregate support.

Batista's command of the armed forces was also challenged from within. The authority of the army chief rested almost exclusively on the sanction of a de facto government lacking national acceptance. Batista was simply one of four hundred noncommissioned officers promoted in the wake of the mutiny whose rank and appointment depended on a political settlement in Havana compatible with—or at least not hostile to—the new army command. As long as the *septembrista* officer corps remained identified with a government lacking a national mandate and the de jure credentials with which to underwrite effectively the fruits of September 4, the new army commanders, as Welles reminded Batista, risked sharing the ultimate fate of a regime opposed at home and abroad. Batista's own position, in short, depended on his ability to legitimize the commissions granted in 1933 through a political settlement satisfactory to organized political and economic groups and Washington. Many army commanders agitated for a stabilization of the national political order, seeking an administration capable of institutionalizing the new officer corps. By early December, a very strong movement within the armed forces had developed among influential army leaders to replace Grau with a government made up of all political factions under Carlos Mendieta.[13] As long as the Grau government lacked the ability to validate the new commissions in any sort of permanent fashion, the integrity of the *septembrista* officer corps remained susceptible to the vagaries of political intrigue against the administration.

Welles's invitation to Batista to create a new government, preparing in advance its political, economic, and diplomatic bases, provided the army chief with the opportunity to at once disassociate himself from the Grau government and ratify his military position by being party to the new settlement. In early December, Welles reported that Batista was "actively seeking a change in government" owing to the apprehension of a movement within the army directed against himself, the constant and "inevitable" attempts at revolution, and fear of an American armed intervention.[14]

The antigovernment activity of the American ambassador continued until mid-December when, having been declared *persona non grata* by Havana, he was replaced by Jefferson Caffery. The preposterous anomaly of appointing a successor to Welles in a country with which the United States had severed diplomatic relations went virtually unnoticed. The new American envoy continued his predecessor's policy, sharing Welles's conviction of the "inefficiency, ineptitude and unpopularity with all the better classes in the country of the de facto government." Unless Grau relinquished power voluntarily, Caffery predicted, a change of government could be produced only by the "armed intervention of the United States" or a "break in the army which is standing strongly behind the government."[15]

Caffery concentrated his efforts on securing the "break in the army." In mid-January Batista asked Caffery directly what the United States "wanted done for recognition." Reiterating Washington's determination to withhold recognition, Caffery repeated to the army chief the invitation to form a new government.[16] After some days of consultation with the American representative and various political factions on the island, Batista agreed to support Carlos Mendieta in forming a government of "national concentration." On January 15, 1934, Batista informed Grau that the armed forces could no longer support his government; after several days of confusion, on January 18, Carlos Mendieta assumed the presidency. Five days later, the United States recognized the new government. Invested with the legitimizing quality implicit in American recognition and the support of the anti-*grauísta* factions, the new administration of "national concentration" ratified the appointments, commissions, and promotions in the army organization produced by the *septembrista* revolt. On February 4, 1934, Decree Number 408 annulled the Military Reorganization Act of 1926, formally dissolving the old National Army and proclaiming in its place the newly organized Constitutional Army. The new army, the government declared, would consist of all officers, noncommissioned officers, and enlisted men on active duty at the time the decree was promulgated.[17]

Consolidation of Army Hegemony, 1934–1940

The Politics of *Septembrismo*

9

The new government of "national concentration" provided the necessary politico-diplomatic legitimacy to validate the *septembrista* order. Supported diplomatically abroad and accepted politically at home, the Mendieta administration accepted—and ratified—the expansion of military authority. Itself a product of a "break in the army," the new government returned to the Presidential Palace weak civilian factions without popular mandate or national legitimacy. Political institutions lay prostrate. The last ostensibly free election had been held in 1925. Since then, *cooperativismo* had undermined existing parties while new competing organizations, outlawed and driven underground, had not yet secured a national constituency upon which to develop political power. In this atrophied political order, the accession to power of civilian factions in post-Machado Cuba often lacked any relationship to national strength. The distribution of portfolios of government simply acknowledged that a handful of men had participated in the struggle against the previous regime. The splinter organizations composing the Mendieta government, including the ABC, *menocalistas, marianistas,* and Mendieta's own *Unión Nacionalista,* failed to confer on the authorities in Havana a political base resting on a national consensus.

In addition, the political factions making up the Mendieta government did not possess the institutional fulcrum upon which to balance growing army authority. As long as stability continued to elude administration leaders and defy a political settlement, the government continued to entrust its fate to the ability of the armed forces to suppress disorders. As stability developed increasingly into a military problem, the breach between the estranged civilian and military representatives of the state widened. Colonel Batista assumed greater responsibility for order and stability, appropriating in the process national influence commensurate with the extent to which civil leaders relied on the armed forces. Those who clamored for order, seeing little value in civilian administration, addressed themselves to the army command. Effective power came to reside in the military establishment. The Cuban government, the American Embassy reported, had a "supine attitude" toward growing agitation, encouraging "terrorist elements" to become more audacious in their acts. "The military authorities," Caffery wrote, "deprecate the attitude of the Government, as they very well realize that the whole onus of putting down an outbreak would fall on them."[1]

The army chief won support for the armed forces among commercial, financial, and diplomatic sectors. Solicitous of the needs of foreign economic interests, army leaders between 1934 and 1935 dedicated a large number of armed troops to the suppression of radical activity, political disorders, and labor agitation. Batista, as one official observer reported, had "done more than anyone else to correct the drift toward radicalism which was so unfair and distressing, not only to foreigners, but also to Cuban business interests."[2] The military's suppression of radical activity was perceived as the most encouraging development in Cuban politics.[3] American consular districts throughout the island reported with considerable satisfaction that there was complete cooperation from local army commands. "The military," wrote the American vice consul in Matanzas, "continues to be most solicitous of the needs of the Consulate and any help or cooperation they can give is always extended graciously and efficiently."[4] By mid-1934, the American ambassador had concluded that Batista was the "one real force" on the island "standing between a reasonable respect for property rights and chaos."[5]

Batista applied army strength specifically against labor agitation. In instances where military coercion, violence, and arrests failed to persuade strikers to return to work, the army leadership approved the employment of soldiers as strikebreakers. When utility and transportation workers called a strike in Santiago de Cuba, the armed forces maintained normal services; a strike of government employees in 1934 found soldiers discharging civilian administrative responsibilities. In addition, the armed institution developed an effective antistrike device in a newly created military reserve. The government compelled all public employees to enlist in the reserve, thereby subjecting potential strikers to direct military authority upon the declaration of martial law.[6]

Large private-sector employers hastened to take advantage of the new military reserve. In Santiago de Cuba, the Compañía de Electricidad recruited most of its male employees from the ranks of the reserve.[7] Similarly, in Cárdenas, the district commander "enlisted" all the employees of the local branch of the Compañía de Electricidad into the military reserve.[8]

The armed forces continued to lend maximum protection to sugar production. During the *zafra* of 1935, one thousand troops from Havana served in the eastern provinces on garrison duty.[9] Havana dispatched an infantry company from Santiago de Cuba into the interior to protect United Fruit Company properties; in Camgüey an artillery company served the same purpose. At the request of provincial military authorities, landowners prepared lists of local agitators and radical leaders, permitting army officials to arrest key political activists before the onset of the harvest.[10] In the end, the government suspended constitutional guarantees for the duration of the harvest throughout the island.[11] The 1935 *zafra*, one observer reported, was "the quietest in many years."[12]

The continuing expansion of army authority expressed itself as well on provincial and municipal levels. Havana's past use of military superviosrs had effectively undermined civil authority at a local level. More specifically, the wide range of political uses to which Machado had applied the armed forces in the effort to bolster his faltering regime had pre-empted provincial and municipal civilian authority. Positions filled normally through electoral mandates passed under the jurisdiction of army officers appointed by Havana. The sudden fall of Machado compounded the crisis of regional civilian authority. The hasty flight of civilian *machadista* officeholders in the interior, the murder by mobs of some, and the arrest of still others created a vacuum in local government filled by army officials appointed by Havana pending political reorganization and elections. Immediately after the fall of Machado, the armed forces assumed charge in many districts of supervising municipal and provincial administration. In Matanzas regional army commanders served as acting governor and *alcalde* of the province and its capital;[13] in Antilla the local Rural Guard lieutenant assumed control of the municipality.[14] Throughout the island, local and provincial government passed under the auspices of army officials awaiting directives from Havana before relinquishing authority to civilian representatives.

In relieving their superiors of command, the sergeants at once ousted the leaders of the army and displaced the officials charged with administrative responsibilities at various levels of municipal and provincial government. Since military and civil authority was assumed conjointly, one became the natural extension of the other. Together with the need to protect the military gains of the revolt of September 4, the new officers acquired a vested interest in political, bureaucratic, and administrative affairs.

In 1933, the Cuban army ceased to function in behalf of existing political organizations. It acquired purposes of its own. Whereas earlier the army intervened electorally to promote the interests of political parties, after 1933 it supervised national activites to prevent political changes that might prove harmful to its interests.

After 1933, the political system reorganized around the armed forces. Old *machadista* officeholders, in search of political affiliation after the collapse of the *cooperativista* parties, found in the new army the support necessary to continue in government. The new military command legitimized the credentials of otherwise discredited *machadista* representatives and guaranteed their return to public office. As political creations of *septembrismo,* and without alternate sources of support, these officials served as the most active collaborators of the army command. Between 1934 and 1940, almost two hundred *machadista* officials assumed elected positions at national, provincial, and municipal levels of government.[15] At the same time, representatives of the new post-Machado political organizations, not yet able to mount a successful civil campaign for public office, turned to regional military leaders for assistance. Stepping into the breach between the old and the new, the military served as the effective power broker on the island.

The provincial commands formed the underpinnings of the *septembrista* order. The military command of Oriente Province, typically, under Lieutenant Colonel Diego Rodríguez, supervised virtually every aspect of provincial affairs. Civil administration served as the means through which to gird the regional military order and conformed at all times to the needs and vagaries of army politics. The military command exercised complete jurisdiction over civil appointments at every level.[16] Politics became an extension of military will, the civilian facade behind which army leaders articulated and defended their interests. "The local commanders," one observer reported, "have absorbed or dominate the judiciary, executive and legislative branches. Mill owners, business, commercial and professional men, realizing this situation, render obeisance to their local commaners, whether he is a Lieutenant Colonel, Sergeant or Corporal."[17] In 1935, Lieutenant Colonel Rodríguez, judging a number of civilians "not the type of citizens that the Army wanted to represent the Government ticket," summoned a number of alternates to his headquarters to offer them the positions on the government slate.[18] "In the event the attitude of any national candidate indicates a threat to the future of the present army organization," the American consulate noted, "there will certainly exist a very potent motive to influence the army against him at the polls."[19] Assessing the impact of the armed forces in Oriente, the American consul in Santiago de Cuba reported:

> The army's strength has grown to such proportions that not only are the civilian law enforcement officers supervised by army officers, but provincial and municipal officers of all grades are said to hold their appointments indirectly through the Lieutenant Colonel in command of the military in Oriente Province. The Military Commander is, in reality, Governor, Mayor and Police Chief of Santiago. The army's tentacles have grown until they reach out to the control of insignificant municipal jobs, such as the appointment of street sweepers and other jobs of similar category. These appointments are said to be distributed to close relations and friends of officers and soldiers. There are many of this class of employees in the Municipal Government of Santiago. Slowly but effectively the Military are replacing the mayors of many municipalities in this Province. Small villages are assigned to the commander of Sergeants and larger places to Lieutenants carrying the title of Supervisor of Police. Military Mayors are Captains and First Lieutenants.[20]

Many new officers used recently acquired military authority and political influence to pursue personal interests. Corruption pervaded the armed forces. That the army retained a remarkable cohesion and loyalty to Batista during the 1930s was in no small measure the result of the army chief's tacit endorsement of his officers' private activities. Corruption worked powerfully to co-opt potentially dissident commanders. From the senior army command to the distant Rural Guard outpost, the former sergeants used their new positions to acquire personal wealth. Colonel José Pedraza, the inspector general of the army and chief of the national police, deposited the fifty thousand dollars he secured monthly from the numbers rackets into his swelling bank account; Major Jaime Mariné, the chief adjutant to Colonel Batista, introduced into Cuba's gambling casinos some twenty-five hundred slot machines.[21] At the provincial level, army leaders pursued similar if slightly more modest enterprises. In Oriente, Colonel Rodríguez persuaded mill owners to donate to the provincial command some thirty-five thousand dollars.[22] At the remote Rural Guard stations, local army commanders terrorized the surrounding populace, confiscating merchandise, livestock, and produce. Control of the army, the military attaché concluded, "is similar to that practiced by American gang-leaders; that as long as the Chief of Staff can obtain certain emoluments, financial, political and military, for his Lieutenant Colonels, and guarantee their immunity to punishment, he can command their loyalty and obedience as a body."[23]

During the mid-1930s, military authority on the national level advanced irregularly, more in response to opportunity than a consequence of policy. In one instance, a general strike in March 1935 accelerated centralization of national authority under the armed forces. Initially a student movement objecting to educational conditions, the project acquired antigovernment dimensions when endorsed by political factions, including the Auténticos, and national labor organizations. In the end, the demonstrators directed the strike specifically against the *batistiano* hegemony on the island.[24] The strike affected virtually every level of national activity. Striking telephone employees, truck and bus drivers, stevedores, hospital workers, and ice and milk deliverymen paralyzed Havana. In the interior, work stoppages on mills crippled the sugar industry. Transportation strikes isolated the three eastern provinces. By mid-March, some two hundred thousand workers had joined the movement.

Administration leaders again surrendered the fate of the government to the armed forces. On March 11, the administration declared martial law, delegating to military leaders the responsibility of maintaining order and stability. Military supervisors quickly appropriated provincial and municipal authority throughout the island. Soldiers operated stricken services, including transportation and utilities.[25] In the interior, the military coerced strikers back to work. Courts-martial were in perpetual session. Of far-reaching impact, the armed forces purged all striking civil servants, bringing civil service under army control. The military measures applied against the general strike converted the armed forces into dispensers of appointive government positions; patronage hitherto reserved for national political organizations was pre-empted by the armed forces. One resident journalist in Havana reported that "military authorities wrested power from nearly every branch of the government" during and after the general strike.[26]

During the crisis of March 1935 the armed forces further raised their prestige as agents of stability. Little credit for the suppression of the strike, Ambassador Caffery suggested, "can justifiably be claimed by the civilian authorities, whose procrastination during several preceding weeks permitted the movement to gain such dangerous momentum"; conversely, "the prestige of the army in general, and of Colonel Batista in particular," the ambassador concluded, "had emerged on a new high level."[27]

The political repercussions of the general strike weakened further the civilian underpinnings of the Mendieta government. By March 1935 the coalition making up the government of "national concentration" had collapsed, when the the ABC, *menocalistas,* and the Acción Republicana withdrew. Political defections left Mendieta to govern on the precarious base provided by his own feeble political party, the Unión Nacionalista. And even this caricature of a political organization was substantially weakened when, during the strike, nine members of the cabinet resigned in protest against army excesses. In late 1935, Mendieta himself resigned, appointing José Barnet as provisional president to supervise national elections in 1936.

The Civil-Military Crisis of 1936:
The Triumph of Army Preeminence

In the presidential election of 1936, the first in eleven years, Miguel Mariano Gómez won national office. Representing a tripartite coalition formed by the Acción Republicana, the Unión Nacionalista, and the Liberal party, Gómez became the first chief executive since Machado not to owe becoming president to direct military intervention.[28]

Almost immediately, Gómez clashed with the army chief of staff. He assumed office prepared to exercise presidential power as defined by the Constitution and determined to recover for the office the authority surrendered by past presidents. This necessarily involved constitutional authority over the armed forces. Within weeks of his inauguration, Gómez criticized the size of military expenditures approved by his predecessor.[29] In addition, he reorganized the command of the armed forces by appointing his two brothers-in-law, Comandante Manuel Espinoso and Colonel Julio Morales de Coello, chief of the army and navy, respectively.[30] As leader of civilian parties long deprived of political patronage, Gómez dismissed some three thousand civil servants, the large majority of whom were military reservists, to provide positions for party functionaries. Batista reabsorbed the dismissed personnel into the military bureaucracy, but not before he hastened to express publicly his vigorous disapproval of the president's action.[31]

Strained civil-military relations erupted in late 1936 when the Presidential Palace vetoed legislation supported by Colonel Batista. In the closing months of the Barnet administration, government authorities had approved a Batista project designed to extend an education network to the rural population under the aegis of the armed forces. To finance the education experiment, the army command proposed adding a nine-cent tax on each bag of sugar produced. The new president opposed the sugar-surcharge bill, arguing that such jurisdiction as the army sought was properly invested in the Ministry of Education, not the Department of War. The issue in the end transcended the legislation in question and developed into a test between civil and military authority. Unable to mobilize sufficient political strength to stop the bill in the legislature, Gómez applied his last option, returning the bill to Congress with an executive veto.

Batista reacted immediately to the president's opposition. The army command's initial impulse centered on a direct military intervention to oust the noncompliant Gómez government. Preliminary to military action, however, Batista approached the American Embassy seeking to learn Washington's disposition toward an army seizure of power.[32] The ambassador discouraged army plans and reported having "personally strongly counselled and even warned the military authorities against violence." Instead, Caffery secured assurances from Batista that all contemplated actions were "certain to be legal and constitutional."[33]

Within the "legal and constitutional" framework insisted upon by the American Embassy, the chief of staff mounted his assault on the Presidential Palace by persuading civilian legislative leaders to inaugurate impeachment proceedings against Gómez. The Congress to which Batista directed his request consisted largely of officials elected under the auspices of regional military authorities if not, in fact, chosen directly by army commanders. Indeed, half the Cuban Senate in 1936 consisted of former *machadista* legislators. In addition, military authorities harassed and intimidated lawmakers known to be hostile to the impeachment design. "Certain forms of intimidation," Caffery acknowledged, were "being employed in certain cases."[34] Moreover, widely circulated rumors of a military coup, raising the specter of a suspension of constitutional guarantees and the dissolution of Congress, forced those unwilling to censure the president to reconsider and choose between a limp parliamentary stystem or none at all.[35]

Army authorities also mobilized popular support for impeachment proceedings. The army command in Havana ordered interior regiments to organize mass demonstrations against the president and for impeachment. In Matanzas, the provincial command persuaded local businesses to proclaim public support for Gómez's removal.[36] Elsewhere in the interior, local political leaders, anticipating the change of government, abandoned the doomed president and rallied around the impeachment cause.

Without an effective counterpoise to thwart the military-directed legislative coup, Gómez appealed to Washington for support. In mid-December, the secretary of agriculture, a close personal friend of President Gómez, solicited from the American Embassy a public statement pledging American support for

Gómez "no matter what happened."[37] Several days later, another cabinet official appealed to Caffery for American "moral intervention" in the civil-military struggle on the island.[38] In Washington, the Cuban ambassador petitioned the White House for assistance, suggesting to Roosevelt that the outcome of the dispute would determine the future of the island for years thereafter.[39] Roosevelt responded positively, if without enthusiasm, instructing the embassy in Havana "to point out to the appropriate persons" that Gómez's veto was consistent with the authority exercised by presidents in other democracies. Beyond this statement, however, Washington disclaimed any "intention of intervening, either morally or otherwise in the Cuban crisis."[40]

In its ambiguity, Washington's instructions allowed the embassy considerable latitude to negotiate the political crisis. Caffery responded cautiously. In mid-December, the ambassador reported that he had "taken the liberty of pointing out" the substance of President Roosevelt's message, "but that the opposition to President Gómez had given little heed to observation."[41] "Pointing out" and submitting an "observation" hardly represented convincing testimony that the ambassador, who earlier had "strongly counselled" and "warned" Batista against direct military action, received Washington's advice with any enthusiasm. In fact, Caffery possessed sufficient insight into power relations on the island to dismiss summarily the lofty principles articulated in Washington about presidents in democracies. Once the issues had been stated, the civil-military conflict was reduced to a personal power struggle between Gómez and Batista. Defiance of military counsel had earned the Cuban president the enmity of the army leaders, producing considerable pressure within the armed forces on Batista to depose the chief executive. As early as December 19, Caffery reported that many officers were "almost hysterical" in their opposition to Gómez.[42] Batista informed Caffery that owing to the intense agitation and feeling generated by the controversy, his own position would be endangered if he were defeated in the struggle.[43] "Feeling in the Army against the President runs so high," reported the American military attaché, "that they want Batista to immediately remove him."[44]

The very alleged precariousness of the army chief's position compelled the embassy to support the army in the controversy. Since 1933, Caffery had found Batista mindful of American policy needs and interests on the island. According to the military attaché, the army chief "listened willingly to and almost invariably followed the sound advice of the American Ambassador in such matters as were of sufficient importance to justify the Ambassador's interest, and this gave stability to [past] governments."[45] Caffery, moreover, supported the rural school project. Lamenting the difficulty in containing army influence over civilian affairs, he expressed the hope that the education project, which promised to absorb much of Batista's energy and attention, would permit civil authority to recover.[46]

By the end of December 1936, Congress had concluded impeachment proceedings against President Gómez. With a strong sense of relief, Caffery reported that the Cubans "were all very careful in everything they did to act strictly within existing law and the present Constitution."[47]

The new president, Federico Laredo Bru, assumed office fully sensitive to power relationships on the island. Arranging a cabinet consistent with the wishes of the army command, Laredo served as the pliant accomplice to military rule for the remainder of the 1930s.

Social Aspects of *Septembrismo*

The collapse of the Gómez government routed whatever civil force remained capable of confining the range of army authority. The faltering civil system created a vacuum into which the army moved to appropriate greater authority and broader responsibilities. By the late 1930s, the armed forces directed a shadow government. In early 1937, Laredo Bru ratified the controversial sugar-tax bill and conferred on the armed forces the responsibility for the education of rural Cuba. The civic-military school system appointed sergeants to serve as schoolmasters and distributed the army teacher corps throughout the Cuban countryside. These *misiones educativas,* designed to disseminate agricultural and hygiene information to rural communities, inaugurated a rudimentary education network in the interior.[48] Colonel Arístides Sosa de Quesada, the chief auditor of the army, proclaimed in 1938 that Cuban militarism had converted the armed forces into agents of culture, guiding the people to reaffirm the integrity of the nation and the "crystallization of justice." Cuba was not a large barracks, Sosa insisted; rather, the barracks served as one great school.[49] By 1937, the military operated one thousand schools in the interior, with the construction of an additional thousand projected for the following year. The rural education network, devoting day sessions to children and three evenings a week to adults, served an estimated one hundred thousand persons throughout the island.[50]

By the end of the decade, the extramilitary functions of the armed institution had spawned an enormous army bureaucracy. A Section of Culture was created within the army to supervise the rural education project. And, inspired by the success of the *septembrista* revolution, the Cuban chief of staff announced the army's Three-Year Plan. This plan, Batista proclaimed in 1936, marked the watershed of the army revolution; the moment had arrived to disseminate the gains of *septembrismo*, hitherto confined exclusively to the military, throughout the nation.[51] In March 1936 Decree Number 707 was enacted, establishing the Instituto Cívico-Militar, an organization authorized to care for orphans of deceased farmers, workers, and soldiers and to oversee the education of invalid children. The Instituto was administered by the Consejo Corporativo de Educación, Sanidad y Beneficencia (Corporate Council of Education, Health, and Welfare), composed of a captain of the army and another officer from the navy chosen by the army General Staff, a captain of the national police designated by the minister of defense, a representative of the Public Health Service, a worker selected by the minister of labor and a peasant chosen by the Department of Agriculture.[52] The Consejo supervised the entire army social experiment. Throughout 1936, it spawned a host of affiliate agencies designed to provide specialized services. The Corporación Nacional de Asistencia Pública, established in 1936, to which the Consejo assigned army and navy officers, a representative of the National Red Cross, and members of the offices of Health and Welfare, distributed funds to hospitals, organized care for the aged, and supported private and public welfare agencies. The Consejo Nacional de Tuberculosis, under the authority of the *fiscal* (attorney) of the Supreme Court, a senior army officers, an army physician, a professor of medicine from the University of Havana, and a physician from the National Red Cross, devoted its attention to the prevention of tuberculosis and the provision of care for patients.[53] Lastly, the Three-Year Plan added an agricultural education program to the rural military-civic schools, a program aimed to "rescue the *campesino* from ignorance," improve his living conditions, and uplift his "spiritual satisfaction."[54]

The impact of the military's new incursions reached fruition before the expiration of the decade. The uniformed sergeant-teachers provided an entire generation of Cubans with its only educational experience; in most instances, the sole medical care and public assistance known in the interior had been administered by the armed forces. Civil projects reinforced army preeminence. Military authority emerged increasingly palatable to sectors traditionally hostile to the armed institution. The civic-military education mitigated much of the past antimilitary sentiment among the rural communities.[55] Throughout the island, army efforts allayed hostility against the armed forces.[56] In addition, the Three-Year Plan boosted Batista's popularity. Many, in fact, viewed the plan as the basis of the chief of staff's presidential aspirations.[57]

The Military Aspects of *Septembrismo*

The new responsibilities assumed by the armed institution, particularly the rural education experiment, provided the *raison d'etre* for an army consisting of some fourteen to fifteen thousand officers and men.[58] The extraordinary growth of the armed forces and expanding military services converted the armed institution into the effective government on the island.[59] By the end of the 1930s, all agencies hitherto independent of military control had passed under army influence. In 1936, municipal treasuries were placed under army authority.[60] In Havana, the armed forces assumed supervision of customs collections. By 1937, the armed institution had absorbed control of the national lottery. The military increased its authority over agents of state force by nationalizing, in 1935, the Havana police force. In the following year, the army command created the National Police Corps, integrating the island's municipal police into an armed force under the authority of a senior army officer.[61]

Within a politico-military context, the structure of the army network responded to the requirements of political stability. Throughout the 1930s, Cuba continued to urbanize. The completion of the rail system and the Central Highway after 1931 encouraged rural migration into urban centers, particularly Havana.[62] By 1943, 54.6 percent of the population lived in cities.[63] In 1919, Cuba had had only two cities with a population above fifty thousand; by 1943, there were seven cities of this size.[64] Havana dominated the island's urban matrix; in 1943 the metropolitan area included almost 21 percent of the island's population[65]

Urbanization contributed to a radical modification in the style of political protest. The urbanization of political opposition, a process commencing in the late 1920s, with a concomitant reliance on mass mobilization, terror, assassination, and bombing, along with the political reverberations of general strikes aptly demonstrated in August 1933 and again in March 1935, underscored the magnitude of the challenge inherent in urban agitation and city mass movement.

The implications of mass mobilization within an urban setting, specifically in Havana, necessitated in a recasting of the army's theory of combat to conform to the demands of political stability. Military authorities became increasingly sensitive to the political repercussions of crowds and disorders in an urban milieu. The urban axis of the political protest resulted in a concomitant urbanization of the armed forces. The nationalization of municipal police agencies under military authority centralized urban law enforcement departments. The army mission, moreover, evolved slowly but effectively into enforcing public order in the cities. Military training during the late 1930s prepared soldiers to discharge police duties in an urban setting. Military preparation of new recruits consisted almost exclusively of close and extended order drill, with considerable emphasis on rifle marksmanship. Cuban military commanders anticipated in the mid-1930s that the primary function of the army was police duty rather than field operations. The army command, consequently, concentrated on discipline and marksmanship rather than field problems and maneuvers.[66] Organized primarily to suppress internal disorders, the Cuban army, moving into urban centers as a new setting, had no theory of tactical deployment, no idea of cooperation with the field forces of the army, the navy, or the air corps.[67]

Urban infantry units girded the politico-military regimen. The Rural Guard, once the armed support of Havana, now became an unimportant appendage of the urban-based armed institution. Rural troops served as garrison details, guarding mines, plantations, and machinery; reinforced by urban troops, they also supervised the *zafra*.

The urbanization of the Cuban armed forces gave the military a new orientation. Between 1933 and 1941, the army had increased by about two thousand officers and men, that is, from twelve to fourteen thousand. Urban politics determined the distribution of this increase. Of the eight military districts, regiments in Oriente, Camagüey, and Santa Clara increased only by a mere 34. The Matanzas regiment actually fell by 30. Military installations in the Havana metropolitan area, that is, Regiment Number 5 ("Martí"), Regiment Number 6, Camp Columbia, and Regiment Number 7 (La Cabaña), increased by 244, 586, and 303, respectively. The most significant increase was registered in infantry units in Camp Columbia. In Havana, the locus of the island's political power, the armed forces increased by some thousand officers and men in an eight-year period.[68] By the early 1940s, several tank companies had been installed in Camp Columbia. Urban army forces also increased in the large provincial cities, including Santiago de Cuba, Camagüey, and Cienfuegos. Together with the nationalization of the police forces, the army command had organized a formidable urban fighting force.

The countryside passed under the protection of a mere handful of Rural Guards, commanded in general by personnel relatively advanced in age. The Rural Guard was assigned to patrol what was perceived by Havana during the 1930s and 1940s to be the politically and militarily valueless rural regions of the island.

The Civilian Interregnum, 1940–1952

10 ### The Batista Incumbency: the Restoration of Civil Authority

Between 1936 and 1939, the army chief of staff broadened his political appeal. Army-inspired social programs had forged for Batista a civilian base from which to launch his nonmilitary political career. An official visit to Washington in 1938, during which Colonel Batista's presidential aspirations received the tacit endorsement of the State Department, further raised the army chief's prestige on the island.[1] American diplomatic officials perceived the Batista candidacy as a means of resolving the anomalous political arrangement in which effective power lay outside the institutional framework of the Constitution. A Batista presidency offered the opportunity to reinvest republican institutions with some of the authority that had accrued personally to the army chieftain.[2] Whatever may have been discussed in Washington, Batista returned to Havana sufficiently inspired to participate more directly in national politics.[3]

In Cuba, the chief of staff fulfilled the military and political preliminaries required for his candidacy. In November 1939 a law prohibiting officers with less than twenty years of service from retiring on pension was amended to permit holders of the Cruz de Honor (Medal of Military Merit), capable of demonstrating their retirement to be of "public necessity," to collect full pension, irrespective of years in the armed services. Congress designed the modification to meet the needs of the **116** outgoing chief of staff, the only officer in possession of the

Cruz de Honor.[4] On December 6, 1939, the army leader accepted the presidential nomination of a political coalition, the Coalición Socialista-Popular (CSP), which was composed of the Unión Nacionalista, Unión Revolucionaria-Comunista, Partido Nacional Revolucionario (Realista), Conjunto Nacional Democrático, and the Liberal party.[5]

Batista's election in 1940 inspired a gradual restoration of civil authority. To be sure, the new President's inauguration did not herald an immediate return of civilian ascendency. The election results themselves were challenged by civilian opposition leaders who charged military intervention, army intimidation and violence, and electoral fraud.[6] The army command, moreover, had secured in advance from opposition candidates guarantees that they would respect the integrity of the armed forces, extracting pledges that they would not advocate a reduction either in military appropriations or in the size of the armed forces.[7] Nevertheless, the 1940 contest provided the setting against which Batista, the civilian candidate, emerged assailable politically. The election infused life into a hitherto moribund national order, stimulating competitive political interaction for national power. Batista's pursuit of national office moved him into a new orbit of civilian relationships. Functioning as a civilian *político,* the former army leader labored to put together a viable civilian political coalition capable of supporting his candidacy. Convinced that the progovernment parties already in control of Congress lacked political value, the former chief of staff, casting about for civilian alliances, promoted new political organizations capable of investing his candidacy with a truly national endorsement.[8] The CSP coalition organized around the Batista candidacy such unlikely allies as Communists, *machadistas,* and retired *septembristas.* To a considerable degree, Batista relied on the old *machadista* machines. Four of the six CSP senators had served in the Machado legislative assemblies.

It was a supreme irony of the decade that the individual singularly responsible for army preeminence during much of the 1930s came to occupy the office which he had worked so powerfully to undermine. In his elected position, Batista acquired a supporting constituency whose needs transcended the one-dimensional military requirements to which he had responded previously as chief of staff. Political organizations, in the national Congress and at the provincial and municipal, level, formed the underpinnings of Batista's civil authority, linking the body politic to the Presidential Palace. Patronage now emerged as a means of maintaining civilian support. As president, Batista moved into competition with the leaders of the armed forces. Forced by the nature of his position, the new chief executive began to assert the presidential authority long relinquished by his predecessors. As the ranking elected official in Cuba, Batista acquired obligations to his civilian partisans. These commitments often meant that patronage and the delegation of authority impinged on the sphere of influence over which the armed forces had long presided. The interests of Batista the president no longer necessarily coincided with the needs of Batista the army chief of staff.

Well before relinquishing command of the armed forces, Batista instituted changes designed to guarantee the army's loyalty to the political order over which he planned to preside. The most insolent and untrustworthy *septembrista* elements in the armed forces passed into retirement. Lieutenant Colonels Diego Rodríguez and Desiderio Sánchez, provincial commanders of Oriente and Matanzas, resigned. Lieutenant Colonel Manuel Benítez, military chief of Pinar del Río, was transferred to Matanzas. In addition, promotions, transfers, and retirements weakened the political authority and military influence of unreliable *septembrista* commanders. Trusted officers received key appointments. Colonel José E. Pedraza assumed command of the army. Lieutenant Colonel Bernardo García became chief of the national police. Lieutenant Colonel Manuel López Migoya was appointed inspector general of the army. Colonel Ignacio Galíndez assumed command of the important Camp Columbia.

Determined to exercise the full scope of civilian executive power, Batista carried into the Presidential Palace the national authority and influence he had wielded as chief of staff. The atrophic civilian order over which the armed institution presided gradually but effectively recovered the authority lost during the 1930s.[9] The new government slowly reduced army influence by withdrawing administrative posts from military supervision and returning them to civilian control. In January 1941 the administration restored custom houses and lighthouses, long under naval jurisdiction, to civilian authority. The Ministry of Treasury assumed supervision of the maritime police. The civic-military rural education project passed into the hands of the Ministry of Education. The 1940 election, moreover, carried members of the Batista coalition into national, provincial, and municipal offices. Officials of the new national order looked to Batista's civilian leadership for support. The political influence of regional military chieftains declined in direct proportion to the successful reassertion of presidential authority. As early as 1938, Colonel Batista had instructed district commanders to confine their interests strictly to military matters as a means of reducing the political influence of regional chieftains over municipal and provincial affairs. Batista simply did not want regimental chiefs discrediting his administration.[10]

The realignment of civil-military relationships orchestrated from the Presidential Palace came as a rude jolt to the *septembrista* commanders, long accustomed to the exercise of unchecked authority. Many army leaders had looked upon Batista's candidacy as the logical conclusion of army preeminence, convinced that the new president would continue to underwrite the reigning military order.[11] The growing subordination of military prerogatives to civil authority, however, very quickly raised some consternation and concern among senior officers. Army confidence in the new president weakened. Friction between the Presidential Palace and the military command increased throughout the early months of Batista's term and erupted ultimately into an army challenge of executive authority. In early 1941, disagreement between Chief of Police García and the president over the suppression of illegal gambling led to the summary dismissal of García. Batista's action angered Pedraza, the army chief, who protested the unilateral nature of the president's dismissal of the police chieftain. Naval commander Angel González, soliciting army assistance in recovering jurisdiction over custom houses and lighthouses, sources of vast smuggling revenue, supported the army chief of staff. Pedraza demanded Batista reconsider the dismissal, warning the president that he could not rely upon the army and navy, which stood unanimously behind the military command.[12] Not coincidentally, only after Batista threatened to suppress corruption within the armed forces did the *septembrista* consensus shatter.

Army leaders sensed correctly the drift of the new administration. From the very outset Batista had been under considerable pressure from politicians, civilian leaders, and cabinet

members to reduce army influence in national life. Discon-
certed army commanders protested that Batista had proceeded
too hastily. The reduction of army and navy influence, the
suppression of illegal gambling, and the dismissal of García had
aroused widespread uneasiness in the military establishment.
Many commanders, moreover, feared that the president's retirement of the police chief portended the dismissal of increasing numbers of senior officers.[13]

The fate of the Batista government in February 1941 remained uncertain. Secretary of Defense Domingo Ramos immediately apprised the American Embassy of the administration's position, disclosing that the "President was in the Palace
quite helpless."[14] The embassy exercised its influence both in
Havana and in Washington in behalf of the challenged government. Ambassador George S. Messersmith informed Ramos
that Washington

> could conceive of nothing more disastrous for Cuba than to permit
> revolution, civil strife or disorder to occur at this time. After a period of
> years, Cuba had returned to Constitutional Government. The President
> had been duly elected and had taken office under the Constitution. It
> would be for Cuba, and in the whole Inter-American picture, a great
> disaster if Constitutional Government should be overthrown. We were
> in a serious situation internationally and the peace of the Americas was
> definitely threatened. At such a time, social or political disorders in any
> of the American Republics could have the most undesirable consequ-
> ences.[15]

At that moment in history, the ambassador insisted,
Washington had a "great interest" in the political stability of the
strategic island.[16]

The American endorsement of the administration worked
powerfully against the military threat. Batista mobilized the
strength inherent in American support to contain the spread of
insurrection in the armed forces. Disclosure that the embassy
opposed the army rebellion counteracted the momentum of the
military plot. Moreover, the American military attaché informed Lieutenant Colonel Ignacio Galíndez, commander of
the strategic regiment in Camp Columbia, that the United
States, standing on the threshold of a world war, could not
permit the breakdown of order and stability on the island.[17]
The Havana garrison, in the end, remained loyal to Batista. On
the evening of February 3, 1941, Batista entered Camp Colum-

bia and assumed personal command of the army, dismissing Pedraza and González.[18] The army's challenge to civil authority had been suppressed.

The collapse of the Pedraza revolt raised presidential authority to a new high. "There is no doubt," the American Embassy reported, "that the authority of the President and of the civil Government has tremendously increased."[19] Batista retired scores of *septembristas* in the wake of the stillborn plot.[20] In early 1942, army strength was reduced.[21] The administration reshuffled military commands and entrusted key army posts to academy-trained officers. The junior officers of the former National Army who had remained in the armed services after September 4, 1933, secured strategic appointments. Lieutenant Colonel Francisco Tabernilla, for example, assumed command of La Cabaña fortress. Lieutenant Colonel Manuel Benítez was appointed chief of the national police. The administration, moreover, reduced the military capacity of army garrisons to challenge the national government. Havana divested provincial commands of reserve ammunition to reduce to a minimum their potential threat in the event of a military rebellion.[22]

Between 1941 and 1944, Batista presided over the gradual restoration of national civilian authority. The administration purged *septembrista* elements most contemptuous of civilian authority. The political influence of *septembrismo,* one Havana weekly proclaimed confidently, had been "liquidated"; Batista had rendered an enormous service to the republic by recovering for the presidency "an authority which had been lost."[23]

Auténticos and the Army, 1944–1952

After eleven years out of power, Ramón Grau San Martín returned to the Presidential Palace as the head of the Auténtico party. The Batista administration and the changes it effected in the armed forces contributed significantly to the viability of the Auténtico administrations. Only four years earlier, during the 1940 campaign, the *septembrista* command of the army had viewed the candidacy of Grau with considerable dismay and suspicion. Army Chief Pedraza, in fact, was unwilling in 1940 to accept an Auténtico victory under any circumstances.[24] By 1944, earlier purges of many *septembristas* had made the prospect of a Grau administration somewhat more acceptable to the armed services—not, to be sure, without conditions. Army leaders secured from the Auténtico candidate satisfactory assurances that he would respect the corporate integrity of the military institution. As early as 1943, Police Chief Benítez had predicted "a slight hope for the avoidance of revolution" only if Grau would talk "to two or three of the leading military commanders" prior to the national elections.[25] In addition, Batista cautioned his successor that the armed forces would support the Auténtico government only "if he kept his hands strictly off them" during his administration.[26] In August 1944 senior army commanders reminded Grau of the importance of "doing nothing to disturb the present existing organization and powers of the armed forces."[27]

The new Auténtico administration gradually won the confidence of the armed forces. Government leaders attempted to instill a new professionalism in the armed services. New military schools expanded professional programs available to the officer corps. Increased American military assistance afforded greater opportunity to attend United States service academies.[28] A general reorganization removed still more *septembristaa* linked politically to the previous regime. By the end of 1944, the government had retired some two hundred officers, among them numerous generals, colonels, and lieutenant colonels. Between 1944 and 1945, General Francisco Tabernilla, chief of La Cabaña, Colonel Ignacio Galíndez, commander of Camp Columbia, Lieutenant Colonel Pedro Díaz, chief of Army Direction, and Army Chief of Staff Manual López Migoya retired. In the navy, Colonels Gaspar Maspón Jordán, inspector general, Rolando Peláez Boch, chief of the Navy Department of Direction, and Rafael de la Paz, chief of the Oriente naval district, resigned. The Auténticos discharged the entire command of the national police and dismissed another four hundred noncommissioned officers and patrolmen of the Havana police force.[29]

The Auténtico government suppressed virtually all traces of *septembrismo* in the armed forces. The Fourth of September flag, commemorating the mutiny, was banned. All September Fourth medals and military decorations were abolished, and the national anthem replaced the September Fourth hymn. September 4 as a military holiday was replaced by "Soldiers' Day," celebrated on December 15.[30]

A general reshuffling of commands placed officers trusted by the Auténticos in key positions. Colonel Genovevo Pérez

Dámera, Grau's aide-de-camp in 1933, assumed command of the army. Transfers separated commanders of uncertain loyalties from important posts. General Ignacio Galíndez, the long-time *batistiano* commander of Camp Columbia, was transferred to staff duty before he retired altogether. Colonel Abrahim Godínez, Batista's brother-in-law and the military chief of Havana province, was also assigned to army headquarters. The Auténticos sought to assign academy officers to top commands. The critical Havana regiments moved into the commmand of carefully selected officers. Almost every officer to emerge with a middle grade or above immediately after the September mutiny retired between 1940 and 1945. *Grauísta* appointments, on the other hand, had gained only junior ranks in the wake of the 1933 sedition; subsequent promotions during the intervening years were earned through academy preparation.[31] The Grau administration, moreover, attempted to create an officer corps loyal to the Auténtico order. By the end of 1944, an estimated 150 officers had been promoted, and 300 sergeants with over twenty years of service had received commissions. These promotions, in turn, benefited some 2,000 noncommissioned officers who moved up.[32] Another 300 enlisted men received corporal's chevrons.[33] In the early years of his administration Grau devoted a great deal of time to the armed forces, attending luncheons, addressing military commands in the interior, and participating in military exercises and ceremonies.[34] The government raised the salaries of enlisted men. Army appropriations remained constant, an estimated thirty million pesos annually, roughly 20 percent of the national budget.[35]

The government of Carlos Prío Socarrás continued the army policy of the previous Auténtico administration. To a greater extent than his predecessor, Prío endeavored to keep army commands in close contact with Havana. He frequently visited provincial garrisons to address the regiments in the interior and often attended army social functions, at which he was generally the invited guest of honor. The chief executive, in fact, socialized more often with the armed services than had Grau and Batista.[36] Similarly, Minister of Defense Segundo Curti conducted inspection tours of the island's military commands. These visits, Curti asserted, promoted a "better understanding" of the mutual needs of both the armed forces and the president, and heralded the "government's new spirit of *com-*

pañerismo."[37] The army chief of staff also kept Havana in close contact with the needs of interior commands. The government inaugurated a system of semiannual inspections in which the army command visited remote detachments to learn firsthand the needs and conditions of provincial outposts.[38]

In addition, Prío promoted programs to reduce army idleness. The armed forces helped commemorate national holidays by recreating the marches made by the Ejército Libertador during the war for independence. The government also encouraged army participation in nonmilitary programs. The air corps transported education missions throughout the island, cooperated with the Civil Aeronautics Institute, aided cartographical programs, and assisted agricultural missions. The navy, too, participated in civil functions, employing the warship *Yara* as a floating laboratory to study means of improving sponge-fishing, measuring ocean depths, and analyzing water content.[39]

The Collapse of the Auténticos

In national affairs Auténtico leadership between 1944 and 1952 discredited civilian administration. Embezzlement, graft, corruption, and the rapacity of public officials permeated virtually every branch of national, provincial, and municipal government. The island was overshadowed by political instability and personal insecurity. The word *gangsterismo* entered the Cuban lexicon to describe the tenor of the national political order, a climate characterized by violence on university campuses, running gun battles on Havana streets, kidnappings, and assassinations. Disorder dominated the capital in the face of the government's inability to arrest its spread.[40] *Grupos de acciones* (armed political bands), when not engaged in sanguinary internecine struggles, frequently fought army and police units on the streets of the capital.[41] Accusations of rampant corruption and graft and the inability of administration leaders to halt widespread violence undermined national confidence in the Auténtico order. Law enforcement in urban centers increasingly involved military assistance. Police cars patrolled city streets with one patrolman and one soldier in full combat dress.[42] Attacks on members of the press turned many news organs against the administration.[43]

Auténtico misgovernment cost the party national unity. The break between Eduardo Chibás and the Auténticos and the subsequent formation of the Ortodoxo party badly fragmented the government party. Perhaps the most gifted politician of the era, Chibás articulated national grievances and crystallized public discontent against the Auténtico regime.[44] The Ortodoxo leader inaugurated an antiadministration campaign that was symbolized by a broom, promising a clean sweep of government. The campaign thrived on spectacular accusations and disclosures of malfeasance on the highest levels of national government. Chibás's histrionics contributed powerfully to a final discrediting of the incumbent administration, undermining moral confidence in national leadership. The Ortodoxo campaign animated political emotions and heightened popular expectations with a vision of a new national order devoted to public integrity and administrative honesty. Chibás's suicide in 1951 produced a mass disillusionment that found ultimate expression in a national dejection characterized by a cynicism of resignation and indifference. The Prío government, however, remained substantially weaker after its bout with the fallen Ortodoxo leader; thoroughly discredited, it presided over a demoralized body politic.

National politics reverberated ultimately throughout the armed forces. Disclosures of graft among senior officers of the army command jolted large numbers of junior officers. In 1946, the armed forces learned that a personal friend of the chief of staff in Camagüey had contracted troops under his command to a commercial construction project, keeping for himself the money designed to pay for civilian labor.[45] Further disclosures of widespread army corruption in the late 1940s increased demoralization among the academy-trained officers. In 1948, the government discovered the existence of army companies drawing pay for eight-four members when, if fact, they consisted of fifty-four soldiers, the difference being passed on to General Staff officers. The quality of food and clothing distributed to the armed forces deteriorated as some officers detected in substitute purchasing a lucrative method of supplementing army pay.[46] In late 1948, retired General Abelardo Gómez accused the chief of staff of having embezzled two million pesos from the armed forces' retirement fund.[47]

During the 1940s, in addition, the strains and stresses of the preceding decade overtook the military establishment. Increasingly, sectors of the army command contracted inward around their respective origins. The traditional rivalry between young academy graduates and older *septembristas* flared anew. Auténtico governments, on the other hand, relied for support on still a third group: officers who were *septembrista* in origin but professional in orientation. These splits were compounded as the Auténtico-Ortodoxo divisions reached the officer corps. Several prominent Ortodoxos, including Roberto Agramonte, Herminio Portell Vilá, and Rafael García Bárcena, occupied key teaching positions at the Escuela Superior de Guerra (War College). These Ortodoxo instructors, with access to sectors of the army command, came into frequent contact with military leaders and established a lasting association with the deputy director, Major Ramón Barquín. The group around Barquín, the *puros,* represented a growing number of dissident officers—drawn largely from the island's service academies—who were attracted to Ortodoxo politics and opposed to the old *septembrista* command.[48] Fearful of the Ortodoxo-*puro* nexus, Prío labored to reduce the *barquinista* influence in the army. *Puros* in command of strategic units received assignments abroad as military attachés. Barquín himself served in the Cuban Embassy in Washington. Other *puros* took over desk jobs or assumed command of remote interior posts.[49] By the early 1950s, having eliminated a source suspected of antigovernment intrigue, the Auténtico also removed an important obstacle to the return of the *septembristas.*[50]

The national climate during the last months of the Prío government generated further instability and uncertainty. The betrayal of public trusts and disclosures of high-level corruption in civilian administration and the armed services had a disquieting impact on the junior academy-trained officers.[51] Assassinations and *gangsterismo* exposed the inability of civilian leadership to underwrite order and stability, discrediting the government and senior army commanders in the eyes of the young professional officers.[52] In addition, rumors that the Auténicos planned a coup with senior officers to forestall the predicted Ortodoxo victory in the 1952 elections further disillusioned junior commanders.[53] In late 1951 a number of junior officers, impatient with the state of affairs in Cuba and disillusioned with civilian authorities, banded together to plot the overthrow of the Auténtico order. The conspirators planned to install in office a military junta long enough to restore order and convoke national elections to return power to responsible civilian authorities.[54] The officers originally contemplated placing Colonel Barquín at the head of the junta, an idea subsequently abandoned for fear the *puro* leader lacked the national support necessary for the success of the movement. Instead the conspirators invited Batista—seeking in 1952, apparently unsuccessfully, another term in the Presidential Palace—to head the movement against the Auténtico regime. Batista's participation in the conspiracy, dissident officers expected, promised to confer on the movement a broader base of support both within the armed forces and among civilian political and economic sectors.[55] By early 1952, all necessary conspiratorial liaisons had been completed.

The Restoration of Army
Preeminence, 1952–1953

11 The Army Seizure of Power

The *cuartelazo* of March 10, 1952, was an accomplishment of
consummate organizational skill. The axis of the conspiracy
passed through the military installations of the capital. From
control of the Havana garrisons, the rebel armed forces moved
into the capital itself, reached the suburban approaches to the
city, and ultimately captured provincial commands.

Key military installations in Havana fell under the control of
army conspirators without resistance. With the cooperation of
Captain Dámaso Sogo, officer of the day, Batista gained entrance to Camp Columbia. Garrison commanders were immediately arrested.[1] Troops were aroused and assembled to
listen to the promises and harangue of the former president.[2]
Another group led by retired General Francisco Tabernilla, in
a similar fashion, secured control of the general's former
command of La Cabaña. Retired naval Captain José E. Rodríguez Calderón entered and quickly dominated Castillo de la
Punta, the island's most important naval station and seat of the
navy command. Finally, Lieutenant Rafael Salas Cañizares, of
the Havana National Police, captured the motorized section of
the capital police force and seized control of the radio dispatch
center. By 2:30 A.M., insurgent military units had secured
control of the capital's armed forces garrisons.[3]

Army conspirators attached success of the movement to the
effective seizure of Havana. All hope of winning the endorse-

128

ment of provincial commands, in fact, depended entirely on presenting the interior with a *fait accompli* in the capital. Having secured the support of Havana detachments, officers and troops moved onto the city to garrison key positions. All public services passed under military command. Bus and rail stations, airports, docks, electricity plants, radio transmitters, banks, and offices of government ministries were placed under army guard. Military roadblocks sealed major arteries to and from the capital.[4] Havana radio stations, under the supervision of the armed forces, were ordered to continue normal programming without, however, broadcasting any news; police and soldiers occupied control booths throughout the city's radio stations to enforce the news blackout.[5] Later that morning citizens awoke amidst rumors of a *cuartelazo* and turning to radio broadcasts heard only uninterrupted music.[6] Army units assumed control of the Cuban Telephone Company and monitored virtually all conversations among members of the beleaguered Auténtico government, including those of the president.[7] The conspirators similarly attempted to interrupt all communications with the interior until Havana was under full army control.[8] Rebel military authorities suspended publication of opposition newspapers. Throughout the city, points of potential mass mobilizations and demonstrations against the new military junta fell under army and police guard. Local headquarters of the Confederation of Cuban Workers and offices of the Communist party passed under military supervision.[9] Military forces occupied the national university. Union leaders were detained and arrested. All constitutional guarantees were suspended and Congress dissolved. Within days, the new government ordered the "reorganization" of all political parties.

Effective domination of Havana garrisons guaranteed the success of the movement. From army headquarters in Camp Columbia a military junta constituted itself as the new government, appointing Batista chief of state and supreme commander of the armed forces. The junta then appealed for national support of the new political order.[10] Havana radio broadcasts promised pay raises for all members of the armed forces.[11] From Castillo de la Punta, the new navy chief José E. Rodríguez Calderón announced possession of the naval service and ordered navy units throughout the island to endorse the junta.[12] Rafael Salas Cañizares, the new chief of the national police, directed officers, noncommissioned personnel, and patrolmen to enforce order, assuring the police that the new government would fully support their efforts.[13] From Camp Columbia the Havana military command exhorted provincial detachments to join the movement.

Control of the capital worked powerfully for the military junta. Numerous commanders in the interior, without direction and the political support necessary to combat the *cuartelazo* or fearing the consequences of not joining, swore allegiance to the new politico-military order in the capital.[14] Officers refusing to pledge support to the new government in Havana were displaced by pro-junta subalterns. Colonel Eduardo Martín Elena, military chief in Matanzas, was arrested by Comandante José Aguiar, who immediately placed the regiment at the service of the Havana command.[15] The commander of the Camagüey regiment, Colonel José de la Fuente, relinquished the garrison to Lieutenant Colonel René L. Chipi Córdova, who quickly proclaimed allegiance to the junta. In Oriente, Colonel Manuel Alvarez Margolles was deposed by sergeants and corporals who proceeded to announce support of Havana.[16] In several instances, particularly in remote army detachments in the interior, noncommissioned officers and junior grade commanders, animated by the prospect of quick promotions and pay raises, cast their posts with the pro-junta forces.

News of Batista's penetration of Camp Columbia aroused the sleeping president at his estate. Prío rushed immediately to the Presidential Palace only to find his advisors and cabinet members in a state of panic and indecision.[17] Having lost support of the Havana garrisons, he established contact with provincial commands and learned that the eastern regiments remained loyal to the constitutional government.[18] The Auténtico leader attempted to reach the provincial commands, he later explained, to lead the "loyal troops" in Matanzas, Las Villas, Camagüey, and Oriente against Havana.[19] Prío's flight eastward, however, was anticipated by defections of the interior commands. Upon arriving in Matanzas, he learned that Colonel Elena had already relinquished command; and as he prepared to move further east, he received the news that Las Villas and Santiago de Cuba had fallen to rebel officers and soldiers. Prío finally capitulated, taking political asylum in the Mexican Embassy.

The speed and efficiency of the insurgent forces in securing control of key garrisons provided the conspirators with the opportunity to organize a new army command to represent the junta to the interior. The very swiftness of the *cuartelazo* immobilized resistance. Within an hour and seventeen minutes the army presented the nation with a *fait accompli* in the capital.[20] The speed and surprise of the coup, *Bohemia* editorialized, produced "stupor in the citizenry."[21] Jorge Mañach described the national response as a "sensation of momentary paralysis."[22] Political reporter Carlos Lechuga suggested that the rapidity of the *cuartelazo* had produced a "cold indifference" among those condemning the act.[23] In the end, the toppled Auténtico government was not invested with the moral creditability to solicit national support. Its fall did not warrant public outrage. One observer accurately measured the duality of national reaction as oscillating between regret and joy, satisfaction and displeasure.[24] The *cuartelazo,* José Antonio Portuondo later wrote, "found a nation disgusted with eight years of Auténtico misgovernment."[25]

The military conspirators exploited this national ambivalence skillfully. Within days of the coup, junta spokesmen announced the discovery of new and sensational cases of Auténtico corruption. Did those deposed officials, the spokesmen asked rhetorically, men who condoned and encouraged graft, corruption, and *gangsterismo,* merit the support of the people? No, responded the military leaders; the army intervention was designed to "save the country from the tragedy" of Auténtico misgovernment.[26]

The de facto government quickly consolidated itself, emerging as an attractive alternative to its predecessors in the eyes of the national sectors most desirous of order and stability. Mario Lazo, a Havana business attorney, later wrote that for many of his friends "the essential thing was that Batista had brought order out of chaos, had given the country the stability it greatly needed."[27] Members of the executive board of the Association of Landowners of Cuba paid respects to the new chief executive to offer their cooperation to secure "order and tranquility" to avoid interruption of that year's *zafra*.[28] The prestigious Economic Society of the Republic, lamenting the usurpation of civil authority, nevertheless urged the nation to accept the regime until the restoration of the "rule of the Constitution."[29] Representatives of the Association of Industries visited General Batista to offer the new government open credit.[30] Within five days of the coup, the government announced that the Havana

Exchange, industrialists, *colonos,* banking firms forming the Association of Banks of Cuba, and the Havana Clearing House had pledged their support of the government which had "emerged to save the nation from the disintegrating factors" threatening the republic.[31]

The De Facto Government and Army Politics

The very success of the *cuartelazo* transfigured the objectives inspiring the original conspiracy. The sentiments driving officers into intrigue failed to survive the coup. The conspiracy, organized originally to save the republic, emerged as a movement proclaiming the salvation of the armed forces from the grip of rapacious civilian leaders. General Jorge García Tuñón later suggested that the army intervention in 1952 had responded primarily to the "state of perturbation in which the Republic lived."[32] Junior officers organized a coup, Colonel Pedro Barrera Pérez wrote, to express a collective revulsion against state corruption and *gangsterismo*; the army planned to impose order, convoke national elections, and return civilians to power.[33] Batista's participation, however, added personal political ambitions to a movement designed initially to restore order. Running a poor third in a three-way contest for the presidency, Batista seized the army plot as an alternative route to power.

An army movement conceived to revive a bankrupt order, in fact, returned to power a new Batista government dependent almost entirely on the support of the armed forces. The new administration, seeking army endorsement of the de facto order, invested the *cuartelazo* with purely military objectives. Military intervention, Batista explained, had responded to the "lack of guarantees for soldiers and the police" in their attempt to end disorders and illegalities.[34] General Francisco Tabernilla, the newly appointed chief of staff, deplored the oversight of civilian political parties in ignoring the three other "parties"—the yellow, the blue, and the white, the uniform colors of the army, police, and navy.[35] The new army chief predicted the necessity of reorganizing the armed forces, for the military had been "completely abandoned" during the preceding years of Auténtico misgovernment. It was necessary for the army to return to its "military functions." Tabernilla pledged that civilian exploitation of the armed forces, including the use of soldiers as bricklayers, carpenters, and gardeners on private homes and estates had ended; "we want the soldiers," he emphasized, "to be solely military."[36]

The yellow, blue, and white parties formed the substructure of the new order. Official spokesmen of the administration exalted the military unanimity of purpose behind the government. The regime boasted that an "army monolith" was underwriting the Batista renovation. Some months after the coup, Minister of Education Andrés Rivero Agüero reminded opposition factions that the "rifles" were on the side of the government.[37] The armed forces "to a man," Tabernilla proclaimed confidently, loyally supported General Batista and were committed to maintaining order and peace and enforcing the laws of the land.[38] Minister without Portfolio Leonardo Anaya Murilla warned antigovernment sectors contemplating the use of violence against the administration that "we of the government have the force."[39]

Political dependence on the armed forces necessarily increased the participation of military officials at all levels of national and local administration. Much of the authority delegated to the armed forces by the conspiracy leadership during the seizure of power developed into a permanent feature of the new government. Navy officials, after a decade, recovered control of custom houses. Regional army commanders displaced governors, municipal *alcaldes,* and *ayuntamiento* presidents. Military authorities served as censors. Army officers represented the government in labor disputes. In 1953, Lieutenant Colonel Pedro Barrera Pérez acted as military interventor in a Havana bus strike. Two years later, Lieutenant Colonel Félix Pérez Montoya and Comandante Máximo Robaina represented the Ministry of Communications during a telegraph strike. Government agencies passed under the supervision of military personnel. The Immigration Administration was placed under the jurisdiction of Lieutenant Jesús Sosa Blanco. The Office of Stevedores, a division of the Ministry of Labor, was headed by Comandante César Docampo who, in turn, staffed administrative subdivisions with junior officers.

Seizing power through a military intervention and without the active aid of the civilian organizations that had supported his earlier administration, Batista relied extensively on the "party" strength of the yellow, blue, and white. A political order came to serve the armed forces. Indeed, the most important constituents of the new regime were the three "parties." Officers loyal to the new administration received the appropriate recognition. A mass purge removed commanders suspected of being unsympathetic to the *batistiano* order, and the openings provided the opportunity to reward military supporters of the new government. The entire command serving the displaced Auténtico resigned. Hundreds of middle and junior grade officers, including those who had withheld support of the *cuartelazo*, were discharged. The new government, Tabernilla pledged, would eliminate from the armed forces all elements that had not supported the army revolt.[40] A wave of promotions rewarded the participants of March 10.[41] Every grade in the armed forces shared the fruits of the coup. One executive decree, not atypical of the orders issued from the Presidential Palace in the aftermath of the coup, commissioned some 155 noncommissioned officers and enlisted men.[42]

The de facto government quickly offered the yellow, blue, and white parties evidence of its devotion to the armed services. Several weeks after the coup the administration announced substantial pay increases for all members of the armed forces.[43] Retirement pensions increased. In August 1952 the government announced the availability of employment for scores of relatives of servicemen in different ministries, a moved designed to provide military families with "economic assistance."[44]

Havana attended closely to all the professional needs of the armed forces. Barracks, housing, and recreational facilities improved. Virtually every provincial command inaugurated housing projects for officers and enlisted personnel. Participating in ground-breaking ceremonies for a housing development in Ciudad Militar, Camp Columbia, Tabernilla pledged that the project augured a national program to be completed in "every regimental district in the nation."[45] Throughout the early 1950s, the Cuban army received the latest American military equipment. Tanks, armored personnel carriers, jeeps, bazookas, and a miscellaneous assortment of small arms, rifles, and ammunition enhanced the army arsenal.

The government converted the aviation corps into the Fuerza Aérea del Ejército (Air Force).[46] The reorganized service received modern equipment and sophisticated air hardware, including F-47 fighters which, the army command admitted with some embarrassment, its pilots did not know how to fly.[47] Air force personnel assumed supervision of the school of aviation mechanics. The administration ordered the construction of airfields to serve all provincial commands. The field in Camp Columbia alone cost an estimated $950,000.[48]

The navy also received benefits from the new regime. New training facilities for recruits and advanced schools expanded naval programs. The Naval Training Center, proclaimed a "model of its type for Latin America,"[49] contained twenty-four technical programs, including training in electricity, sanitation, machinery, administration, artillery, signal, refrigeration, radio operation, and radar. The government established a naval aviation corps endowed with six aircraft. In addition, the navy secured new bases, more ship facilities, service hospitals, and a new staff headquarters.

The administration did not overlook the national police. An estimated two thousand new openings were created. Policemen already in the service were encouraged to invite friends and family to join.[50] The national law enforcement agency received new arms and equipment, including some 150 new police cars and 100 motorcycles.

Havana further established a variety of government services to meet the personal needs of the members of the armed forces. In October 1952 the administration created the Instituto Militar Juvenil to provide "technological education," specifically in electronics, mechanics, construction, plumbing, and cabinet-making, to servicemen's children between fourteen and sixteen years of age.[51] At the same time, the government formed the Caja de Seguros y Anticipos de las Fuerzas Armadas, an insurance fund for members of the armed forces.[52] Two months later, the Organización de la Vivienda Económica de las Fuerzas Armadas (OVEFA) was founded to organize the construction of low-cost homes and low-renting apartments to meet the needs of military families.[53]

Symbols and ceremonials of the new martial order prevailed throughout the island. The *marcista* order revived the hagiolatry of *septembrismo*. The Fourth of September flag adorned military installations. The hymn of September 4, military decorations commemorating the sergeants' revolt, and the annual celebration of September 4 formed an integral portion of the ceremonial activities of the armed forces. The military calendar, in addition, was vastly augmented. March 10 assumed its place beside September 4. December 15, the Soldiers' Day instituted by the Auténticos, remained. November 8 was declared Day of Military Mourning to honor soldiers, sailors, and policemen who had fallen in the line of duty. May 14 was established as the Day of the Pilot.

By the mid-1950's, the exaltation of martial virtues, the sense of importance infused into the armed forces by the administration, and the official patronizing of the military institution had resulted in a new insolence among the armed services. The army establishment lay above and beyond criticism and reproach. The subject of the armed forces was a theme prohibited to the antigovernment press and opposition groups.[54] Those who criticized the armed forces incurred the risk of harassment and arrest.[55] Pelayo Cuervo, a prominent Ortodoxo spokesman, was detained by the armed forces for having spoken against the military. Alluding to the Pelayo Cuervo arrest, Andrés Domingo y Morales del Castillo, minister of the president, warned all members of the opposition against confusing "freedom of speech" with "grave accusations against the high Chiefs of the Armed Forces."[56]

Patterns of Resistance: The Armed Forces and Opposition, 1953–1958

Civilian Resistance

After March 10, opposition organizations solicited army assistance in the struggle against the Batista government. The relative ' importance of the military to antigovernment conspiracies developed in direct proportion to the administration's reliance on the armed institution. Opposition factions, conspiring in an urban setting, perceived army support vital to any enterprise plotting the overturn of the *marcista* order. As early as August 1952, Havana uncovered a conspiracy led by Aureliano Sánchez Arango, minister of education in the Prío government, involving members of the armed forces.[1] The abortive plot sought to coordinate a movement between military personnel in Camp Columbia and La Cabaña and several air force pilots assigned to hijack planes and bomb military installations in Havana.[2] In November 1952 ex-Colonel Lázaro Landeira, former chief of the Ninth Armored Division, was arrested for attempting to enlist the support of former colleagues for an armed uprising against the government.[3] A month later, the administration discovered a naval conspiracy in which former officers, including ex-Navy Chief José A. Aguila Ruiz, were charged with fomenting discontent within the navy.[4] The Movimiento Nacionalista Revolucionario (MNR) attempted still another army-oriented coup against Batista in April 1953. Organized in May 1952 by Rafael García Bárcena, the former Ortodoxo instructor at the Escuela Superior de Guerra, the MNR

137

consisted largely of students and representatives in the armed services. García Bárcena formulated antigovernment strategy around the capture of key Havana garrisons, particularly Camp Columbia, with the inside assistance of MNR military supporters.[5] In April 1953 García Bárcena and an MNR cadre attempted to occupy Camp Columbia with the aid of army contacts within the garrison.[6] The movement collapsed when the MNR leader and twenty-one followers were captured outside Camp Columbia while seeking entrance to the military installation.

The axis of the initial response to the March coup passed through plots designed to enlist army support against the *marcista* order. Opposition efforts adopted an urban-Havana strategy calculated to turn one or more of the important military regiments against the government. The attack by Fidel Castro on the Moncada Barracks on July 26, 1953, represented, in many ways, a continuity of opposition tactics. Instead of Havana, the *fidelistas* chose Santiago de Cuba as their urban base; instead of expecting army cooperation to deliver the military post to the opposition, the rebels opted for a seizure of the installation by force.[7] The assailants selected Moncada over Camp Columbia largely because of the Oriente post's notorious military weakness and lax discipline.[8] Upon the capture of Moncada, the *fidelistas* planned to distribute arms and ammunition to the civilian population, hoping ultimately to inspire a mass mobilization across the island against the government from the base in Santiago.[9] Rebel commandos launched a simultaneous siege on the military post at Bayamo to impede the passage of army reinforcements from Holguín to Santiago de Cuba.[10]

The Moncada assault failed, like previous urban efforts, precisely because it challenged the armed forces to a type of combat for which they had been most adequately prepared. Havana responded to the uprising in Oriente with a massive reinforcement effort. Government units, transported by land, air, and sea, poured into Santiago. Within hours, order had been restored in the eastern capital.

From City to Countryside: The Army and Guerrilla Warfare

After a three-year hiatus of armed struggle, the *fidelistas* returned to Cuba in December 1956 prepared to deliver the mortal blow to the *batistiano* order. The "Twenty-Sixth of July" movement, organized after the attack on Moncada, continued to combat the government within an urban setting. Castro and his expeditionaries aboard the *Granma* entrusted the fate of their disembarkation and, in fact, the entire enterprise, to the success of the urban insurrection planned in Santiago de Cuba. The organizers of the November 1956 uprising, which was scheduled to coincide with the arrival of the *Granma* expedition, assigned to Santiago primary responsibility for creating *focos conflictivos* (centers of armed conflict) to engage government forces and prevent them from reaching the site selected for the *Granma* landing on the Manzanillo coast.[11] In virtually every other aspect, however, the 1956 rebellion contained the objectives and approaches of the abortive 1953 Moncada attack. The rebels planned to capture the eastern capital by dominating government forces in the city. To obstruct all movement to and from Moncada, insurgents installed a mortar placement on the roof of the nearby Instituto de Santiago.[12] The assault coordinated the shelling of Moncada with a siege on all national and maritime police stations. Another rebel unit freed political prisoners. The Twenty-Sixth of July planned to seize a radio transmitter to issue a general call to arms, exhorting the *santiagüero* population to the streets to receive the weapons taken by the insurgent forces.[13] The thrust of the *Granma*-Santiago uprising, as in the earlier Moncada assault, was mastery over Oriente through control of Santiago.[14]

Government forces quickly suppressed the Santiago uprising. Within several days, paratroopers and infantry units from Havana under Colonel Pedro Barrera Pérez reestablished government control of the eastern capital. Discovered at sea by naval patrols and its point of disembarkation located by air force reconnaissance units, the *Granma* expedition barely survived the landing.[15]

The armed forces reacted lamely to the rural *foco* implanted by the surviving *Granma* expeditionaries, revealing incomprehension of the guerrilla dimensions of armed struggle. The army command dispatched an artillery battalion to Oriente to suppress the *fidelistas*. The artillery unit from La Cabaña promptly established its headquarters in Niquero and proceeded to construct fortifications in the apparent anticipation of a rebel attack.[16] Only after the General Staff replaced field commands and ordered active pursuit did army forces encounter, on December 5, rebel survivors of the *Granma* expedition.[17] The casualties inflicted on the insurgents at the battle of Alegría de Pío, together with those sustained earlier, reduced the original band of eighty-two men to between twelve and twenty survivors.[18]

After several days of unsuccessful pursuit, the government suspended operations. On December 11, Havana ordered a cease-fire and offered the remaining insurgents a guarantee of their lives upon surrendering. After several days without a rebel response, the army command withdrew its tactical units. Given the "scarce numbers of insurrectionary element" in complete retreat, army spokesman Comandante Policarpo Chaviano announced, the army command no longer felt the need to maintain any units in the field. "This General Staff," Chaviano concluded, "considers the insurrectional outbreak over."[19] Captain Juan Moreno Bravo, the field officer commanding government troops at Alegría de Pío, reported upon returning to Havana that a "good part of the enemy" had dispersed after the battle.[20] In the course of the following weeks, all evidence convinced Havana that army operations had indeed been successful. The expeditionaries had apparently dissolved and abandoned the revolutionary struggle.[21] By the end of December, Havana's first offensive in Oriente had ended with government proclamations of victory.

In January 1957, however, surviving expeditionaries reappeared and launched their first offensive action against the Rural Guard post at La Plata in southeast Oriente. In Havana, the military command responded immediately by concentrating local army forces against the guerrillas. By the end of January, Havana had deployed an infantry unit consisting of some fourteen hundred officers and men under Colonel Pedro Barrera Pérez in the foothills of the Sierra Maestra.[22] The second offensive against the Twenty-Sixth of July consisted of three primary objectives. First, the government attempted to establish an armed cordon around the Sierra to contain insurgent operations. In addition, army units sought to seal all approaches leading to the mountain range to impede recruits from joining the guerrillas.[23] Finally, field units inaugurated pacification programs—described by Havana as "social labor"—to construct homes and schools, provide health services, and extend medical attention to the mountain population. By April, the field command announced with some pride that an estimated six thousand persons, largely women and children, had been treated by army medical units attached to the forces of operation.[24]

The military mission of the campaign, however, remained unfulfilled. After four months of patrol, army chief Tabernilla announced that the insurgent band, "reduced to ten to twelve men," had been completely humbled.[25] A government press release reported that the guerrillas, reduced to "less than twenty men" scattered and in desperate condition, had declined to make hostile contact with army units. Hence, the administration concluded, the "zone of operations is practically normalized."[26] From the field, Colonel Barrera Pérez reported no contact with rebel forces, suggesting that they had disappeared months before.[27] In mid-April, the government ended the fruitless four-month campaign against the elusive guerrillas in Oriente. "All operations in the Sierra Maestra," reported Barrera Pérez confidently, "have been completed."[28] The second Havana effort against the Twenty-Sixth of July had ended without engaging the insurgent forces.

A month after the army withdrew from the Sierra Maestra, the *fidelistas* overwhelmed a Rural Guard detachment at El Uvero. The government launched its most formidable offensive to date. Infantry, naval detachments, and air forces carried the government campaign back to the Sierra Maestra. The General Staff announced that the army offensive was designed to force the guerrillas into battle, inaugurating a "progressive military plan" intended to defeat Castro by forcing him to fight.[29] Colonel Barrera Pérez, again appointed to direct government operations, announced his plans to suppress the guerilla *foco* through starvation by surrounding suspected centers of rebel activity.[30] In mid-June, the government launched its "campaign of extermination" against the insurgents. The armed forces, Batista vowed, had undertaken "operations to finish with that insurrectionary outbreak."[31]

Extraordinary measures accompanied the third offensive. The army command converted the Sierra Maestra into a "free fire zone." Government forces undertook the mammoth task of evacuating and relocating peasant families from the Sierra range. Government troops moved an estimated two thousand families, together with their livestock, crops, and personal possessions to deprive the guerrilla force of the aid of the *montuño* (mountain) population.[32] Airplanes, trucks, and ships relocated families to hastily constructed detention centers in Bayamo and Santiago de Cuba. These measures, Batista explained, were necessary to protect peasant families.[33]

The forced relocation of peasants alienated a large portion of the mountain population against government forces. Havana's campaign in Oriente revived memories of the Spanish policy fifty years earlier of herding Cubans into reconcentration camps. The repercussions were similar. Many refused to leave their homes and fled to join the guerrilla columns.[34]

The armed forces shelled the ostensibly clear Sierra Maestra in an effort to draw the guerrillas into combat. Once the rebels left their mountain sanctuary, Colonel Barrera Pérez predicted, they would be destroyed in a "question of hours."[35] Artillery barrages, offshore naval batteries, and air force saturation bombing with napalm failed, however, to produce the expected confrontation.[36] By July, Barrera Pérez admitted that the army had not made contact with the rebel forces. After some 133 days of operations, the government abandoned the plan to draw the guerrillas into combat.[37] In November, Havana announced that the "total extermination" of the insurrectionary *foco* was in sight.[38] A month later, the administration proclaimed the suspension of operations in Oriente, declaring the insurgency at an end. "Operations have been suspended," a presidential spokesman announced, "since the objective of crushing the insurrectional outbreak has been achieved."[39] The third offensive against the Twenty-Sixth of July had again failed to suppress the insurgency in Oriente.

Successful insurgent attacks on Rural Guard stations marked important guerrilla victories over the armed forces. In waging war against the Rural Guard, the rebels immediately attacked the provincial underpinnings of the Batista regime and the symbolic expression of Havana's presence in the Sierra Maestra region. For decades, arbitrary Rural Guard commanders had terrorized rural communities in Oriente.[40] And however modest rebel successes against the isolated and remote rural constabulary may have seemed, they did, in fact, strike at Havana's politico-military authority in Oriente province. After the attack at Uvero, in fact, Havana virtually conceded to the guerrilla force mastery over the region by dismantling the Rural Guard stations distant from major army posts.[41]

Havana had proven incapable of subduing the guerrilla movement during its formative phase—its most vulnerable gestation period—largely due to an ignorance of insurgency. Senior military commanders and government officials lacked an appreciation of the nature of the struggle building up against the administration. They repeatedly refused to assign any political or military importance to a handful of armed zealots in the wilderness of the Sierra Maestra. The refusal of the rebels to engage government forces served only to confirm official views of the harmlessness of the rural insurgents. The rebel force, Batista noted with some frustration, only ran and hid. "From the military or national security point of view," he remarked, "that group has no significance at all."[42] Justifying later the premature withdrawal of army units after La Plata, Batista noted derisively that those who had come to fight would not offer battle.[43] The government had misread the rebels' early no-fight strategy during the first days of the insurgency.

Political factors may also have contributed to the apparent inability of Havana to suppress the insurgency. The presence of armed opposition in the field in the politically and militarily insignificant and remote regions of Oriente gave Batista the excuse to tighten his control in the capital. Rafael Guas Inclán, Batista's vice-president, later charged that the chief executive did not suppress the insurrection within twenty-four hours of the *Granma* landing so that he could raise and maintain the specter of revolution with which to dominate the four political parties and dispose of emergency funds without restrictions.[44] Colonel Samuel G. Kail, the American military attaché, similarly suggested that "it was to Batista's advantage to have Fidel running loose in the hills, because with this happening he could take many political actions in Cuba that he might have had trouble explaining without a whipping boy (Fidel)."[45]

The Generalization of Opposition

During the mid-1950s the Batista government came under increasing attack. Opposition groups directly assailed the armed forces, at once the most important and most visible expression of the *marcista* regime. Assassination of army officers and police chiefs became common. In October 1956 Antonio Blanco Río, chief of army intelligence, was assassinated in Havana. Several days later, Police Chief Salas Cañizares died of wounds sustained in a gun battle in the capital. Within a month, a Twenty-Sixth of July action squad assassinated Colonel Fermín Cowley, the commander of the military garrison at Holguín.[46] In April 1956 an insurgent Auténtico group attacked the Goicuría army barracks at Matanzas.[47] A year later, a student revolutionary organization, the Directorio Revolucionario, carried the armed struggle directly to the president. The Directorio attacked the Presidential Palace attempting to assassinate Batista and capture a Havana radio station to issue a national call to arms.[48] The failure of the attack on the palace and the subsequent deaths resulting from the abortive mission virtually destroyed the leadership cadre of the Directorio. Survivors later regrouped and, repudiating urban resistance, took the struggle to the Escambray mountain range in Las Villas where they organized the II Frente Nacional del Escambray.[49]

A stillborn general strike called by the Twenty-Sixth of July leadership in April 1958 marked the end of significant revolutionary efforts in urban centers. The failure of the general strike and the government's subsequent success against urban opposition leaders crippled organized resistance in the cities. When asked two months later if the Twenty-Sixth of July had been affected adversely by the failure of the strike, Castro admitted that the organization had suffered in the cities.[50] In Havana alone, an estimated ninety-one *fidelistas* were killed in the days immediately following the unsuccessful strike.[51] The orientation of antigovernment operations now shifted away from the cities to the mountains. Arms used in the urban struggle passed clandestinely into the interior, now the center of operations.[52] The *fidelistas* were presently convinced that only a general engagement with the armed forces, not underground urban operations, would topple the regime.[53]

By mid-1958, virtually every opposition faction had abandoned urban warfare. The armed forces had demonstrated their efficiency in an urban setting. The position of the government behind the shield of the urban force had remained virtually unassailable. Castro recalled that it later seemed absurd to have men fight in the streets against a disciplined army which had "technical preparation and recourse to tanks, planes, pursuit cars, arms of all types and which had organization and experience." The army, Castro indicated, had the particular expertise "to kill people in the streets and disorganize groups and crush public demonstrations."[54]

Origins of Military Dissension

Against a backdrop of growing armed opposition and behind the government's boast of unanimous military support, divisions and fissures—resulting from the contradictions in the March 10 *cuartelazo* and made acute by growing civilian opposition—emerged in the armed forces. The much vaunted "army monolith" was more apparent than real. The split that had occurred earlier between professional academy officers, the *puros,* and political appointees survived into the *batistiano* armed services. *Puro* officers who supported the movement of March 10 to end Auténtico excesses very early came to feel that the Batista government had betrayed the objectives of the coup. Many officers had expressed keen disappointment in the composition of the new administration.[55] General Jorge García Tuñón, an original conspirator in 1952 and forced by disagreement with Tabernilla into retirement, complained that the government had failed to respond to the problems initially inspiring army intervention.[56]

Junior and middle grade officers grew increasingly impatient with the military establishment under Batista. Within weeks of the coup, the new government had virtually dismantled the professional officer corps. All commanders suspected of being unsympathetic to the new order were retired. More than ever, political credentials determined commissions and promotions. In the space of twenty-four months, the Batista government had counteracted twelve years of professional development. In the haste to fill army ranks with supporters of the regime, the government consistently violated the army code regulating promotion and appointment. The number of commissions awarded to noncommissioned officers and enlisted personnel rankled academy-trained officers. Demoralization spread to the military service academies as well. Cadets in the Escuela de Cadetes questioned with some cynicism the value of spending years in the academy only to see enlisted men commissioned overnight.[57]

The new government sacrificed the tenuously institutionalized professionalism of the armed forces for political expedients. Despite Batista's earlier pledge that his administration would not recall to active service officers retired by previous administrations,[58] scores of *septembristas* returned to assume key positions in the new military order. The *lumpen-proletariat* in uniform returned to active duty. General Franciso Tabernilla became chief of staff. Lieutenant Pilar García, who had retired in 1944, assumed command of the Las Villas regiment. Colonel Carlos M. Cantillo, dismissed by Grau, returned to active service. Captain José E. Rodríguez, retired in 1945, assumed charge of the navy in 1952. Lieutenant Manuel Larrubia, a victim of the early Auténtico purges, assumed command of the air force. Colonel Ramón E. Cruz y Vidal, the former private of Camp Columbia, returned to head the Servicio de Inteligencia Militar after eight years in retirement. In 1958, even José E. Pedraza, the *septembrista* gambling czar during the 1930s and Batista's one-time foe, returned to active service. Ex-*septembrista* commanders also assumed positions within the nonmilitary sectors of the *marcista* order. Former Colonel Rolando Peláez was appointed subsecretary of national defense. Ex-Lieutenant Colonel Juan Rodríguez Alonso returned to public service as chief of the merchant marine division of the Cuban Maritime Commission. Braulio Eligio Fernández, a retired naval captain, was appointed military interventor in the Empresa Naviera de Cuba. Many *septembristas* similarly returned to command provincial-level departments. Lieutenant Colonel Rogelio Rojas Meis, a former *machadista* officer who joined the sergeants, assumed command of the national police headquarters in Camagüey.

The return of *septembrista* commanders demoralized *puro* officers. Many professional commanders, irked by the quality of promotions and appointments, grew increasingly restive in the armed institution. Proud of their academy preparation and professional credentials, young officers were offended by their subordination to the political appointments of former sergeants.[59]

Nepotism within the *septembrista* command, converting the armed forces into the patrimony of a handful of families, specifically the Tabernillas, further contributed to undermining the army *esprit de corps*. The progeny of the *septembrista* command had come of age, demanding grades in the armed forces commensurate to the relative importance of their surnames. The three sons of Chief of Staff Tabernilla, retired in 1944, returned to active service after March 10. Francisco Tabernilla Palmero, recalled to duty as a lieutenant on March 22 rose immediately to the rank of comandante; on April 19 he was promoted to lieutenant colonel, emerging several years later as brigadier general in command of the Mixed Tank Regiment. Carlos Tabernilla, formerly a lieutenant, was immediately promoted to captain upon returning to active duty on March 22; by May he had reached the rank of colonel. In 1955, Carlos was appointed chief of the air force, ultimately leaving the island as a brigadier general. Marcelo Tabernilla, returning to the army on March 22, was promoted to captain on the same day. By May 3, he had reached the grade of comandante. By 1958, Marcelo had reached the rank of lieutenant colonel and commanded the Air Force Bomber Squadron.

Army Chief of Staff Tabernilla's brother-in-law, Brigadier General Alberto del Río Chaviano, served as military chief of Oriente Province. In addition, representatives of the Tabernilla group assumed key commands throughout the island, much to the disgust of the original conspirators of March 10 and junior academy officers. The brother of Batista's wife, Roberto Fernández Miranda, had a meteoric career, rising from lieutenant to brigadier general in five years. Brigadier General Rafael Salas Cañizares brought three brothers into the command hierarchy of the national police. His son served as deputy director of army intelligence. Lieutenant Colonel Pilar García promoted the interests of his two sons, Captain Rolando García Báez, an air force pilot, and Captain Irenaldo R. García Báez, a member of the General Staff. Brigadier General Carlos Cantillo, the brother of General Eulogio Cantillo, later the chief of military operations in Oriente, commanded the Matanzas regiment.

Quite apart from their growing disillusionment with developments in the armed forces, dissident officers could not remain unaffected by growing opposition to the government. The army deed of March 10, 1952, returned to haunt the professional ranks. In the eyes of the opposition, the armed forces held full responsibility for placing and sustaining in power an unpopular government. As in 1933, the fate of the post-Batista army became an increasing source of concern to those officers unattached politically to the regime. By the mid-1950s, sectors of the officer corps, now prepared to abandon an inexpedient alliance, were receptive to conspiratorial overtures.

The much vaunted "monolithic unity" of the armed forces

dissolved in full national view with the discovery of a far-flung army conspiracy in April 1956. Led by *puro* Colonel Ramón Barquín, with the collaboration of civilian opposition sectors, the plot implicated the most distinguished professional officers in the Cuban military establishment. Barquín himself had received the American Legion of Honor and had represented Cuba in the Inter-American Defense System. A graduate of national service academies, Barquín had received additional preparation abroad, including training at the Escuela Superior de Guerra in Mexico and service with American army intelligence.[60] Barquín's co-conspirators, too young to have had any association with *septembrismo* but not sufficiently senior to suffer in the post–March Tenth purges, likewise possessed impressive credentials. Captain José Ramos Avila had recently completed advanced studies in army administration in the United States. Lieutenant Colonel Manuel Varela commanded the Army Tank Battalion. Comandante Enrique Borbonet directed the paratroopers. Comandante José J. W. Orihuela was a leading artillery expert in the Cuban army. Lieutenants Manuel A. Villafaña, René Traviesa Pla, and José Planes de la Torre had recently returned from the United States after successfully completing air force flying programs. In all, some two hundred twenty officers and men were implicated in the planned overthrow of the government.[61]

The *puro* conspiracy came as a rude jolt to political leaders dependent upon military support. Batista later wrote that the movement had "greatly surprised" his administration.[62] The army command perceived the full implication of the plot. During the subsequent courts-martial, the army prosecutor charged that the conspirators had "caused a great [deal of] damage to the armed institution which could be considered irreparable. They were teachers, they were men of talent, they were mentors of the military generation." By their youth and professional preparation, the prosecutor went on, "they were the true masters of the Army. They were the ones who formed the spirit of many of our brothers."[63]

The administration turned immediately to the task of repairing the shattered army consensus. Batista secured congressional authority to retire, promote, and transfer—entirely at his discretion—officers and enlisted men for a period of forty-five days. One source predicted some four thousand "movements" within the armed forces as a result of the president's determination to reconstruct the "army monolith."[64] Scores of retirements, in fact, accompanied the discovery of the *puro* conspiracy. Numerous officers resigned their commissions after the trials; others were dismissed by executive decree.[65]

The Barquín conspiracy, above all, exposed the exalted army monolith as a fraud. The long-whispered rumors of dissension within the armed services surfaced into full national view. The April plot started a process in which the president's confidence in the armed forces gradually crumbled. Government obsession for political loyalty drove into retirement an entire sector of professional officers. At the precise moment the administration would require the services of its most talented and respected military leaders to lead the army against the guerrilla columns, it inaugurated a mass purge of professional officials. Batista grew increasingly reliant on his political officers to maintain control of the armed forces.[66] The army passed under the authority of officers who lacked the professional credentials to command the respect of subordinates; professionally trained officers, on the other hand, after April 1956 failed to win the confidence of their superiors. Open dissension in the armed forces, moreover, inspired opposition factions to continue probing the military armor of the regime in search of further pressure points.

Within a year, antigovernment factions had again pierced the military defenses of the *batistato,* this time in the navy. On September 5, 1957, mutinous officers and sailors captured the naval installation at Cayo Loco, Cienfuegos. The naval rebels threw the base open to collaborating units of the Twenty-Sixth of July and the armed wing of the Auténticos, which distributed arms to civilian participants.[67] Insurgent naval contingents, revolutionary groups, and armed civilians moved on Cienfuegos, attempting to capture the city. All the important objectives except the local military detachment passed under rebel control. Within hours, the Las Villas port was under the sway of revolutionary forces.[68]

Rebel mastery over Cienfuegos proved short-lived. Government reinforcement, preceded by heavy air attacks, immediately began the task of recapturing the insurgent-held city. Within twenty-four hours, an estimated two thousand troops, supported by tanks and armored personnel carriers, had subdued the revolt.[69] By September 6, government forces had reoccupied the city.

Subsequent government investigation into the naval uprising uncovered a conspiratorial network of far-reaching proportions, implicating every branch of the armed forces. Cayo Loco represented only one dimension of a far-flung conspiracy in which naval stations throughout the island, including bases in the cities of Pinar del Río, Mariel, Havana, and Santiago de Cuba, planned a concerted strike against the regime. The original plot called for seizing vessels anchored in Havana and training naval guns on key army installations in the capital to force the government to relinquish power.[70] A last-moment suspension of plans, however, the news of which never reached Cayo Loco, halted the nationwide conspiracy.

Further investigations uncovered an air force conspiracy independent of naval activity. The government learned that air force pilots had refused to fulfill their missions when ordered to bomb and strafe the rebel-held city in Las Villas. The first wave of bombers discharged their loads off-target and at sea.[71] Before a military tribunal, Comandante Enrique Carrera Rojas, an air force squadron chief, recounted that during his missions against the guerrillas in the Sierra Maestra he foresaw an occasion when pilots would be ordered to attack urban centers in Oriente. In the face of this prospect, Carrera and his fellow pilots pledged to disobey any command requiring the bombing of open cities. When orders arrived to attack Cienfuegos, Carrera and other flyers agreed to release their bombs at sea. Upon returning to Havana, they were arrested.[72] In the end, two majors, three captains, and five lieutenants were implicated in the aftermath of the Cienfuegos uprising.

Army investigators further discovered the involvement of the medical corps in the conspiracy. Numerous army doctors, such as the leader of the conspiracy, Captain Teobaldo Cuervo Castillo, had served earlier in the Sierra Maestra campaigns. Attending to the needs of wounded officers and men, Cuervo "gathered their complaints and discontents," impressing upon wounded soldiers the urgency of resolving the national crisis.[73] In the course of the government probe, army investigations discovered army and naval medics prominently involved in the coordination of the Cienfuegos uprising.[74]

Coming within a year of the Barquín plot, the Cienfuegos uprising and the conspiracies in the other branches of the armed forces shattered the credibility of the Army's monolithic unity. Since 1933, reported Ruby Hart Phillips from Havana,

Batista had been "confident that the Army, Navy and police force were solidly behind him. Today he is not so sure."[75] And Ambassador Earl E. T. Smith later wrote that the president and other administration officials realized "they were no longer able to count on the blind support of the army forces, which Batista had previously completely depended upon."[76]

A wave of purges, retirements, and transfers followed the Cienfuegos uprising. The government launched a general loyalty check throughout the armed forces. Army detachments patrolled the installations of the less-trusted navy. Toward the mid-1950s the government's military order revealed the stresses of national tensions.

The Final Confrontation:
The Eclipse of the *Marcista* Order,
1958–1959

13 The suppression of organized resistance in the urban rear guard of the *batistiano* politico-military order permitted Havana to concentrate its resources in the Sierra Maestra. The collapse of the general strike inspired in government circles the belief that the end of armed resistance was imminent. Batista, Ambassador Smith later wrote,"apparently felt he was in the ascendancy."[1] From the Sierra Maestra, Fidel Castro recognized that the government had "seen its morale improved" and predicted that the administration was "getting ready to come over us with all its might."[2] To make good official claims that the revolution had, in fact, been suppressed, Havana moved to crush the guerrilla *foco* in Oriente. By April 1958 the insurgents in the Sierra Maestra had assumed a symbolic value out of proportion to their military capability. The Twenty-Sixth of July had come to represent a defiance, a tribute to the revolutionary will compelling Havana to leave the cities to end the rural insurrection.[3] Any "delay in fighting the guerrillas with adequate tactics," Batista later recalled, threatened to undermine confidence in government authorities. The president mobilized government resources to deliver "an effective blow" to create "the impression that the days of the Sierra Maestra affair were numbered."[4]

In late May 1958, a month after the abortive general strike, the government launched its fourth and most formidable offensive against the guerrilla *foco* in Oriente. Every service of the armed forces participated in the offensive. An estimated

152

twelve thousand troops moved on the guerrilla columns. Air force squadrons bombed and strafed suspected rebel-held regions in the Sierra Maestra. Naval offshore units pounded the southeastern mountain range. Within three months, the government offensive ended unsuccessfully. In the face of this failure, the guerrilla columns launched a counteroffensive movement leading ultimately to Havana and the collapse of the Batista government.

The Collapse of the Cuban Army

Military Dimensions

The armed forces inaugurated the spring campaign alienated from the body politic and discredited for defending a regime held in national scorn. Contempt for the uniform manifested itself everywhere soldiers came into contact with civilians. Whatever self-view soldiers held—whatever perception they had of the cause for which they fought—suffered in the looking-glass image refracted by the civilian population. Comandante José Quevado, ultimately defecting to the Twenty-Sixth of July, lamented the lack of national support extended to the army effort. "We felt," Quevado complained, "as if we were an army of occupation."[5] An enlisted man in Bayamo discovered to his dismay that soldiers "were simply hated"; the women, the recruit noted dolefully, "did not even look at us."[6]

Fidelista propaganda contributed further to the demoralization of the armed forces. Designed to at once undermine the soldier's allegiance to the regime and destroy his confidence in the army command, insurgent exhortations contributed powerfully to the collapse of the army's will to oppose the insurgent columns.[7] From the very outset the Twenty-Sixth of July directed propaganda specifically at the government forces in the field. The guerrillas denied antimilitary sentiments and encouraged soldiers and officers not guilty of crimes to join the insurgent units. The Twenty-Sixth of July carefully avoided singling out the soldier as the enemy, depicting him instead as a co-victim of an oppressive order. As early as February 1957 a manifesto from the Sierra Maestra reminded soldiers that "Batista's sons do not come to the mountains, Tabernilla's sons do not come to the mountains, the sons of ministers and senators do not come to the mountains, the sons of millionaires do not come to the mountains"; precisely for this reason, Castro proclaimed, the Twenty-Sixth of July could not "feel hatred against the soldiers."[8] The establishment of Radio Rebelde in the Sierra Maestra, carrying the impassioned exhortations of the rebel chieftain behind enemy lines during the spring offensive, further weakened army will. The Twenty-Sixth of July, Castro insisted, "was not at war with the armed forces but against the dictatorship."[9] "The Armed Forces and the Revolution whose interests are not—nor is there any reason for them to be—opposed, can solve the problem of Cuba together. We are at war against the tyranny, not against the Armed Forces."[10] Castro admonished the army to unfasten itself from the "cadaver" of a dying regime and redeem the integrity of the military institution.[11] He pledged in addition that the new revolutionary government would "divorce the army from politics and . . . . guarantee the non-political status" of the military.[12]

Rebel treatment of army prisoners further raised the prestige of the Twenty-Sixth of July among government troops. Wounded soldiers received medical attention, and prisoners were treated cordially. After some "revolutionary instruction," prisoners were released unharmed, less arms and ammunition.[13] By the end of the spring offensive, the guerrillas had set free an estimated five hundred prisoners.[14] The policy of the Twenty-Sixth of July toward the armed forces proved particularly effective during the government offensive. The return of army prisoners unharmed belied administration allegations of rebel torture of captured soldiers.[15] Many soldiers concluded that it was far wiser to fall prisoner than to risk their lives resisting insurgent advances.[16]

The government offensive collapsed through defections, desertions, and a simple unwillingness among large numbers of officers to continue supporting Havana in the field. After the failure of the spring offensive, the army virtually ceased to resist the drives of the rebel counteroffensive. The army, tired and weakened by two years of a prolonged campaign, "had completely lost its combat power."[17] Camilo Cienfuegos, leading his guerrilla column into Las Villas, reported to the rebel command that an army patrol, discovering the presence of his unit, did nothing to impede their passage. This, Cienfuegos concluded, was the "most palpable demonstration" that the army no longer wished to fight.[18]

Desertions and defections became commonplace. By the

autumn of 1958, Batista wrote, "the surrender of Army units to rebel groups by certain officers in command in the zones of operation occurred with surprising frequency."[19] Comandante José Quevado took his entire field command over to the rebel line. A fifty-three man reconnaissance patrol under Leiutenant Rodolfo Villamil, unable to secure adequate support and proper arms, defected to the insurgent cause.[20] Numerous air force pilots defected to the United States. As early as April 1958 some fifteen flyers had applied for political asylum in Miami. Others had been arrested in Havana for refusing to fly missions over the Sierra Maestra.[21] Many who did remain deliberately sabotaged the government's air war against the guerrilla forces by releasing their bombs off-target.[22] Paratroopers were also reported unwilling to serve in the front lines.[23]

Demoralization resulting from reversals in the field contributed still further to undermining the government campaign. Four offensives and two years later, the insurgents continued to defy all government military efforts. The Cuban army had lost its capacity to wage war in the countryside. Batista had reached military maturity in a political setting where urban resistance dominated all forms of challenge to the constituted order. Between 1935 and 1958, opposition to the political system had found its most formidable expression almost entirely in an urban setting; two general strikes, two urban uprisings in Santiago de Cuba, the capture of Cienfuegos, the attack on the Presidential Palace, and several military conspiracies revolving around the seizures of Camp Columbia and La Cabaña conformed to past patterns of resistance. The Cuban army had developed into a formidable urban armed force, supported by an equally efficient national police. In a rural setting, this military establishment crumbled. The last significant rural uprising suppressed by the army had occurred in 1931.

The mold in which the American Military Defense Assistance Program (MDAP) cast the Cuban military, moreover, weakened the rural effectiveness of the army. Prepared to meet an illusory Soviet assault on the Western Hemisphere, the Cuban military institution may very well have conducted itself commendably against a Russian invasion of the island. Tank battalions, armored personnel carriers, motorized divisions, antiaircraft equipment, heavy artillery, and jet aircraft prepared the Cuban armed forces adequately for conventional war. The "emphasis of the United States Military Missions," one military observer wrote, "was placed on those forces that had Hemispheric defense missions, such as sea and coastal patrols."[24]

The historic evolution of the armed forces and the Hemispheric mission assigned to the Cuban military by the cold war military planners in Washington hindered counterinsurgent effectiveness. "Fighting in the mountains," former Ambassador Arthur Gardner admitted, "was not what the Cuban troops were ever taught."[25] Colonel Clark Lynn, Jr., the chief of the American military mission in Havana, conceded that instruction in guerrilla operations was "limited."[26] And Batista himself later attributed the fall of his government to the lack of military preparation needed "to meet the guerrilla tactics of the rebels."[27]

Havana's frustration in Oriente forced the government to adopt measures designed for immediate returns. Troops most familiar with the eastern terrain and countryside, reported too friendly with the local population, were replaced by units from Havana.[28] These troops, in a good many instances, could not endure the rigors of countryside campaigning. Physically weak and poorly trained, these soldiers lacked the preparation for a prolonged campaign in the mountain countryside.[29] In 1958, the regime revived obligatory military service, defunct since World War II. Thousands of youths between eighteen and twenty-five years of age were drafted. Hastily trained and inadequately armed, recruits were hurled against the guerrilla veterans. During the ceremonies celebrating the completion of basic training for one group of enlisted men, a soldier noted with considerable if misplaced pride that the recruits had finished in thirty days a program requiring ordinarily six months.[30] By December 1958 the military had recruited an estimated ten thousand youths under twenty years of age, and Havana continued to dispatch them to the Sierra Maestra with only weeks of training.[31] Inmates of juvenile detention centers were inducted into the army and promptly assigned to the Sierra Maestra.[32] One infantry company trained by North American advisory units was transferred to the eastern front before completing its training program.[33] The almost summary collapse of these poorly prepared combat units in battle further demoralized the armed forces.[34]

The use of such army units, routed easily by the guerrilla columns, was a boon to the insurgent war effort. A veritable arsenal fell to the Twenty-Sixth of July. One rebel victory alone, for example, yielded the insurgents fourteen Springfield rifles, nine machine guns, forty-eight rifle grenades, one .30-caliber Browning machine gun, and eighteen thousand rounds of ammunition.[35] In the wake of the government's failure, retreating forces left behind over five hundred arms, armored cars, cannons, tanks, and bazookas, and thousands of rounds of ammunition.[36] Batista later claimed, in fact, that the guerrillas had achieved "actual superiority in arms over the Cuban Army."[37]

The military command launched the offensive at a season particularly inauspicious for the type of campaign the Cuban army was capable of conducting. Required to protect sugar during the *zafra* between January and May, mass troop mobilization of the magnitude required for the general offensive was possible only between June and December—the island's rainy season.[38] Rain seriously impeded the army's forward progress, frustrating any meaningful penetration of the Sierra Maestra. Motorized detachments and armored units came to a slow, grinding halt in the field. As early as June, dispatches from the front in Oriente indicated that the offensive had become "stuck in a sea of mud."[39] Several days later, virtually all army movement was reported "paralyzed by the torrential downpours," interrupting communications and curtailing army patrols.[40]

Fear of conspiracies, specifically in the Havana garrisons, contributed to the weakening of the administration's military effort. Plots that had occurred in the past were taking their toll in 1958. Batista's most trusted officers—those loyal politically—remained in command of the vital regiments in the capital. The army leadership refused to transfer prominent *marcista* commanders to remote provincial units to assume charge of the government campaign. Batista insisted on keeping his trusted brother-in-law, General Roberto Fernández Miranda, in command of La Cabaña. General Francisco Tabernilla remained at Camp Columbia for fear of the presence of *barquinistas* awaiting the opportunity to strike again.[41] The president could not confidently detach his most trusted officers and, equally important, the large reserve of well-trained troops from Havana garrison duty to the theater of operations.[42] Batista found himself compelled to assign battle commands to young field officers not necessarily linked politically to Havana, very likely the products of the island's service academies, not entirely convinced of the righteousness of the cause for which they fought, and, hence, most susceptible to the appeals delivered from Radio Rebelde. The administration entrusted its fate to raw recruits and young field officers while politically dependable commanders and well-trained troops remained in Havana.

Diplomatic Dimensions (I)

The drama in Cuba unfolded in an anomalous diplomatic context. The Cuban insurgency, almost from its inception, received considerable attention in the United States. Herbert Matthews's penetration of the Sierra Maestra wilderness to interview the guerrilla chieftain in 1957 fastened the Cuban insurgency onto the North American consciousness.[43] Thereafter, journalists, photographers, and film reporters, in the tradition of their predecessors during the Spanish–Cuban—American War, undertook clandestine missions to Oriente in search of the guerrillas, keeping the North American reading public abreast of the Cuban struggle.

The rebellion in the provinces evolved in a fashion reminiscent of early twentieth-century insurrections. Rebels exploited Havana's international responsibilities. The destruction of property—specifically, foreign-controlled industries—assumed tactical priority in the guerrilla campaign. In February 1958 the Twenty-Sixth of July announced plans to cripple sugar mills, tobacco factories, public utilities, railroads, and refineries.[44] The destruction of the sugar harvest emerged as an integral part of the guerrillas' "definitive plan."[45] "Either Batista without the zafra or the zafra without Batista," vowed the Twenty-Sixth of July. By March 1958 the insurgents reported having applied a torch to every cane-producing province on the island, destroying an estimated two million tons of sugar.[46]

Insurgent tactics placed still additional strains on the government campaign. Rebel operations against property compelled the government to assign large numbers of troops to garrison duty. Soldiers otherwise available for combat protected property.[47] It behooved Havana, seeking to retain diplomatic support, to demonstrate its capacity to govern effectively. Within the context of United States–Cuban relations, this necessarily involved safeguarding foreign lives and property. In March 1958 Batista reassured Ambassador Smith of his government's ability to "control the situation" and provide "proper protection of American lives and American property."[48] During the second government offensive in Oriente, Colonel Barrera Pérez, having found "tranquility reigning" in the Sierra Maestra foothills, deployed more than half his force to augment the military detachments in Manzanillo, Bayamo, Palma Soriano, and Santiago de Cuba to patrol the countryside during the *zafra*.[49] Shortly after launching government operations for the third time in the Sierra, after the attack at El Uvero, the army spent much of its time in the field lending protection and assistance to the coffee harvest.[50] At the start of the 1958 spring offensive, the military requirements of the *zafra*, still only two-thirds completed, necessitated the presence of numerous army units at sugar production centers.[51] Francisco Tabernilla later accused Batista of crippling the 1958 campaign by assigning troops to protect "sugar *centrales*, mining companies, the aquaduct of the United States Naval Base in Guantánamo, rice mills, coffee fields, private *fincas* [farms], etc., instead of dedicating all those forces to the persecution of the enemy."[52]

The guerrilla command skillfully exploited American influence in Havana. In June and July, during the most severe phase of the government offensive, guerrilla units of the Second Front in Oriente under Raúl Castro kidnapped some forty Americans and Canadians in an effort to halt government air strikes.[53] The internment of the North American hostages in the zone of government operations forced Havana to suspend hostilities pending their release. The prisoners were released slowly, several at a time, prolonging the inactivity of the government effort.[54] In the end, the kidnapping—known in revolutionary terminology as *"operación antiaérea"*—and the subsequent halt of the government campaign, provided a respite vital for the Second Front to reorganize and redeploy its forces, all later considered critical for subsequent guerrilla victories.[55]

Public attention to Latin America in 1958 after Vice-President Nixon's disastrous peregrinations through South America catapulted the struggle in Cuba onto an inter-American stage. In many ways, Batista came to serve as the sacrificial victim of North American penitence for a decade of collaboration with dictatorships. American diplomatic officials redefined the Cuban political reality to conform to the newly proclaimed *démarche* of extending a handshake to dictators and an *abrazo* (embrace) to democrats. In this context, Batista had to apply sufficient force and violence to suppress the opposition but with care not to exceed an undefined limit capable of alienating United States support.[56]

In March 1958, sensitive to the drift of American hemispheric policy, Batista reorganized his cabinet with the objective of renewing Washington's support of his faltering regime. On March 7, the Cuban president announced his "cabinet of peace," in which the Prime Ministry had been assigned to Emilio Núñez Portuondo. The important credentials of the new prime minister consisted almost entirely in his serving as ambassador in Washington and representing Cuba at the United Nations where he vigorously supported the American international position.[57] Batista reordered his cabinet, appointing a zealous anticommunist as prime minister, to win the support of Secretary of State Dulles.[58] By March 12, however, the new ministry collapsed. On March 14, the United States declared an embargo on arms to the Cuban government.

The arms embargo came as a jolt to the Havana war effort. Politically the embargo was tantamount to a withdrawl of American support and undermined even further the government's internal position. Coming as it did on the eve of the spring offensive, moreover, it shattered whatever moral support existed for the army in the belief that the United States endorsed the government campaign. In addition, the State Department protested the use of American military aid, provided to Cuba only for hemispheric defense projects, without Washington's prior consent. State Deparment officials asked Havana to withdraw from the theater of operations an infantry battalion trained and equipped by the Military Defense Assistance Program and requested Cuban authorities to pledge to discontinue the use of MDAP bombers against rebel-held cities.[59]

The arms embargo and the subsequent protest over the use of army units trained and equipped by the United States contributed powerfully to the final collapse of morale within the Cuban armed forces. Throughout the 1950s army *esprit de corps* had been reinforced by American military decorations awarded to senior Cuban officers, including Ramón Barquín, Francisco Tabernilla, and Carlos Tabernilla. North American military personnel frequently participated in official army functions as invited guests of honor. Several hundred Cuban officers had received training in the United States. The military establishment had been created, trained, provisioned, and armed by the United States; its highest military honor emanated from Washington, and for almost a half a century it had been invested with North American support. Thus the arms embargo could crush at once the army's self-confidence and its faith in the constituted government. Repeatedly Batista had invoked American support that manifested itself in American arms, equipment, and the presence of MDAP missions.[60] Evidence that the United States no longer backed the government's war effort, Ambassador Smith later suggested, "had a devastating psychological effect" on the armed forces. The American ambassador subsequently concluded that the embargo "was the most effective step taken by the Department of State in bringing about the downfall of Batista."[61] Batista himself conceded that the suspension of arms delivery "weakened the faith and will to fight of our men."[62]

Popular Dimensions

The *marcista* order did not crumble as a result of a military defeat inflicted by the expanding columns of the Rebel Army. Rather, the government's inability to restore a political consensus and the continued operation of the guerrilla *foco* contributed to the creation of a revolutionary situation. The conditions produced by the ability of the guerrillas to elude the government contributed powerfully to the fall of Batista. This lesson, in fact, Che Guevara and Castro inferred from the Cuban revolutionary war: the conditions for revolution could be created by a guerrilla *foco*.[63] As early as 1957, Castro had informed Robert Taber that the guerrillas did not expect to overthrow the government singlehandedly but rather planned to produce a "climate of collapse."[64]

The guerrilla *foco* did, in fact, produce this "climate of collapse." During the offensive, the guerrilla forces—never more than three hundred strong—withstood the fiercest government attack.[65] The failure of the campaign, exposing the vulnerability of the political authorities, added impetus to the "climate of collapse." Between the government offensive and Batista's flight, uprisings throughout the island anticipated the insurgent counteroffensive. In December 1958 the army command in Santiago de Cuba reported that some 90 percent of the population in the eastern capital supported the guerrillas.[66] In late 1958, popular uprisings in Camagüey threatened army control of the province; assassinations, strikes, and growing civil participation in the struggle against Batista grew in direct relation to the success of the guerrilla operations.[67] In the decisive battle of Santa Clara, the guerrilla columns secured decisive assistance from the local population.[68] In Las Villas generally, in fact, an estimated 80 percent of the population supported the advancing guerrilla columns.[69] By the end of the year, the provinces were in virtual alliance with the Rebel Army.

The combination of government failures and guerrilla victories produced the conditions encouraging mass participation against a faltering regime. The triumph over Batista, Claude Julien later suggested, was "not exactly a military victory" but rather a "moral and popular victory."[70] Castro subsequently claimed that some 98 percent of the population participated in the revolutionary struggle.[71] Former army Chief of Staff Tabernilla, when questioned if the army could have stopped the *fidelistas* from entering Habana, replied, "It could but not for a long time because by that time the people of Cuba were already against the regime of Batista, and there is no army, once the people get up in arms, that can suppress it." When asked further if the "people themselves" supported the revolution, Tabernilla responded, "Completely."[72]

Diplomatic Dimensions (II)

The insurgency ultimately undermined Havana's international position. By late 1958, Washington had lost all confidence in the ability of Cuban authorities to restore order. Political stability on the island had collapsed. More specifically, Cuban disorders had placed the lives and property of foreigners in increasing jeopardy and had paralyzed business and commerce. Guerrilla operations against property had cost millions of dollars; the armed forces were simply unable to prevent the destruction of property.[73] In a cable to New York, Ruby Hart Phillips reported that commerce, industry, and capital, "which have wholeheartedly supported President Batista since he took over the Government in 1952, are growing impatient with the continued violence in the island."[74]

In the fall of 1958 Batista attempted to recover lost Amercian support by holding long-deferred elections. The Cuban government sought to demonstrate to Washington that democratic processes, civil war notwithstanding, were still viable on the island. To the surprise of few, the government candidate, Andrés Rivero Agüero, won the election.

The November electoral hoax, rather than strengthening the regime, further weakened the government's position both at home and abroad. The imposition of the official candidate disillusioned many who, placing their hopes in the election to provide a pacific denouement to the political crisis, had earlier supported the government.[75] Moreover, Batista may well have conceded the margin of military superiority in a politico-diplomatic gamble. At the precise moment the government was sustaining its most serious reversals in the war, Batista took the extraordinary measure of detaching an estimated twenty thousand troops—presumably all capable of combat service—for poll duty during the election.[76] Officers loyal personally to Batista, finally, disheartened by the prospect of an imminent transfer of executive power, lost some enthusiasm in the fight to defend a leader already ousted at the polls. "Faced with the prospect of your retirement," Francisco Tabernilla Palmero wrote to Batista, "the whole system began to collapse after the election on November 1."[77]

The 1958 election also failed to rally support abroad. Washington repudiated the continuity of power orchestrated by the Presidential Palace and announced in advance plans to withhold diplomatic support of the Rivero Agüero government. Within weeks of the election, Rivero called upon the American Embassy to learn the policy the United States planned to follow toward the Cuban government.[78] Ambassador Smith informed the Cuban president-elect that Washington "would not give aid and support to [his] . . . government when installed because we did not feel he could maintain effective control of the country."[79]

Word that the United States had refused to endorse the Rivero Agüero government undermined the army's commitment to a political order whose future at that moment appeared bleak. Conditions in the armed forces continued to deteriorate. Some officers, Batista later wrote, indicated "they would not continue fighting for a government that was doomed."[80] By mid-November, the American ambassador reported to Washington that the Batista government "was on its last legs."[81]

Repudiating the constituted government and rejecting in

advance the administration of Rivero Agüero, the United States assumed the direction of imposing a settlement in Havana consistent with its vision of Cuban and American needs. In late 1958, Washington attempted to block the distrusted Twenty-Sixth of July from seizing power. In early December, the State Department dispatched William D. Pawley, a former American financier in Cuba, to undertake a covert quasi-official mission to Havana to persuade Batista "to capitulate to a caretaker government unfriendly to him, but satisfactory to us, whom we could immediately recognize and give military assistance to in order that Fidel Castro not come to power."[82] On December 9, Pawley held a three-hour conference with Batista, offering him an opportunity to live unmolested in Daytona Beach with his family. The American agent informed the president that "we would make an effort to stop Fidel Castro from coming into power as a Communist, but that the caretaker government would be men who were enemies of his, otherwise it would not work anyway, and Fidel Castro would otherwise have to lay down his arms or admit he was a revolutionary fighting against everybody only because he wanted power, not because he was against Batista"[83] The American ambassador agreed and informed Batista that Washington believed him incapable of maintaining effective control—he should retire.[84] Though his term would expire shortly—on February 24, 1959—Batista refused to relinquish power.

Washington's announcement of its decision to withhold support of the Rivero government may well have served as the signal to army leaders to seek an alternative solution more acceptable to the United States. By late fall, conspiracies and counterconspiracies wracked that armed forces. The army responded to the crisis with a search for a political arrangement of its own. In November, the administration uncovered an antigovernment plot based in Camp Columbia. Led by General Martín Díaz Tamayo, chief of army operations, the conspiracy involved some thirty officers. Several weeks later, another plot implicating important naval chieftains, including Commodore Joaquín Pablo Varela, chief of the navy air corps, was uncovered.[85] In December, Chief of Staff Tabernilla, his brother-in-law General Alberto del Río Chaviano, and his son Carlos Tabernilla, paid a visit to the American Embassy to offer the ambassador a solution to the crisis. The Tabernilla patriarch proposed to form a military junta composed of senior army and navy commanders to replace the Batista government. The visit, the army chief indicated, was designed to learn the probable American response to such an arrangement.[86] At the same time the Tabernillas plotted, General Eulogio Cantillo, chief of army operations in Oriente, General Carlos Cantillo, commander of the Matanzas regiment, Colonel José M. Rego Rubido, chief of the Santiago regiment, and Colonel Florentino Rosell Leyva, chief of the army corps of engineers, banded together to establish a junta in order to "guarantee stability and public order." The conspiracy collapsed when uncovered by government agents forcing a number of key officers to flee into exile.[87] In another antigovernment plot, General Eulogio Cantillo entered into negotiations with the Twenty-Sixth of July command on December 28, promising to arrest Batista and relinquish power to the guerrilla leader. Castro received Cantillo's assurances that the Santiago regiment would unite with the Rebel Army after which Castro expressed hope that the remaining army units would support the guerrillas.[88]

Diplomatic, political, and military pressure, culminating in the Cantillo-Castro pact, forced Batista to flee on January 1, 1959. Rather than surrender to the Twenty-Sixth of July, however, Cantillo assumed leadership of the army, determined to continue the war effort under the presidency of Supreme Court Justice Carlos Piedra. The insurgent leadership repudiated the political machinations in Havana and, pledging to continue the struggle, exhorted the population to join the revolution and organize a general strike.[89] With the news of Batista's flight, army units throughout the island simply ceased to resist the rebel advances. Cantillo complained to the American Embassy that he had inherited the command of a "dead army."[90] Seeking to reanimate the moribund government war effort, Cantillo summoned the imprisoned Colonel Barquín and relinquished command of the army to the *puro* officer.[91] The new military chieftain ordered a cease-fire, saluted the insurgent "Army of Liberation," and surrendered command of Camp Columbia and La Cabaña to Camilo Cienfuegos and Ernesto Che Guevara.[92] On January 13, 1959, the provisional revolutionary government ordered the reorganization of the armed forces and suspended the Organic Law of the Army, allowing the incumbent authorities to reshape the armed forces in a fashion consistent with the needs of the new order.[93]

The Cuban Army, 1898–1958:
In Retrospect

14 In January 1959 the last underpinning of a frail national order collapsed. In the course of about fifty years, the Cuban army had experienced a skewed institutional development. Between 1898 and 1899, the Cuban Army of Liberation, linked organically to the island's historical processes, had been dissolved under the direction of United States occupation authorities seeking to eliminate a potential challenge to American politico-military hegemony. This corporate expression of Cuban nationalism—the Ejército Libertador—organized to call into existence an independent Cuba, had failed to survive the American occupation.

United States interventions, first from 1898 to 1902 and later from 1906 to 1909, laid the groundwork for the emergence of the republic's armed forces. The 1898–1902 occupation endowed the island with the Rural Guard, assigned by the occupation officials to protect rural properties. The American provisional government between 1906 and 1909 left behind the Permanent Army, designed to underwrite the Platt Amendment by giving Havana the politico-military support that the Rural Guard had failed to provide during the 1906 insurrection.

The centralization of national authority during the early decades, a process vastly accelerated during the *machadato*, vitiated the precarious viability of national institutions. Rival centers of authority, provincial and municipal autonomy, legislative prerogatives, and judicial controls collapsed in the expan-

166

sion of executive power in Havana. Civilian leaders had undermined national institutions well before the first direct intervention of the army in 1933. Indeed, national institutions in Cuba had little relation to the reality of national politics and simply could not without compromising their integrity serve the aspirations of Cuban leaders. Cuban national institutions, assaulted from above by leaders, lost legitimacy from below within the body politic. Ignacio García, the protagonist in Carlos Loveira's novel *Generales y doctores*, asks Cuban legislators if they understand the cynicism inherent in their rhetoric when they invoke the concept of patriotism. The *doctores* and *generales* "have placed the nation in danger a hundred times with their electoral hoaxes, their government terrorism, under the pretext of re-establishing the rule of law and justice, when basically it has been nothing else than the desperate defense of partisan interests, the struggle to preserve positions, political patronage, and leadership."[1]

The legitimacy of existing political institutions declined almost from the inception of nationhood. Whatever consensus upheld the constituted order in the young republic collapsed by the early 1930s, thereby preparing the way for the military intervention of August 1933. Similar conditions prevailed in 1952 and 1958. In many ways Cuban history lends support to the observation of Gino Germani and Kalman Silvert that military "intromission in the political power structure always indicates, of course, at least a relative inability of other social institutions to marshall their power effectively, and at most an advanced state of institutional decomposition."[2] Similarly, postwar army politics in France, as described by John S. Ambler, sheds some light on the Cuban experience:

> First, and most important, the French experience from 1942 to 1962 lends added weight to the theory that military intervention in politics is closely related to the degree of *legitimacy* of existing civilian political institutions, i.e., the strength and breadth of the national political consensus which supports them. Had government leaders in Paris enjoyed solid authority and the backing of a more united nation, in all probability there never would have been a serious threat to civilian control in France.[3]

The military organizations created by the American provisional governments were, in many ways, inconsistent with Cuban national institutions. United States authorities designed the armed forces to set the limits of the institutional interaction of Cuban politics to conform to American policy needs on the island. Stability was reduced to the preservation of the prevailing order—until it no longer served Washington's interests. Supported by North American insistence upon stability as articulated in the Platt Amendment, the Cuban army emerged as a counterforce to political change beyond the control of the leaders entrusted by Washington to govern the island. Like other armed forces created in the course of American interventions in Nicaragua, Haiti, and the Dominican Republic, the army in Cuba represented the front line of U.S. interests.

The diplomatic context in which the Cuban state evolved placed additional strains on the army. As Machado, and later Batista, discovered, the public opinion to which Havana responded resided in the United States. The final measure of stability around which American support revolved consisted in the protection of the lives and property of foreigners. This external fulcrum of power determined the mission of the Cuban armed institution.

The diplomatic and economic sinews on which the Cuban political order rested were measured in direct proportion to the stability provided by the armed forces. When opposition stepped beyond prescribed political behavior and exceeded the army's capacity to keep order, the very diplomatic underpinnings supporting the government turned against Havana. Both Machado and Batista had made a peaceful settlement of the crises impossible; both had produced radical responses to reactionary policies. The Welles and Pawley missions attempted to remove the apparent source of instability and obviate the imposition of a domestic radical solution. Against this diplomatic background, the Cuban army formed the keystone of a national order acceptable to the United States. The army served as an American lever in Cuban politics. Twice, in 1933 and 1958, changes in U.S. policy caused the armed forces to scramble in an effort to offer the embassy the political settlement sought by Washington.

Internally, the Cuban military organization developed in response to the partisan needs of the dominant political parties. From its inception, the Cuban armed institution passed under the command of officers appointed for their political predilections rather than for military competence. The armed forces emerged as simply another arena in which competing political factions played out their schemes for national hegemony. Very quickly political parties, starting in 1909 with the Liberals, expanded the mission of stability invested initially in the armed forces to include underwriting a partisan ascendancy. From this point it was a short and natural step to appoint army commanders with loyalties consistent—or at least not inimical—to the constituted administration in order to establish the military foundation of the political order.

The deterioration of political parties, which underwent continual fragmentation, splintering, and reorganization around dissident and ambitious leaders, and the relative meaninglessness of suffrage reduced the value of civilian political organizations. The armed forces quickly filled this vacuum, emerging ultimately to replace entirely the traditional party structure. First by partisan appointments to the army command and later by applying the armed forces directly to political tasks, national leaders created in the military institution a national organization capable of giving civilian politicos the power so coveted.

Developing increasingly as the bulwark of the constituted order, relied upon for election, reelection, and, in the end, the continuation of illegal power, the armed institution ultimately acquired its own interests. As the 1920 electoral contest suggested, the army developed vested interests in the outcome of elections, independent of the political needs of the incumbent administration. These interests grew in direct proportion to the army's involvement in national politics—a process orchestrated by civilian leaders. As the political institutions of the state atrophied from lack of use and abuse, the armed organization grew stronger and its political mission enlarged. Hence when the overthrow of a political order which the military had served appeared imminent, the armed institution felt compelled to intervene to protect its interests long vested in the threatened political arrangement. In the course of twenty-five years, the armed forces moved closer to the vortex of the national political system. By 1933 and thereafter, the army's stake in the existing political order made it impossible for the military to remain on the margin of political change. The army survived the threat in 1933; it failed in 1958.

Increasing military participation in national processes, necessitated by the political mission assumed by the army, conferred on the armed forces vested interests in the partisan order. The armed institution emerged ultimately as the instrument of national politics, aptly described by General Tabernilla as the yellow, blue, and white parties. Political success revolved around the control of the army. Every administration securing power electorally had an organic link with its predecessor. Each president chose his successor and committed the armed forces to carrying out the partisan decision. As frail national institutions yielded to the concentration of executive authority, and provincial and municipal autonomies collapsed under political pressure from Havana, the army emerged as the sole national institution capable of delivering effective power.

Lacking national tradition, the Cuban body military could look back to but not claim ties with the Ejército Libertador. In its origins, development, and mission, the Cuban military did not respond to national needs. On the contrary, it too often met policy needs articulated by American officials in Havana and Washington. In this *a parenti* relationship to extranational authorities, the armed forces, lacking historicity, grew increasingly estranged from national traditions. The army developed into something of an anomaly in the institutional order, never quite able to identify or define a legitimate national purpose for its existence. In its search for a place in the national order, it gravitated toward repression. The quest ended ultimately in an unusual army seizure of power, a mutiny of the noncommissioned officers and enlisted men, which the officers corps proved incapable of withstanding.

Entering into a vacuum created by thirty years of republican misgovernment, the early Batista army provided services that civilian rulers had ignored. Civilian management of the republic had been a disaster.[4] In the social science lexicon of today, the early Batista-led army emerged as a modernizing elite. It devoted much of its resources, talent, and energy to national health and education projects, setting up public assistance programs and national literacy campaigns. Through programs designed specifically for rural Cuba, the army became involved in a national reconstruction effort. In 1934, it was instrumental in the readjustment of the island's international relations, when Havana and Washington negotiated the abrogation of the Platt Amendment. In addition, the army supervised the modernization of the political order. Against the setting of army hegemony, a constituent assembly met to nullify the anachronistic charter of 1901 and frame the progressive Constitution of 1940. Equally important, elections for the constituent assembly revived the moribund political system. According to MacGaffey and Barnett:

> Batista's decision to hold elections for a constituent assembly in 1939 opened a debate in which all the major political groups of the 1930's participated for the first time. The move greatly increased his popularity and advanced his goal of becoming constitutional president. It also afforded the opposition the first real opportunity to make its view effective in national life. For the first time, the Auténtico party headed by Grau San Martín was strongly represented in an arena where major political decisions were made. The recently legalized Communist party and all the more traditional parties were also represented.[5]

In the service of the discredited Machado government during the early 1930s, the armed forces grew further apart from the island's ascending political classes. Alienation climaxed when the sergeants severed the army completely from the political and social elites. The problem of legitimacy became acute after the revolt. The deposed officers had, if only tenuously, represented continuity in the personal association of senior- and middle-grade officers with the Ejército Libertador. As veterans of the Army of Liberation, they conferred on the republican armed institution the prestige attending participation in the nineteenth-century struggle for independence. Through consanguinity and social association, moreover, the old army command had linked the body military to the island's political elite. Henceforth, army leadership was politically and socially afloat, lacking roots of legitimacy in the political, economic, and social sources of power on the island. Not trusting representatives of these traditional sectors to represent and promote the interests of the new officer corps, the former sergeants moved the armed institution closer to the foreign fulcrum of power, making the army increasingly responsive to the needs of American interests as a means to national hegemony.

The viability of the new military order—and, concomitantly, the political system dependent on that order—rested precariously, again, on sources outside the nation. American support of a political order so utterly dominated by the armed forces and the willingness of the United States to collaborate with the army command provided the vital margin of legitimacy necessary to underwrite military preeminence. The Cuban army represented no group other than its own corporate interest. Insofar as the armed forces derived considerable legitimacy from Washington, the arms embargo crippled the body military. And because the army institution defended no class interests, it could disintegrate to the cheers of virtually all sectors of Cuban society. All it could offer was stability. When it failed in this minimum mission, it was dispensable. Perhaps the army command sensed this intuitively, for on two occasions, in 1933 and 1958, it responded hastily to any solution offering to end political disorders.

Throughout the 1930s, to undercut further and neutralize the authority of traditional ruling groups, the military command moved directly into almost every aspect of national life in pursuit of corporate security. The army developed into a quasi-political party, acquiring features of a mass-based rural organization dedicated to nonmilitary enterprises in the interior. One result was the emergence of Batista from the military organization into political leadership.

Part of the facility in overturning the political order based on a military foundation between 1956 and 1958 lay precisely in the alienation of the Cuban military from the rest of society. By the 1950's, the armed forces had abandoned their rural projects. When Washington withdrew its support, the military establishment found itself virtually isolated. The struggle against the armed forces during the 1950s assumed qualities of a national liberation movement against, as Comandante José Quevado perceived, an "army of occupation." Almost thirty years after the former sergeants had taken command, the army demonstrated a singular incapacity to survive political change. For the third time in sixty years, the Cuban armed forces were subjected to a far-reaching reorganization.

Batista was ousted in 1958 by a military intervention designed to save the order his continued presence threatened. The Cantillo maneuver failed, in part, because the insurgent leadership, recalling the events of 1933, refused to accept a political settlement imposed by the military in Havana. The national prominence of Fidel Castro, moreover, enabled the insurgents to mobilize mass opposition, including a successful general strike, against the post-Batista regime.[6] The final rebel victory transcended a military triumph. By intervening to restore order and offering to oust Batista to propitiate the insurgent drive, the army chieftains opened the floodgates to mass participation by fulfilling the first demand of the revolution—the removal of the president. The former sergeants displaced Batista in much the same way as their superiors in 1933 had ousted Machado—and for the same reasons. In 1958, however, it marked the beginning of a revolution, not a climax. The military architects of the anti-Batista coup lost the war in a peculiarly nonmilitary fashion. By 1958, a rival source of national authority, much more powerful than the discredited order in Havana, had emerged in the Sierra Maestra.

NOTES : BIBLIOGRAPHY : INDEX

Notes

Chapter 1: Genesis of the Cuban Army (I)

1. General S. B. M. Young to adjutant general, June 29, 1898, Correspondence File, General Joseph Wheeler Papers, Alabama Department of Archives and History, Montgomery, Alabama. Charles H. Brown, *The Correspondents' War: Journalists in the Spanish–American War* (New York, 1967), p. 336.

2. José Müller y Tejeiro, *Battles and Capitulations of Santiago de Cuba*, Office of Naval Intelligence, War Note No. I, Information from Abroad, United States Congress, 1st sess., Document no. 388, ser. 3876 (Washington, 1900), p. 145.

3. Major General William R. Shafter to Secretary of War R. A. Alger, July 29, 1898, United States Congress, Senate, *Report of the Commission Appointed by the President to Investigate the Conduct of the War Department in the War With Spain*, 56th Cong., 1st sess., ser. 3859–66 (8 vols., Washington, 1900), II, p. 1052 (hereafter cited as *RCAP*).

4. Brigadier General Leonard Wood, "Report of Brigadier General Leonard Wood, U.S. Volunteers, Commanding Department of Santiago," August 9, 1899, United States Department of War, *Annual Report of the War Department, 1899*, United States Congress, House, 56th Cong. 1st sess., House Document no. 2, ser. 3899–3904 (3 vols., Washington, 1899), II, part 1, p. 302 (hereafter cited as *ARWD/1899*).

5. General Leonard Wood to secretary of war, September 9, 1898, File 139813, Records of the Adjutant General's Office, National Archives, Record Group 94 (hereafter cited as RG 94).

6. Brigadier General James H. Wilson, "Report of Brigadier General James H. Wilson, U.S. Volunteers, Commanding the Department of Matanzas and Santa Clara," February 18, 1899, *ARWD/1899*, I, part 1, p. 156.

7. Fitzhugh Lee, *Special Report of Brigadier General Fitzhugh Lee on the Industrial, Economic and Social Conditions Existing in the Province of Havana and Pinar del Rio* (Quemados, Cuba, 1899), p. 3.

8. Emilio Roig de Leuchsenring, *La lucha cubana por la república, contra la anexión y la Enmienda Platt, 1899–1902* (Havana, 1952), p. 23.

9. Rafael Martínez Ortiz, *Cuba, los primeros años de independencia* (2 vols., 3d ed., Paris, 1929), I, pp. 32–33. Horacio Ferrer, *Con el rifle al hombro* (Havana, 1950), pp. 135–37.

One Cuban historian suggests that the Ejército Libertador increased after the cessation of hostilities with Spain in anticipation of a conflict with the American occupation forces. See Enrique Collazo, *Los americanos en Cuba* (Havana, 1905), pp. 189–90.

10. *New York Times*, February 4, 1899, p. 2.

11. Franklin Matthews, *The New-Born Cuba* (New York, 1899), pp. 42–43.

12. *New York Times*, September 9, 1900, p. 14.

13. Lieutenant J. W. Heard to adjutant general, August 21, 1898, United States Department of War, *Annual Report of the War Department: Report on the Major-General Commanding the Army, 1898*, United States Congress, House, 55th Cong., 3d sess., House Document no. 2, ser. 3745 (Washington, 1898); pp. 375–76 (hereafter cited as *ARWD/ 1898*).

14. General H. W. Lawton to adjutant general, August 16, 1898, File 116542, RG 94.

15. Adjutant General H. C. Corbin to General H. W. Lawton, August 16, 1898, *RCAP*, II, p. 1098. Hamilton V. Bail, "The Military Government of Cuba, 1898–1902," (unpublished manuscript, Hoover Institution for War and Peace, Stanford, California, 1943), pp. 11–12.

16. General William R. Shafter to adjutant general, August 16, 1898, *RCAP*, II, p. 1099.

17. General John R. Brooke to Secretary of War R. A. Alger, February 9, 1899, File 243539, RG 94.

18. Henry Adams to Elizabeth Cameron, February 26, 1899, in Worthington Chauncy Ford, ed., *Letters of Henry Adams* (2 vols., Boston, 1930–1938), II, p. 20.

19. General John R. Brooke to adjutant general, June 2, 1899, File 248666, RG 94.

20. Hermann Hagedorn, *Leonard Wood, a Biography* (2 vols., New York, 1931), I, p. 255.

21. Leonard Wood, "The Military Government of Cuba," *The Annals of the American Academy of Political and Social Science*, 21 (March 1903), p. 154.

22. Roig, *La lucha cubana . . .* , pp. 16–17.

23. P. E. Betancourt, civil governor of Matanzas, to Colonel G. M. Randall, May 27, 1899, File (1899) 3100, Records of the Military Government of Cuba, National Archives, Record Group 140 (hereafter cited as RG 140).

24. In Hagedorn, *Leonard Wood, a Biography*, I, p. 256.

25. General James H. Wilson, commander of Matanzas and Santa Clara and a vocal opponent of the recruitment of Cubans, suggested that the military governor had simply "hired the 'Cuban Army.' " General James H. Wilson to Colonel Bluford Wilson, April 28, 1899, James Harrison Wilson Papers, Personal Letters, Box 44, Library of Congress, Manuscript Division.

26. J. A. Porter to Adjutant General H. C. Corbin, September 29, 1898, File 132052, RG 94.

27. "Memoria de la primera Comisión enviada a Wáshington," in Joaquín Llaverías and Emeterio S. Santovenia, eds., *Actas de las Asambleas de Representantes y del Consejo de Gobierno durante la Guerra de Independencia* (5 vols., Havana, 1932), V, pp. 152–53.

28. Máximo Gómez to William McKinley, March 4, 1899, in Ramón Infiesta *Máximo Gómez* (Havana, 1937), pp. 227–28.

29. Elihu Root to William McKinley, August 17, 1899, William McKinley Papers, Library of Congress, Manuscript Division.

30. General Leonard Wood to Theodore Roosevelt, August 18, 1899, Theodore Roosevelt Papers, Library of Congress, Manuscript Division.

31. David F. Healy, *The United States in Cuba, 1898–1902* (Madison, 1963), p. 105.

32. Captain H. J. Slocum, "Report of Captain H. J. Slocum, 7th U.S. Cavalry,

Superintendent of the Rural Guard and the Cuerpo de Artilleria of the Island of Cuba, for the Period of January 1st, 1902 to May 20th 1902," July 2, 1902, in Leonard Wood, *Civil Report of Brigadier General Leonard Wood, Military Governor of Cuba, January 1st to May 20th, 1902* (6 vols., Washington, 1902), III, p. 67 (hereafter cited as *Civil Report/1902*).

33. General Leonard Wood, "Civil Report of Major General Leonard Wood, U.S. Volunteers, Military Governor of Cuba," United States Department of War, *Annual Report of the Military Governor of Cuba on Civil Affairs*, United States Congress, House, 56th Cong. 2d sess., House Document no. 2, ser. 4080–4087 (2 vols., Washington, 1901), I, part 1, p. 63 (hereafter cited as *Civil Report/1900*).

34. Luis A. Arce, *Emilio Núñez (1875–1922): historiografía* (Havana, 1943), p. 285. Ferrer, *Con el rifle al hombro*, p. 27.

35. Brigadier General William Ludlow, "Report of Brigadier General William Ludlow, Commanding Department of Havana and Military Governor of the City of Havana, Cuba," August 1, 1899, *ARWD/1899*, I, part 1, p. 228.

36. Colonel L. H. Carpenter, "Report of L. H. Carpenter, Commanding Department of Puerto Principe," July 10, 1899, *ARWD/1899*, I, part 1, p. 331.

37. Secretary of War Russell Alger to Major General Francis V. Greene, November 12, 1898, File 2433548, RG 94.

38. "Orígenes de nuestro Ejército," *Boletín del Ejército* (Havana), III (July–August 1952), p. 11.

39. Hagedorn, *Leonard Wood, a Biography*, I, p. 214.

40. General Fitzhugh Lee to Joseph Benson Foraker, November 20, 1899, in Joseph Benson Foraker, *Notes of a Busy Life* (2 vols., 3d ed., Cincinnati, 1917), II, p. 48.

41. Leonard Wood, "The Existing Conditions and Needs in Cuba," *North American Review*, 168 (May 1899), p. 600.

42. *Ibid*. Herminio Portell Vilá, "La intervención militar norteamericana, 1899—1902," *El Mundo* (Havana), May 20, 1952, p. 34.

43. Wood, "Civil Report of Major General Leonard Wood, U.S. Volunteers, Military Governor of Cuba," December 20 1899–December 31, 1900, *Civil Report/1900*, I, part 1, p. 65.

44. Slocum, "Report of Captain H. J. Slocum," *Civil Report/1902*, III, p. 26.

45. Elihu Root, *The Military and Colonial Policy of the United States*, ed. Robert Bacon and James Brown Scott (Cambridge, Mass., 1916), p. 190.

46. Wood, "Civil Report of Major General Leonard Wood, U.S. Volunteers, Military Governor of Cuba," December 20, 1899–December 31, 1900, *Civil Report/1900*, I, part 1, p. 65.

47. Wood to Elihu Root, February 8, 1901, Leonard Wood Papers, General Correspondence, Box 29, Library of Congress, Manuscript Division.

48. "Treaty of Relations between the United States and Cuba, Signed at Habana, May 22, 1903," in James W. Gantenbein, ed., *The Evolution of Our Latin-American Policy: A Documentary Record* (New York, 1950), p. 490.

49. Root to Wood, June 20, 1900, Wood Papers, General Correspondence.

50. Wood, "Civil Report of Major Leonard Wood, U.S. Volunteers, Military Governor of Cuba," December 20, 1899–December 31, 1900 *Civil Report/1900*, I, part 1, pp. 63–64.

51. Slocum, "Report of Captain H. J. Slocum," *Civil Report/1902*, III, pp. 67–70. "Orígenes de nuestro Ejército," p. 35.

52 Comandante B. Peña, Rural Guard of Puerto Príncipe, to Major C. A. P. Hatfield, February 13, 1901, File (1901) 879, RG 140. J. F. Craig, president, Francisco Sugar

Company, to Wood, February 2, 1901, File (1901) 879, RG 140. W. I. Consuegra, acting chief of the Rural Guard, Santa Clara, "Monthly Report for November, 1900," File (1900) 6105, RG 140.

53. José de Jésus Monteagudo, chief of the Rural Guard, to Brigadier General Fitzhugh Lee, October 31, 1900. File (1900) 6105, RG 140.

54. Leopoldo Figueroa, president of the municipality of Cienfuegos, to Wood, January 24, 1901, File (1901) 138, RG 140.

55. Cuba, Guardia Rural, *Memoria explicativa de los trabajos realizados por el Cuerpo durante el año fiscal 1905* (Havana 1906), pp. 89–95. Not infrequently municipalities donated land in the attempt to attract a Rural Guard detachment. Local authorities thus transferred the financial burden of law enforcement onto the central government. See Rafael Armas, president of the Ayuntamiento of Colon, to Wood, June 26, 1901, File (1901) 194, and Alejandro Rodríguez, chief of the Rural Guard, to adjutant general, Department of Cuba, August 28, 1901, File (1901) 194, RG 140.

56. Slocum, "Report of Captain H. J. Slocum," *Civil Report/1902*, III, p. 68.

57. See Eduardo Usabiega to Wood, May 26, 1901, File (1901) 14, RG 140, and Colonel Pio Domínguez to Wood, May 16, 1901, File (1901) 194, RG 140.

58. For enlistment requirements see Camagüey, *Reglamento para el gobierno interior del Cuerpo de Guardia Rural* (Camagüey, 1899), p. 4.

59. Matthews, *The New-Born Cuba*, p. 387.

60. Captain Dwight Aultman, "Project for Combining the Cuerpo de Artilleria with the Rural Guard," in Aultman to adjutant general, Department of Cuba, January 25, 1902, File (1902) 2, RG 140.

61. Herbert G. Squiers to secretary of state, September 29, 1902, no. 215, General Records of the Department of State, National Archives, Record Group 59 (hereafter cited as RG 59).

62. *Ibid.*, August 12, 1902, no. 116.

63. *Ibid.*, June 10, 1902, no. 13.

64. *Ibid.*, June 26, 1903, no. 575.

65. *Ibid.*

66. Matthew Elting Hanna, "The Necessity of Increasing the Efficiency of the Cuban Army," *Journal of the Military Service Institution of the United States*, 35 (July–August 1904), pp. 29–30.

67. *Ibid.*, p. 31.

68. Lieutenant N. A. McNully to commanding officer, April 3, 1903, File B-8-c, Records of the Office of the Chief of Naval Operations, National Archives, Record Group 38 (hereafter cited as RG 38).

69. "Orígenes de nuestro Ejército," p. 41.

70. Victor M. de Peralta, *Conmonitorio de intervención á intervención* (Havana, 1907), pp. 15–16.

71. Pánfilo D. Camacho, *Estrada Palma, el gobernante honrado* (Havana, 1938), pp. 232–33. The "Constitutionalist Army" secured much of its arms from defeated units of the Rural Guard. More important, however, many members of the Ejército Libertador had retained possession of their weapons. Only "an insignificant number of arms," an American officer was informed, was collected between 1898–1899. See F. Pedro Griñan and Francisco de P. Valiente to Major E. F. Ladd, October 30, 1906, in William Howard Taft and Robert Bacon, "Cuban Pacification: Report of William H. Taft, Secretary of War, and Robert Bacon, Assistant Secretary of State, of What Was Done Under the Instructions of the President in Restoring Peace in Cuba," Department of War, *Report of the Secretary of War, 1906*, Appendix E, United States Congress, House, 59th Cong., 2d

sess., House Document no. 2, ser. 5105 (Washington, 1906), pp. 538–29 (hereafter cited as *Taft/Bacon Report*).

72. Cuba, Cámara de Representantes, *Mensajes presidenciales remitidos al congreso, transcurridos desde el veinte de mayo de mil novecientos dos, hasta el primer de abril de mil novecientos diez y siete* (Havana, n.d.), p. 176.

73. Allan Reed Millett, *The Politics of Intervention: The Military Occupation of Cuba, 1906–1909* (Columbus, 1968), pp. 62–63.

74. Frank M. Steinhart to secretary of state, September 8, 1906, *Taft/Bacon Report*, pp. 444–45.

75. Ralph Eldin Minger, "William H. Taft and the United States Intervention in Cuba in 1906," *The Hispanic American Historical Review*, 41 (February 1961), p. 85.

76. William H. Taft to Elihu Root, September 15, 1906, William Howard Taft Papers, Series 8, Letterbook, Secretary of War, Semi-Official File, Library of Congress, Manuscript Division.

77. O. H. Platt, "The Solution of the Cuban Problem," *The World's Work*, 2 (May 1901), p. 732.

78. Root, *The Military and Colonial Policy of the United States*, p. 100.

79. Theodore Roosevelt to Joseph Benson Foraker, September 27, 1906, in Foraker, *Notes of a Busy Life*, II, p. 58.

80. Cuba, Cámara de Representantes, *Mensajes presidenciales . . .* , p. 176.

81. Commander William F. Fullam to secretary of the navy, September 15, 1906, Admiral William Freeland Fullam Papers, Box 4, Library of Congress, Manuscript Division.

82. *Taft/Bacon Report*, p. 457.

83. Commander J. S. Colwell to secretary of the navy, October 4, 1906, Correspondence Relating to the Cuban Insurrection, 1906, Naval Records Collection of the Office of Naval Records and Library, National Archives, Record Group 45 (hereafter cited as RG 45).

Chapter 2: Genesis of the Cuban Army (II), 1906–1909

1. "Final Report of the Advisory Law Commission," in Charles E. Magoon, *Supplemental Report, Provisional Governor of Cuba, For Period December 1, 1908 to January 28, 1909*, United States Congress, Senate, 61st Cong., 1st sess. Senate Document no. 80, ser. 5572 (Washington, 1909), p. 22 (hereafter cited as *Report/1908–1909*).

2. Captain C. F. Crain to Major H. J. Slocum, February 5, 1907, File 064, Records of the Provisional Government of Cuba, National Archives, Record Group 199 (hereafter cited as RG 199).

3. David A. Lockmiller, *Magoon in Cuba: A History of the Second Intervention, 1906–1909* (Chapel Hill, 1938), p. 82. Russell H. Fitzgibbon, *Cuba and the United States, 1900–1935* (Menasha, 1935), p. 134.

4. Charles E. Magoon, *Report of Provisional Administration From December 1st, 1907, to December 1st, 1908* (Havana, 1909), p. 105 (hereafter cited as *Report/1907–1908*).

5. Captain C. F. Crain, "Report on General Conditions in Santa Clara," December 27, 1906, File 104/3, RG 199. Alejandro Rodríguez, "Report of Commanding General, Armed Forces of Cuba," Appendix H, in Charles E. Magoon, *Report of Provisional Administration: From October 13th, 1906, to December 1st, 1907* (Havana, 1908), p. 498 (hereafter cited as *Report/1906–1907*).

6. For an excellent treatment of this theme see Millett, *The Politics of Intervention*.

7. William H. Taft to Charles E. Magoon, October 31, 1906, File 866/16, Record Group 350 (hereafter cited as RG 350).

8. "Report of Conference Between Provisional Governor Magoon and General Guerra, García Velez, Monteagudo . . . . ," November 28, 1906, File 012, RG 199.

9. William H. Taft to Magoon, January 23, 1907, Taft Papers, Semi-Official Correspondence, Series B, Library of Congress, Manuscript Division.

10. Major H. J. Slocum to provisional governor, February 26, 1907, File 866/44, RG350.

11. Captain C. F. Crain to Slocum, February 5, 1907, File 064, RG 199.

12. Rodríguez, "Report of Commanding General, Armed Forces of Cuba," *Report/ 1906–1907*, p. 498.

13. Magoon to secretary of war, November 16, 1906, File 866/16, RG 350.

14. *Report/1906–1907*, p. 20.

15. *Ibid.*, p. 20.

16. *Ibid.*, p. 19.

17. Rodríguez, "Report of Commanding General, Armed Forces of Cuba," *Report/ 1906–1907*, pp. 503–04.

18. "Stenographic Report of the Conference between Mr. Juan Gualberto Gómez, General José de Jésus Monteagudo, General Carlos García Velez, General Ernesto Asbert, Senator Tomás Recio, Senator Alfredo Zayas, and the Provisional Governor . . . ," February 6, 1907, File 062/2, RG 199.

19. "Report of Conference between Provisional Governor Magoon and General Guerra, García Velez, Monteagudo . . . ," November 28, 1906, File 012, RG 199.

20. "Stenographic Report of the Conference between Mr. Juan Gualberto Gómez, General José de Jésus Monteagudo, General Carlos García Velez, General Ernesto Asbert, Senator Tomás Recio, Senator Alfredo Zayas, and the Provisional Governor . . . ," February 6, 1907, File 062/2, RG 199.

21. *Ibid.*

22. "Memorandum of Conference between Secretary Taft and the Liberal Committee," April 8, 1907, File 078/5, RG 350.

23. Slocum to Magoon, February 26, 1907, File 866/44, RG 230.

24. Captain E. Wittenmyer to Slocum, *ibid.*

25. Captain J. A. Ryan to Slocum, February 25, 1907, *ibid.*

26. "Statement made by General Pino Guerra to Provisional Government of Cuba," February 19, 1907, in Magoon to secretary of war, February 19, 1907, File 062/6, RG 199.

27. *Ibid.*

28. Magoon to the president, April 17, 1908, File 222/3, RG 199.

29. "Memorandum of Conference between Secretary Taft and the Liberal Committee," April 8, 1907, File 078/5, RG 199.

30. *Report/1907–1908*, p. 108.

31. *Report/1908–1909*, p. 22.

32. Magoon to the president, April 17, 1908, File 222/3, RG 199.

33. *Ibid.*

34. *Ibid.*

Chapter 3: National Politics and the Cuban Army, 1909–1924

1. Major Henry A. Barber to Major H. J. Slocum, February 3, 1909, File 15984/3, RG 350.

2. Major Henry A. Barber, "The Armed Forces and the President," March 1, 1910,

File 5775, Records of the War Department, General and Special Staffs, National Archives, Record Group 165 (hereafter cited as RG 165).

3. Charles E. Chapman, *A History of the Cuban Republic: A Study in Hispanic American Politics* (New York, 1927), p. 299.

4. Major Henry A. Barber, "General Pino Guerra," April 7, 1909, File 5399/1, RG 165.

5. Major Henry A. Barber, "Armed Forces," June 6, 1910, *ibid.*

6. For the political repercussions of the split between Gómez and Zayas, see Mario Riera Hernández, *Cuba política, 1899–1955* (Havana, 1955), pp. 169–182.

7. Army War College, "Monographs on Cuba: The Infantry," January 26, 1910, File 5775, RG 165.

8. Cuba, Presidente, *Memoria de la administración del Presidente de la República de Cuba Mayor General José Miguel Gómez, durante el periodo comprendido entre el 1° de enero y 31 de diciembre de 1910* (Havana, 1911), p. 109.

9. "Armed Forces of Cuba, 1906–1913," Appendix no. 1, in Lieutenant Colonel C. K. Nulsen to military attaché, Havana, Cuba, July 5, 1934, File 2012–153, RG 165. Damaso Pasalodos, "El gobierno del General Gómez," *Bohemia*, 30 (June 12, 1938), p. 8.

10. James L. Rodgers, consular agent, Havana, "Memorandum," May 24, 1911, 837.00/476, RG 59.

11. Cuba, Cámara de Representantes, *Mensajes presidenciales . . .* , p. 262.

12. Cuba, Guardia Rural, *Memoria explicativa de los trabajos realizados por el cuerpo de la Guardia Rural desde el 21 de enero de 1909 hasta el 30 de junio de 1910, inclusiva* (Havana, 1911), pp. 204–17. Cuba, Presidente, *Memoria de la administración de . . . . Gómez*, p. 126.

13. Major Henry A. Barber, "The Army (Cuba)," January 12, 1910, File 5775, RG 165. John B. Jackson to secretary of state, April 7, 1910, 837.00/366, and April 20, 1910, 837.00/368, RG 59.

14. Jackson to secretary of state, April 26, 1910, 837.00/377, RG 59.

15. Allan R. Millett, "The Rise and Fall of the Cuban Rural Guard, 1898–1912," *The Americas*, 29 (October 1972), pp. 210–12.

16. W. I. Consuegra, *Hechos y comentarios. La revolución de febrero de 1917 en Las Villas* (Havana, 1920), p. 13.

17. Ferrer, *Con el rifle al hombro*, p. 200. Consuegra, *Hechos y comentarios*, pp. 17–19.

18. León Primelles, *Crónica cubana, 1915–1918* (Havana, 1955), pp. 245–46. Raimundo Cabrera, *Mis malos tiempos* (Havana, 1920), p. 187. Ferrer, *Con el rifle al hombro*, pp. 220–21.

19. William Gonzales to secretary of state, February 15, 1917, 837.00/1090, RG 59.

20. Consuegra, *Hechos y comentarios*, p. 27. Ferrer, *Con el rifle al hombro*, pp. 223–24. Primelles, *Crónica cubana, 1815–1918*, p. 250.

21. Cuba, Congreso, Cámaro de Representantes, Octavo Periodo Congresional, *Memoria de los trabajos realizados durante las cuatro legislaturas ordinarias y las dos extraordinarias del octavo periodo congresional, comprendido del dos de abril de mil novecientos diez y siete y siete di abril de mil novecientos diez y nueve* (Havana 1919), p. 817.

22. M. J. Shaw, commanding officer, Seventh Regiment, USMC, Santiago de Cuba, May 17, 1918, File 7082-156, Subject File, 1911–1927, Box 630, RG 45.

23. Major Thomas F. Van Natta, Jr., military attaché, to chief, military intelligence section, *G.S.*, December 6, 1917, 837.61351/68, RG 59.

24. Van Natta to chief, military intelligence section, G.S., January 1918, File 7299–35, RG 165.

25. Cuba, Congreso, Cámara de Representantes, Octavo Periodo Congresional, *Memoria de los trabajos . . . de mil novecientos diez y nueve*, p. 816.

26. Riera Hernández, *Cuba política, 1899–1955*, pp. 263–78.

184 : NOTES TO PAGES 36–38

27. León Primelles, *Crónica cubana, 1919–1922* (Havana, 1957), p. 26.

28. In *ibid.,* pp. 159–60.

29. Major N. W. Campanole, Office of the Military Attaché, "Preliminary Report on Observations 1920 Cuban National Elections," December 1, 1920, File 2657-Q-54, RG 165.

30. *La Lucha* (Havana), August 23, 1920, p. 1.

31. Major N. W. Campanole, Office of the Military Attaché, "Report on Observations of 1920 Cuban Elections in Oriente Province, for Period October 11 to November 15," November 22, 1920, File 2657-Q-54, RG 165.

32. Office of the Military Attaché, Havana, Cuba, to director of military intelligence, G.S., "Political Situation in Province of Oriente for Week Ending November 6, 1920," November 7, 1920, File 2657-Q-50, RG 165.

33. Charles E. Seijo, "Memorandum for Major Stephenson: Political Situation in Camaguey and Santa Clara," October 27, 1920, Enoch H. Crowder Papers, Correspondence, File 266, Western Historical Manuscript Collection, University of Missouri, Columbia, Missouri.

34. E. H. Crowder to secretary of state, February 14, 1921, 837.00/2009, RG 59.

35. Campanole, "Report on Observations of 1920 Cuban Elections in Oriente Province, for Period October 11 to November 15," November 22, 1920, File 2657-Q-54, RG 165, Campanole to director of military intelligence, G.S., "Political Situation in Oriente Province for Week Ending October 30, 1920," October 31, 1920, File 2657-Q-48, RG 165.

36. Lieutenant E. E. Valentini to director of military intelligence, G.S., "Military Supervisors in Cuba in Relation With Observation of Elections in Santa Clara Province," November 3, 1920, File 2657-Q-31, RG 165.

37. Major H. E. Stephenson to Enoch H. Crowder, October 12, 1920, Correspondence, File 263, Crowder Papers.

38. Colonel Paul W. Beck, military attaché, "Office Memorandum for Information of Successor," April 15, 1920, File 2056–196, RG 165.

39. Herpert T. Spinden, "Elecciones espurias en Cuba," *Reforma Social* (New York/Havana), 19 (April 1921), p. 357.

40. Campanole, "Preliminary Report on Observations 1920 Cuban National Elections," December 1, 1920, File 2657-Q-54, RG 165.

41. Campanole, "Report of Observations of 1920 Cuban Elections in Oriente Province, for Period October 11 to November 15," November 22, 1920, *ibid.*

42. Boaz W. Long to secretary of state, October 5, 1920, 837.00/1797, RG 59.

43. *Ibid.*

44. Campanole, "Preliminary Report on Observations of 1920 Cuban National Elections," December 1, 1920, File 2657-Q-54, RG 165. Valentini to director of military intelligence, "Miliatry Supervisors in Cuba in Relation with Observation of Elections in Santa Clara Province," November 3, 1920, File 2657-Q-31, RG 165. Campanole to director of military intelligence, G.S., "The Cuban Army and Politics," October 11, 1920, File 2657-Q-39, RG 165. Campanole to director of military intelligence, G.S., "Notes on Political Situation in Eastern Provinces of Cuba," October 10, 1020, File 2657-Q-40, RG 165.

45. *Havana Post,* September 3, 1920, p. 1.

46. Valentini to director of military intelligence, G.S., "Military Supervisors in Cuba With Special Reference to Santa Clara Province," October 19, 1920, File 2657-Q-31, RG 165. Boaz W. Long to secretary of state, October 19, 1920, 837.00/1819, RG 59.

47. Valentini to director of military intelligence, "Military Supervisors in Cuba in Relation with Observation of Election," November 8, 1920, File 2657-Q-31, RG 165.

Campanole, "Report of Observation of 1920 Elections in Oriente Province, for period October 11 to November 15," November 22, 1920, File 2657-Q-54, RG 165.

48. Office of the Military Attaché, Havana, Cuba, to director of military intelligence, G.S., "Combat Factor," August 23, 1920, File 2012-62, RG 165.

49. United States Department of State, "Memorandum on Cuban Elections," March 31, 1921, 837.00/2095, RG 59. Campanole to director of military intelligence, G.S., September 15, 1920, File 2012-62, RG 165.

50. Charles E. Seijo, "Memorandum for Major Stephenson: Political Situation in Camaguey and Santa Clara," October 27, 1920, Correspondence, File 266, Crowder Papers.

51. Campanole, "Influence of the Cuban Army in the Approaching National Election," September 15, 1920, 837.00/1771, RG 59. Campanole to Colonel A. B. Cox, General Staff, August 20, 1920, File 2657-Q-10, RG 165.

52. Valentini to director of military intelligence, G.S., "Military Supervisors in Relation with Observations on Election," November 8, 1920, File 2657-Q-31, RG 165. Office of Military Attaché, Havana, Cuba, to director of military intelligence, G.S., "Political Situation," September 21, 1920, File 2657-Q-28, RG 165.

53. Campanole, "Preliminary Report on Observations 1920 Cuban National Elections," December 1, 1920, File 2657-Q-54, RG 165. Cf. Major H. E. Stephenson, "Statement of Complaints Concerning Electoral Matters Received from September 1, 1920 by the American Legation, Havana, and their Connection with Military Supervisors," Material on Cuba, File 1216, Crowder Papers.

54. Campanole to director of military intelligence, G.S., "Notes on Political Situation in Eastern Provinces of Cuba," October 10, 1920, File 2657-Q-40, RG 165.

55. Campanole to director of military intelligence, G.S., "Political Situation in Pinar del Rio," September 14, 1920, File 2657-Q-21, RG 165.

56. Campanole, "Influence of the Cuban Army in the Approaching National Elections," September 15, 1920, 837.00/1771, RG 59. Campanole to director of military intelligence, G.S., September 15, 1920, File 2012-63, RG 165.

57. Campanole to director of military intelligence, October 10, 1920, File 2657-Q-40, RG 165.

58. Valentini to director of military intelligence, G.S., "Military Supervisors in Cuba with Special Reference to Santa Clara Province," October 19, 1920, File 2657-Q-31, RG 165.

59. Campanole to director of military intelligence, G.S., "Political Situation in Oriente Province for Week Ending October 30, 1920," October 31, 1920, File 2657-Q-48, RG 165.

60. Director of military intelligence to Campanole, "Political Conditions of Santa Clara Province," September 2, 1920, File 2657-Q-14, RG 165. Campanole to director of military intelligence, G.S., "Political Situation in Province of Oriente, Cuba, for the Week Ending October 17, 1920," October 17, 1920, File 2657-Q-37, RG 165.

61. Valentini to director of military intelligence, G.S., "Military Supervisors in Cuba with Special Reference to Santa Clara Province," October 19, 1920, File 2657-Q-31, RG 165.

62. Office of the Military Attaché, Havana, Cuba, to director of military intelligence, "Political Factor," August 23, 1920, File 2657-Q-11, RG 165. Colonel Berkeley Enochs, General Staff, "Memorandum for War Plans Division, G.S.: Cuban Situation," September 30, 1920, File 2657-Q-30, RG 165. Campanole to director of military intelligence, G.S., "Notes on Political Situation in Eastern Provinces of Cuba," October 10, 1920, File 2657-Q-40, RG 165.

63. Charles E. Seijo, "Memorandum for Major Stephenson: Political Situation in

Camaguey and Santa Clara," October 27, 1920, Correspondence, File 266, Crowder Papers.

64. Harold D. Clum, consul, Santiago de Cuba, to Boaz W. Long, September 23, 1920, 837.00/1782, RG 59.

65. Minutes, Cruces Interviews, March 10, 1921, Material on Cuba, File 1252, Crowder Papers.

66. Clum to Long, September 23, 1920, 837.00/1782, RG 59.

67. Minutes, Sagua la Grande Interviews, March 10, 1921, Material on Cuba, File 1254, Crowder Papers.

68. Valentini to director of military intelligence, G.S., "Military Supervisors in Cuba. A Potent Factor in the Approaching Elections," September 28, 1920, File 2657-Q-31, RG 165.

69. Clum to Long, September 23, 1920, 837.00/1782, RG 59.

70. Office of the Military Attaché, Havana, Cuba, to director of military intelligence, G.S., "Political Situation in Province of Oriente for Week Ending November 6, 1920," November 7, 1920, File 2657-Q-50, RG 165.

Chapter 4: The United States and the Cuban Army, 1909–1924

1. "Stenographic Report of the Conference between Mr. Juan Gualberto Gómez, General José de Jésus Monteagudo, General Carlos García Velez, General Ernesto Asbert, Senator Tomás Recio, Senator Alfredo Zayas, and the Provisional Governor . . . ," February 6, 1907, File 062/2, RG 199.

2. General Staff, G-2, "A Study of the Organization and Administration of the Cuban Government: American Control in the Event of Intervention and Qualifications of American Officials Selected as Advisors in the Coordinate Branches and as Head of the Important Sub-Divisions," March 15, 1922, File 2271-Q-8(2), RG 165.

3. E. H. Crowder to General John J. Pershing, January 30, 1923, File 210.681, Cuba, Project Files, 1917–1925, Records of the Adjutant General's Office, 1917—, National Archives, Record Group 407 (hereafter cited as RG 407).

4. Colonel Frank Parker to chief of military intelligence division, G.S., March 14, 1922, File 2012-93(2), RG 165.

5. Office of the Military Attaché, Havana, Cuba, "Estimate of the Military Situation," April 12, 1924, File 10641-267(3), RG 165.

6. Major J. M. Hobson, military attaché, to director of military intelligence, G.S., May 23, 1921, File 2012-73, RG 165.

7. *Ibid.*

8. Hobson to army chief of staff, G-2, December 13, 1921, File 2012-86, RG 165.

9. Office of the Military Attaché, Havana, Cuba, "Estimate of the Military Situation," April 12, 1924, File 10641-267(3), RG 165.

10. Hobson to chief of staff, G-2, March 10, 1922, File 2012-94. Military Intelligence Report, "Cuba: Estimate of Military Situation," n.d. [received December 17, 1918], File 11002-65(1) RG 165.

11. Office of the Military Attaché, Havana, Cuba, "Estimate of the Military Situation," April 12, 1924, File 10641-267(3), RG 165. Hobson to chief of staff, G-2, March 10, 1922, File 2012-94, RG 165.

12. Major General H. L. Scott to Major Edmund Wittenmyer, February 25, 1921, War Department General Staff, Report Number 11918, RG 165.

13. Colonel H. J. Slocum, military attaché, to director of military intelligence, G.S., May 23, 1921, File 2012-73, RG 165.

14. Colonel H. J. Slocum, "The Commander of the Armed Forces and the Alleged Interference of the Rural Guard in Politics," October 24, 1921, File 7299-1, RG 165.

15. Office of the Military Attaché, Havana, Cuba, "Estimate of the Political-Military Situation," March 1923, File 10641-267(1), RG 165.

16. Theodore Roosevelt to Joseph Benson Foraker, September 28, 1906, in Foraker, *Notes of a Busy Life*, II, p. 57.

17. A. Mitchell Iness, British Embassy, Washington, to secretary of state, June 13, 1912, File 27868/18, General Correspondence, General Records of the Department of the Navy, National Archives, Record Group 80 (hereafter cited as RG 80).

18. Arthur M. Beaupré to secretary of state, June 4, 1912, 837.00/684, RG 59.

19. P. Merrill Griffith, American consul, Santiago de Cuba, to Captain R. R. Belknap, March 15, 1917, File 27868-64, Subject File 1911–1927, Box 629, RG 45. Belknap to commander in chief, Atlantic Fleet, March 1, 1917, File 27868-45, Subject File, 1911–1927, Box 629, RG 45.

20. John H. Parker, "How the Cuban Problem Might Be Solved," *The American Review of Reviews*, 37 (January 1908), p. 66.

21. *Ibid.*, p. 65.

22. Major Thomas F. Van Natta, Jr., military attaché, "Memorandum," December 13, 1921, File 2012-86, RG 165.

23. Parker, "How the Cuban Problem Might Be Solved," p. 66.

24. Beaupré to secretary of state, May 23, 1912, 837.00/598, RG 59.

25. Beaupré to secretary of state, June 4, 1912, 837.00/684, RG 59.

26. Beaupré to secretary of state, June 6, 1912, 837.00/731, RG 59.

27. J. H. Stabler to secretary of state, March 30, 1917, 337.11/763, RG 59.

28. R. E. Haladay to Beaupré, June 13, 1912, 837.00/763, RG 59.

29. Rigoberto Fernández, commander in chief, First District, to Capitán Ramón Calis, Guantánamo, February 24, 1917, File (1917) 800, American Consulate, Santiago de Cuba, Miscellaneous Correspondence, Records, of the Foreign Service Posts of the Department of State, National Archives, Record Group 84 (hereafter cited as RG 84).

30. Commander H. K. Hewitt to secretary of the navy, March 20, 1917, 837.00/1270, RG 59.

31. Beaupré to secretary of state, June 6, 1912, 837.00/731, RG 59.

32. John J. Jackson to secretary of state, October 24, 1910, 837.00/432, RG 59.

33. Secretary of state to Beaupré, June 15, 1912, 837.00/690a, RG 59.

34. Major Thomas F. Van Natta, Jr., military attaché, to chief of military intelligence section, G.S., January 1918, File 7299-35, RG 165.

35. Van Natta to the chief, War College Division, G.S., February 7, 1918, File 7289-35, RG 165.

36. Lieutenant Charles M. Brown, assistant military attaché, to Van Natta, January 28, 1918, File 7299-26, RG 165.

37. Hobson to director of military intelligence, G.S., May 23, 1921, File 2012-73, RG 165.

38. General J. Franklin Bell, chief of staff, "Memorandum for Secretary of War," April 21, 1910, File 1643705, RG 94.

39. Van Natta to the chief, War College Division, G.S., February 7, 1917, File 7298-30, RG 165.

40. Hobson to director of military intelligence, G.S., May 23, 1921, File 2012-73, RG 165.

41. Colonel Frank Parker to chief of military intelligence division, G.S., March 14, 1922, File 2012-93(2) RG 165.

42. See Hobson to director of military intelligence, G.S., May 23, 1921, File 2012-73, RG 165.

43. Pan American Union, *Bulletin of the Pan American Union,* (November 1923), pp. 520–21.

44. Enrique Prieto, "The Organization of the Cuban Army," *The Military Engineer,* 20 (September–October, 1928), p. 388.

45. *New York Times,* February 15, 1917, p. 5. William E. Gonzales to secretary of state, February 12, 1917, 837.24/26, RG 59.

46. *New York Times,* February 20, 1917, p. 3.

47. *New York Times,* February 21, 1917, p. 6.

48. Gonzales to secretary of state, February 14, 1917, 837.24/27, RG 59.

49. Pablo Desvernine, Cuban foreign minister, to Carlos Manuel de Céspedes, Washington, February 14, 1917, 837.00/1093, RG 59.

Chapter 5: Sources of Army Preeminence: The *Machadato,* 1925–1933

1. "Intrigas y secretos del machadato: la casa militar del dictador Machado," *Bohemia,* 26 (February 11, 1934), pp. 16–17. E. H. Crowder to secretary of state, September 8, 1926, 837.20/66, RG 59.

2. Major J. J. O'Hare, military attaché, "Commissioned Officers," G-2 Report, December 2, 1932, File 2012-141(2) RG 165.

3. Cuba, Presidente, *Mensaje del presidente Gerardo Machado y Morales al Congreso de la República referente a los actos de la administración y demostrativo del estado general de la República en 2 de noviembre de 1925* (Havana, 1925), p. 229.

4. Decreto Número 1,100, "Ley Orgánica del Ejército," *Graceta Oficial de la República* (special edition), July 20, 1926, p. 4. Major James C. R. Schwenck, military attaché, "Combat Estimate of Cuba," G-2 Report, March 20, 1928, File 10641-267(15), RG 165.

5. Schwenck to army chief of staff, G-2, October 26, 1928, File 2657-Q-282(2) RG 165.

6. Captain Henry C. Clark, military attaché, "Presidential Decree Providing for the Appointment of Military Instructors in Schools of Secondary Education in Cuba," G-2 Report, September 28, 1926, File 2277-Q-7, RG 165.

7. Cuba, Presidente, *Mensaje del presidente Gerardo Machado y Morales al Congreso de la República referente a los actos de la administración y demostrativo del estado general de la República en 8 de noviembre de 1926* (Havana, 1926), pp. 158–59.

8. Schwenck to army chief of staff, G-2, July 8, 1928, File 10641-267(16), RG 165. Schwenck, "Present Executive: Political Policies, Methods, etc.," G-2 Report, June 15, 1928, File 2657-Q-285(1), RG 165.

9. Gerardo Machado y Morales, *Declarations of General Machado y Morales* (Havana 1928), pp. 31–32.

10. E. H. Crowder to secretary of state, February 14, 1927, 837.00/2626, RG 59.

11. "Memorandum of the Conversation," April 23, 1927, United States Department of State, *Foreign Relations of the United States, 1927* (Washington, 1919), p. 527 (hereafter cited as *FRUS,* with appropriate year).

12. Alfredo Lima, *La odisea de Río Verde* (Havana 1934), pp. 9–10. Lieutenant Elwood R. Quesada, acting military attaché, "Important Problems and Issues Requiring Governmental Recognition and Action," G-2 Report, August 14, 1931, File 2657-Q-330(63), RG 165. Ferrer, *Con el rifle al hombro,* p. 262.

13. Gerardo Castellanos G., *Hacia Gibara* (Havana 1933), pp. 284–85. Rubén de León, *El origin del mal (Cuba, un ejemplo)* (Miami, 1964), pp. 294–95. Quesada, "Armed Revolutionary Movement," G-2 Report, August 21, 1931, File 2657-Q-330(64), RG 165.

14. Waldemar León, "Cómo fueron capturados Menocal, Mendieta y su estado mayor en 'Río Verde,' " *Bohemia*, 59 (January 13, 1967), pp. 105–06, 109.

15. Alberto Lamar Schweyer, *Cómo cayó el presidente Machado* (Madrid, 1934), p. 17. Hamilton M. Wright, "Modern Road Building in Cuba, Argentina, and Colombia," *Bulletin of the Pan American Union*, 63 (February 1929), p. 146.

16. Ralph Lee Woodward, Jr., "Union Labor and Communism: Cuba," *Caribbean Studies*, 3, (October 1963), p. 18. Cf. José Rivero Muñiz, *El movimiento obrero durante la primera intervención (1899–1902)* (Havana, 1961) and *ibid., El movimiento laboral cubano durante el perído 1906–1911* (Havana, 1962).

17. E. Sánchez, secretary of agriculture, commerce, and labor, to director of military intelligence, March 26, 1919, File 2056-171, RG 165.

18. In Raymond Leslie Buell, "Cuba and the Platt Amendment," *Foreign Policy Association Information Service*, 5 (April 17, 1929), p. 42.

19. See Gustave Scholle to secretary of state, October 31, 1917, 837.504/32, RG 59, and E. C. Hendrix to secretary of state, December 9, 1918, 837.504/65, RG 59.

20. Office of the Military Attaché, Havana, Cuba, "The Political Situation," G-2 Report, December 23, 1921, File 2657-Q-107, RG 165.

21. Lieutenant Colonel William Bracket, USMC, to military attaché, December 9, 1918, File 2056-73, RG 165.

22. "Immigration and Labor Matters," February 1, 1927, 837.504/306, RG 59.

23. N. H. Hall, commanding officer, Seventh Regiment, Santiago de Cuba, to commandant, United States Naval Station, Guantánamo, December 17, 1918, File 7082-184, Subject File, 1911–1927, Box 629, RG 45.

24. G. A. Morson to W. J. Maslen, Esq., in Rutherford Bingham to secretary of state, January 13, 1919, 837.504/94, RG 59.

25. Víctor Alba, *Historia del movimiento obrero en América Latina* (México, 1964), pp. 421–22. Raymond Leslie Buell et al., *Problems of the New Cuba* (New York, 1935), pp. 186–87.

26. A. E. Méndez, "Al través de mis lentes," *Boletín del Ejército*, 22 (May 1927), p. 248.

27. Moisés Poblete Troncoso and Ben G. Burnett, *The Rise of the Latin American Labor Movement* (New York, 1960), p. 108. Robert J. Alexander, *Organized Labor in Latin America* (New York, 1965), p. 154.

28. Jaime Suchlicki, "Stirrings of Cuban Nationalism: The Student Generation of 1930," *Journal of Inter-American Studies*, 10 (July 1968), pp. 355–56.

29. Raúl Roa, "Rafael Trejo y el 30 de septiembre," *Granma*, September 30, 1968, p. 2.

30. Major J. J. O'Hare, military attaché, "Important Problems and Issues Requiring Governmental Recognition and Action," G-2 Report, November 11, 1930, File 2657-Q-330(12), RG 165.

31. Luis E. Aguilar, *Cuba, 1933: Prologue to Revolution* (Ithaca, 1972), pp. 119–21. Lamar Schweyer, *Cómo cayó el presidente Machado*, pp. 19–21.

32. Carlos G. Peraza, *Machado, crímenes y horrores de un régimen* (Havana, 1933), p. 217. Buell, *Problems of the New Cuba*, pp. 1–11. Carleton Beals, *The Crime of Cuba* (Philadelphia, 1933), pp. 314–15.

33. Leland H. Jenks, "Cuba Faces a New Deal," in A. Curtis Wilgus, ed., *The Caribbean Area* (Washington, 1934), p. 173.

34. Harry F. Guggenheim to secretary of state, January 20, 1931, 837.00B/36, RG

59. Cf. Nelson Amaro and Carmelo Mesa-Lago, "Inequality and Classes," in Carmelo Mesa-Lago, ed., *Revolutionary Change in Cuba* (Pittsburgh, 1971), p. 363.

35. Guggenheim to secretary of state, February 18, 1932, 837.00/3230, RG 59.

36. "El caso de Zubizarreta," *Bohemia*, 26 (February 4, 1934), p. 20. O'Hare, "Important Problems and Issues Requiring Governmental Recognition and Action," G-2 Report, July 26, 1932, File 2657-Q-330(130), RG 165. Guggenheim to secretary of state, March 5, 1932, 837.00 General Conditions/50, RG 59.

37. Guggenheim to secretary of state, February 7, 1933, 837.00 General Conditions/58, RG 59.

38. J. Martínez, captain, General Staff, chief of personnel, "Relación numérica de oficiales y alistados del ejército, existentes en 31 de julio de 1933," File 2012-153(2), RG 165.

39. "Cuban Budgetary Appropriations for Army and Navy, 1902–1934," Appendix no. 2, in Lieutenant Colonel C. K. Nulsen to military attaché, Havana, Cuba, July 5, 1934, File 2012-153(2), RG 165.

40. *New York Times,* January 4, 1931, sec. 3, p. 6. Cf. Edelmira González, *La revolución en Cuba. Memorias del coronel Rosendo Collazo* (Havana, 1934), pp. 39–40.

41. Lieutenant Colonel T. N. Gimperling, military attaché, "Strength and Composition," G-2 Report, April 27, 1933, File 2012–119 (11), RG 165.

42. Peraza, *Machado, crímenes y horrores de un régimen,* pp. 234–35.

43. Carlos Manuel de la Cruz, *Proceso histórico del machadato* (Havana, 1939), p. 207.

44. Cosme de la Torriente, *Cuarenta años de mi vida, 1898–1938* (Havana, 1939), p. 207.

45. Major J. J. O'Hare, military attaché, "Loyalty," G-2 Report, November 28, 1932, File 2012-133(3), RG 165. O'Hare, "Memorandum," February 7, 1933, File 2012-133(3), RG 165.

46. O'Hare "Loyalty," G-2 Report, February 7, 1933, File 2012-133(3), RG 165.

47. See José A. Tabares, "Guiteras y el alzamiento de abril de 1933," *Bohemia,* 61 (May 3, 1974), pp. 88–96.

Chapter 6: The Politics of Army Interventions, 1933

1. Harry F. Guggenheim to Francis White, November 23, 1932, Francis White Papers, Box 11, General Records of the Department of State, National Archives, RG 59.

2. William Phillips, "Memorandum of Conversation with Cuban Ambassador," May 4, 1933, 550. S.S. Washington/415, RG 59.

3. Secretary of state to appointed ambassador in Cuba, May 1, 1933, *FRUS,* V, 1933, p. 285.

4. Mario Kuchilan Sol, "12 de agosto de 1933," *Bohemia* 62 (August 7, 1970), p. 61.

5. Charles A. Thomson, "The Cuban Revolution: Fall of Machado," *Foreign Policy Reports,* 11 (December 18, 1935), p. 253.

6. Sumner Welles to secretary of state, May 13, 1933, *FRUS,* V, 1933, p. 288, and Welles to Franklin D. Roosevelt, July 17, 1933, *FRUS, V, 1933, p. 324.*

7. Welles to Franklin D. Roosevelt, May 18, 1933, Official File 470, Sumner Welles, Franklin D. Roosevelt Papers, Hyde Park, New York.

8. Welles to Roosevelt, July 17, 1933, *FRUS,* V, 1933, p. 324.

9. *New York Times,* July 27, 1933, p. 1.

10. Welles to acting secretary of state, August 5, 1933, 837.00/3603, RG 59.

11. Welles to secretary of state, August 7, 1933, 837.00/3606, RG 59.

12. Welles to secretary of state, August 9, 1933, 837.00/3626, RG 59.

13. Welles to secretary of state, August 10, 1933, 837.00/13630. Cf. Hugh Thomas, *Cuba: The Pursuit of Freedom* (New York, 1971), pp. 620–21

14. Lieutenant Elwood R. Quesada, acting military attaché, "Banditry, Riots and Similar Infractions of Public Peace and Safety," September 3, 1931, 837.00 Revolutions/56, RG 59.

15. Welles to secretary of state, August 9, 1933, 837.00/3622, RG 59.

16. "I do not believe that the withdrawal of recognition would in all probability force us to intervene," Welles stated. "I think if the President himself was advised that we would withdraw recognition unless he accepted a fair solution of the problem, he would be obliged to accept such solution by most members of his Cabinet, by the Army and by the great majority of Congress." Welles to secretary of state, August 8, 1933, 837.00/3616, RG 59.

17. Welles to secretary of state, August 7, 1933, 837.00/3606, RG 59.

18. "Memorandum by the Under-Secretary of State," August 8, 1933, 837.00/3629, RG 59.

19. Welles to secretary of state, August 8, 1933, 837.00/1616, RG 59. *New York Times*, August 9, 1933, p. 12.

20. *New York Herald Tribune*, August 8, 1933, p. 2.

21. Welles to secretary of state, August 10, 1933, 837.00/3633, RG 59.

22. Gerardo Castellanos G., *Panorama histórico* (Havana, 1934), pp. 1539–40.

23. Welles to secretary of state, August 10, 1933, 837.00/3633, RG 59.

24. *Ibid.*

25. Arthur Krock, "Hull Winds Spurs in Test of State Department in Cuban Crisis," *New York Times*, August 21, 1933, p. 16.

26. *New York Times*, August 12, 1933, p. 1.

27. Thomson, "The Cuban Revolution: Fall of Machado," p. 257. *New York Times*, August 7, 1933, p. 7. Lamar Schweyer, *Cómo cayó el presidente Machado*, pp. 179–80.

28. Under-Secretary of State William Phillips, "Memorandum of Conversation with Cuban Ambassador," July 25, 1933, 837.00/3582½, RG 59. Cf. Enrique Lumen, *La revolución cubana* (México, 1934), p. 78. At the same time, the military attaché, Lieutenant Colonel T. N. Gimperling, informed senior military chiefs that the United States would intervene unless Machado retired. Lamar Schweyer, *Cómo cayó el presidente Machado*, p. 180.

29. Gonzalo de Quesada y Miranda, *¡En Cuba Libre! Historia documentada y anecdóctica del machadato* (2 vols., Havana, 1938), II, pp. 243–44. Ferrer, *Con el rifle al hombro*, pp. 321–22. Orestes Ferrara, "Los últimos días del régimen de Machado," *Bohemia*, 44 (August 10, 1952), p. 114.

30. Welles to acting secretary of state, June 6, 1933, 837.00/3537, RG 59.

31. ABC, *El ABC en la mediación* (Havana, 1934), pp. 46–48. Ricardo Adam y Silva, *La gran mentira. 4 de septiembre de 1933* (Havana, 1947), p. 67. Cf. Lamar Schweyer, *Cómo cayó el presidente Machado*, pp. 179–80.

32. Lieutenant Colonel T. N. Gimperling, military attaché, "Causes of Recent Revolt of Armed Forces Against Machado," G-2 Report, August 21, 1933, File 2012-133(7), RG 165.

33. Lamar Schweyer, *Cómo cayó el presidente Machado*, pp. 179–80.

34. Gerardo Machado to Franklin D. Roosevelt, September 4, 1933, Official File 150, Cuba, 1933–1934, Box 2, Roosevelt Papers. Cf. Rafael Guas Inclán, *El General Gerardo Machado y Morales* (Havana, 1956), p. 23.

35. "Memorandum," August 11, 1933, in Orestes Ferrara to Sumner Welles, August 12, 1933, File (1933) 800, American Embassy, Cuba, Correspondence, RG 84.

36. Sumner Welles, *Two Years of the "Good Neighbor" Policy*, Department of State, Latin American Series no. 11 (Washington, D.C., 1935), pp. 8–9.

37. Ferrer, *Con el rifle al hombro*, p. 316.

38. *New York Times*, August 7, 1933, p. 7.

39. Jorge Quintana, "Fué el 12 de agosto de 1933," *Bohemia*, 41 (August 14, 1949), p. 98. Thomas, *Cuba: The Pursuit of Freedom*, pp. 623–24.

40. Cordell Hull, *The Memoirs of Cordell Hull* (2 vols., New York, 1948), I, p. 314. Cf. Lester D. Langley, *The Cuban Policy of the United States* (New York, 1968), pp. 155–56.

41. Welles to secretary of state, August 19, 1933, *FRUS*, V, 1933, pp. 367–68.

42. Mario G. Menocal to Horacio Ferrer, June 28, 1933, in Ferrer, *Con el rifle al hombro*, p. 304.

43. R. Hart Phillips, *Cuba: Island of Paradox* (New York, 1959), p. 55.

44. Welles to secretary of state, August 19, 1933, *FRUS*, V, 1933, pp. 367–68.

45. Welles to secretary of state, August 24, 1933, President's Secretary's File, Cuba, 1933–1935, 1942–1944, Box 5, Roosevelt Papers.

46. Edwin Schoenrich, American consul, Santiago de Cuba, to Welles, August 26, 1933, File (1933) 800, American consul general, Havana, Cuba, Correspondence, RG 84.

47. Ferrer, *Con el rifle al hombro*, p. 342.

48. See, for example, Decreto Número 1, 262, *Gaceta Oficial de la República*, 31 (August 31, 1933), p. 2914.

49. Céspedes had earlier been a political protegé of the former Conservative president, serving Menocal between 1913 and 1921 as the Cuban minister in Washington.

50. "La espada rota," *El Liberal*, 1 (March 30, 1935), p. 4. Mario Riera Hernández, *Historial obrero cubano, 1574–1965* (Miami, 1965), pp. 87–88.

51. Mario Torres Menier, "Mi diario: Batista, Belisario y yo," *Bohemia*, 26 (February 25, 1934), pp. 12–13.

52. Ferrer, *Con el rifle al hombro*, p. 348.

53. "La espada rota," pp. 4–5. Ferrer, *Con el rifle al hombro*, p. 347.

54. Riera Hernández, *Historial obrero cubano, 1574–1965*, pp. 87–88. Phillips, *Cuba: Island of Paradox*, pp. 87–88.

55. Phillips, *Cuba: Island of Paradox*, p. 89. Manuel Costales Latatu, "Una revolución efímera en el tiempo y gloriosa en los hechos," *Bohemia*, 46 (September 12, 1854), p. 63. Rubén Martínez Villena, "The Rise of the Revolutionary Movement in Cuba," *The Communist*, 12 (June 1933), pp. 567–68.

56. *New York Times*, August 13, 1933, sec. 1, p. 23.

57. Lieutenant Colonel T. N. Gimperling, military attaché, "Loyalty," G-2 Report, August 16 1933, File 2012-133(6), RG 165.

58. Edwin Schoenrich, American consul, Santiago de Cuba, to American Embassy, Havana, Cuba, August 26, 1933, File (1933) 800, American Embassy, Havana, Cuba, Correspondence, RG 84.

59. "Memorandum of Press Conference," August 14, 1933, Department of State, RG 59.

60. Lieutenant Colonel T. N. Gimperling, military attaché, "Causes of Recent Revolt of Armed Forces Against Machado," G-2 Report, August 21, 1933, File 2012-133(7), RG 165.

61. Katherine Chorley suggests that generally during fraternization, revolutionaries link "their grievances to revolutionary propaganda during the period of education and preparation for a revolt. They will exploit discontent with the practical conditions of

service under the old regime suggesting that under a new regime the grievances could be remedied." *Armies and the Art of Revolution* (London, 1943), p. 136.

62. Ferrer, *Con el rifle al hombro,* p. 340.

63. Costales Latatu, "Una revolución efímera en el tiempo y gloriosa en los hechos," pp. 63, 80.

64. "Circular de 3 de septiembre desmintiendo el rumor de la rebaja de sueldos a las tropas," in Ferrer, *Con el rifle al hombro,* p. 347.

65. *New York Times,* September 5, 1933, p. 12.

66. Adam y Silva, *La gran mentira,* pp. 62–63, 75–76.

67. Ulpiano Vega Cobiellas, *La personalidad y la obra del General Fulgencio Batista y Zaldívar* (Havana, 1943), pp. 9394. Mario Riera Hernández, *Un presidente constructivo* (Miami, 1966), p. 6. Torres Menier, "Mi diario: Batista, Belisario y yo," p. 62.

68. In Edmund A. Chester, *A Sergeant Named Batista* (New York, 1954), p. 101.

69. Adam y Silva, *La gran mentira,* pp. 173–74.

70. Lieutenant Colonel T. N. Gimperling, military attaché, "Summary of Army Mutiny of September 4–5, 1933," G-2 Report, September 26, 1933, File 2012-144 (12), RG 165.

71. Adam y Silva, *La gran mentira,* pp. 173–74.

72. Castellanos G., *Panorama histórico,* p. 1558. Lieutenant Colonel T. N. Gimperling, military attaché, "War Department," G-2 Report, October 6, 1933, File 2012-133(15), RG 165.

73. *New York Times,* October 14, 1934, sec. 6, p. 3.

74. Adam y Silva, *La gran mentira,* p. 121. Years later, Cosme de la Torriente, a close friend of then President Batista, disclosed that the former sergeant had told him that the September 4 movement never intended to change governments. *El Mundo* (Havana), July 18, 1952, p. A-7.

75. Rafael García Bárcena, "Razón y sinrazón del 4 de septiembre," *Bohemia,* 44 (September 7, 1952), p. 60. "Such words," García Bárcena recalled, "surprised us when we were under the impression that we were there to depose the Céspedes government" (p. 61).

76. Rubén de León, "La verdad de lo ocurrido desde el cuatro de septiembre," *Bohemia,* 26 (February 4, 1934), p. 29.

77. Francisco Masiques Landeta, "Puntos sobresalientes del septembrismo," *Bohemia,* 31 (September 11, 1949), p. 54. Ramón Grau San Martín, *La revolución cubana ante América* (México, 1936), p. 92.

78. García Bárcena, "Razón y sinrazón del 4 de septiembre," pp. 60–61.

79. Castallanos G., *Panorama histórico,* p. 1559. Céspedes was in the interior, inspecting the damage produced by a hurrican days earlier.

80. M. Franco Varona, *La revolución del 4 de septiembre* (Havana, 1934), pp. 44–51.

81. "La gran tragedia de la verdadera oficialidad cubana," *Bohemia,* 26 (January 7, 1934), p. 36.

82. Adam y Silva, *La gran mentira,* pp. 27–28. Hugh Thomas, "The Origins of the Cuban Revolution," *The World Today,* 19 (October 1963), p. 455. Thomas, *Cuba: The Pursuit of Freedom,* p. 583.

83. Adam y Silva, *La gran mentira,* p. 24.

84. "Relación de oficiales que continuan en el actual Ejército Nacional," File 2012-33(60), RG 165.

85. See Cuba, Estado Mayor General del Ejército, *Lista directorio y escalafones* (Havana, 1916), and "Relación de oficiales que continuan en el actual Ejército Nacional," File 2012-133(60), RG 165.

86. Gimperling, "Loyalty," G-2 Report, October 9, 1933, File 2012-133(19), RG 165.

87. Hartwell Johnson, American vice consul, Matanzas, "Political Affairs in the Province of Matanzas, Cuba," November 27, 1933, File (1933) 800, Matanzas, Cuba, Correspondence, RG 84.

88. Edwin Schoenrich to Samuel S. Dickson, December 26, 1933, 837.00/4593, RG 59.

89. Buell, *Problems of the New Cuba*, pp. 33–34. Cf. Ramón Eduardo Ruiz, *Cuba: The Making of a Revolution* (Amherst, 1968), p. 158.

90. Lieutenant Colonel T. N. Gimperling, military attaché, "Alleged Dissension and Communism in the Cuban Army," G-2 Report, October 30, 1933, File 2012-133(27), RG 165.

91. Alberto Arredondo, *El negro en Cuba* (Havana, 1939), pp. 158–59.

92. Emilio Díaz, *Essay of the Cuban History* (Coral Gables, Ha., 1964), p. 162.

93. Andrés Suárez, *Cuba: Castroism and Communism, 1959–1966*, trans. Joel Carmichael and Ernest Halperin (Cambridge, Mass., 1967), p. 10.

Chapter 7: Diplomacy, Army Politics, and the Collapse of the Cuban Officer Corps

1. The "sudden end of the Céspedes regime," Bryce Wood suggests, "was a suprise, and must have been a great shock to Welles, for in a real sense the Céspedes government was his government, and the mutiny was a blow to his newly-gained prestige no less than an attack on the position of the traditional ruling groups in Cuba." Bryce Wood, *The Making of the Good Neighbor Policy* (New York, 1961), p. 71.

2. Sumner Welles to secretary of state, September 5, 1933, 837.00/3757, RG 59.

3. "Memorandum of Telephone Conversation Between Secretary of State Hull and Welles," September 5, 1933, 837.00/3800, RG 59.

4. In E. David Cronon, "Interpreting the New Good Neighbor Policy: The Cuban Crisis of 1933," *The Hispanic American Historical Review*, 34 (November 1959), p. 546.

5. "Memorandum of Telephone Conversation between Secretary of State and the Ambassador in Cuba," September 5, 1933, 837.00/3756, RG 59.

6. Welles to secretary of state, September 5, 1933, *ibid.*

7. Welles to secretary of state, September 7, 1933, 837.00/3778, RG 59.

8. P. A. del Valle, squadron marine officer, to commander, Special Squadron, September 29, 1933, File (1933) 800, American Embassy, Havana, Cuba, Correspondence, RG 84.

9. Harold L. Ickes, *The Secret Diaries of Harold L. Ickes* (3 vols., New York, 1953–1954), I, p. 87.

10. Hull *The Memoirs of Cordell Hull*, I, p. 313.

11. Lieutenant Colonel T. N. Gimperling, military attaché, to chief, military intelligence, September 29, 1933, File 2012-147(1), RG 165.

12. R. R. Henning, commanding officer, to commander, Special Service Squadron, September 21, 1933, File EF19/P9-2 (330921), RG 80.

13. C. S. Freeman, commanding officer, to commander, September 21, 1933, *ibid*. Freeman reported seeing automobiles displaying signs on the windshields pledging, "moriremos combatiendo la intervencion" ("we will die fighting the intervention"). As Ruby Hart Phillips made an entry into her diary on September 5, she recorded, "A sergeant, broadcasting over the radio, boasts of what the Cuban army will do the American marines if they dare to land." R. Hart Phillips, *Cuba: Island of Paradox*, p. 65.

14. "Memorandum of Telephone Conversation Between Hull and Welles," September 5, 1933, *FRUS*, V, 1933, p. 390.

15. Welles to secretary of state, September 8, 1933, 837.00/3798, RG 59.

16. Welles to secretary of state, October 16, 1933, *FRUS*, V, 1933, p. 489.

17. Welles to secretary of state, September 5, 1933, *ibid.*, p. 379.

18. Welles to secretary of state, September 14, 1933, 837.00/3798, RG 59.

19. Welles to secretary of state, September 12, 1933, 837.00/3847, RG 59.

20. León, "La verdad de lo ocurrido desde el cuatro de septiembre," p. 39. Charles A. Thomson, "The Cuban Revolution: Reform and Reaction," *Foreign Policy Reports*, 11 (January 1, 1936), p. 263.

21. Lieutenant Colonel T. N. Gimperling, military attaché, "Army Officers Defy Present Regime," G-2 Report, September 11, 1933, File 2012-133(8), RG 165.

22. "Memorandum of Conversation Between Secretary Hull at Washington and Ambassador Welles at Habana, by Telephone," September 9, 1933, 837.00/3939, RG 59.

23. *New York Herald Tribune*, September 11, 1933, p. 1.

24. Gimperling, "Army Officers Defy Present Regime," G-2 Report, September 11, 1933, File 2012-133(8), RG 165.

25. Fulgencio Batista, *Piedras y leyes* (Mexico, 1961), p. 19.

26. *New York Times*, September 7, 1933, p. 3.

27. Cronon, "Interpreting the New Good Neighbor Policy: The Cuban Crisis of 1933," p. 550.

28. Eddy Chibás, "Los gobiernos de Cuba: Grau San Martín (1933–1934)," *Bohemia*, 30 (June 5, 1938), p. 95. Riera Hernández, *Un presidente constructivo, pp. 8–9*.

29. In Phillips, *Cuba: Island of Paradox*, pp. 90–92. Cf. Alfredo Betancourt to Secretary of State Cordell Hull, November 5, 1933, Correspondence, Box 5, Cordell Hull Papers, Library of Congress, Manuscript Division.

30. Welles to secretary of state, October 24, 1933, 837.00/4289, RG 59.

31. Lieutenant Colonel T. N. Gimperling, military attaché, "Commissioned Personnel," G-2 Report, September 9, 1933, File 2012-133(9), RG 165. Ruby Hart Phillips similarly recalled hearing rumors that the American Ambassador had promised intervention if the hotel were attacked by government forces. Phillips, *Cuba: Island of Paradox*, p. 71.

32. Welles to secretary of state, September 9, 1933, 837.00/3807, RG 59.

33. Torres Menier, "Mi diario: Batista, Belisario y yo," p. 6.

34. Lieutenant Colonel T. N. Gimperling, military attaché, "Battle at National Hotel, on October 2," G-2 Report, October 6, 1933, File 2012-193(19), RG 165.

35. "Relación de los nombramientos y ascensos hechos durante el desgobierno de los Auténticos," File 2012-133(60), RG 165.

Chapter 8: The Diplomatic Imperative and the Rise of Fulgencio Batista

1. Sumner Welles to secretary of state, September 12, 1933, 837.00/3847, RG 59.

2. Charles W. Taussig to Franklin D. Roosevelt, November 16, 1933, Caribbean Files, File Number 34, Box 37, Charles W. Taussig Papers, Hyde Park, New York.

3. Welles to secretary of state, September 21, 1933, 837.00/3982, RG 59, Major P. A. del Valle, squadron marine officer, to commander, Special Squadron, September 29, 1933, File (1933) 800, American Embassy, Havana, Cuba, Correspondence, RG 84.

4. Samuel S. Dickson, chargé d'affaires, to secretary of state, January 4, 1934, 837.00/4581 RG 59. Hartwell Johnson, "General Survey of Political and Economic Conditions in the Matanzas Consular District," December 22, 1933, File (1933) 800, American Consulate, Matanzas, Cuba, Correspondence, RG 84.

5. C. S. Freeman, commanding officer, to commander, September 21, 1933, File EF19/2(330921), RG 80.

6. Welles to secretary of state, September 21, 1933, 837.00/3982, RG 59.

7. Lieutenant Colonel T. N. Gimperling, military attaché, "Loyalty," G-2 Report, October 9, 1933, File 2012–133(12), RG 165.

8. Lieutenant Colonel T. N. Gimperling, military attaché, "Strength of Grau's Position as President," G-2 Report, October 23, 1933, File 2012-133(25), RG 165.

9. Secretary of state to Welles, October 5, 1933, 837.00/4131, RG 59.

10. Welles to secretary of state, October 5, 1933, *ibid.*

11. Welles to secretary of state, October 4, 1933, *ibid.*

12. Welles to secretary of state, October 7, 1933, 137.00/4146, RG 59.

13. Welles to acting secretary of state, December 7, 1933, 837.00/4480, RG 59.

14. Welles to acting secretary of state, December 5, 1933, 837.00/4475, RG 59.

15. Jefferson Caffery to acting secretary of state, January 10, 1934, 837.00/4591, RG 59.

16. Caffery to acting secretary of state, January 13, 1934, 837.00/4605, RG 59.

17. Decreto Número 408, *Gaceta Oficial de la República,* 32 (February 9, 1934), p. 1915.

Chapter 9: Consolidation of Army Hegemony, 1934–1940

1. Jefferson Caffery to secretary of state, September 18, 1934, 837.00/5456, RG 59.

2. Lieutenant Colonel T. N. Gimperling, military attaché, "Resignation of Cabinet Members," G-2 Report, June 23, 1934, File 2657-Q-330(288), RG 165.

3. Lieutenant Colonel T. N. Gimperling, military attaché, "Communists and Auténticos Arrested," G-2 Report, September 28, 1934, File 2657-Q-330(31), RG 165.

4. Hartwell Johnson to American Embassy, April 10, 1934, File (1934) 800, American Consulate, Matanzas, Cuba, Correspondence, RG 84.

5. Caffery to secretary of state, May 4, 1934, 837.00/5055, RG 59.

6. Major E. W. Timberlake, military attaché, "Data for Revision of Combat Estimate," G-2 Report, April 12, 1938, File 10641-267(32), RG 165.

7. Sheridan Talbot, American consul, Santiago de Cuba, to Caffery, August 26, 1935, File (1935) 800, American Consulate, Santiago de Cuba, Miscellaneous Correspondence, RG 84.

8. Milton Patterson Thompson, American vice consul, Matanzas, to Ellis O. Briggs, September 4, 1935, File (1935) 800, American Embassy, Havana, Cuba, 1935, Correspondence, RG 84.

9. Lieutenant Colonel T. N. Gimperling, military attaché, "Public Order and Safety," G-2 Report, January 18, 1935, File 2655-Q-81, RG 165.

10. Lieutenant Colonel T. N. Gimperling, military attaché, "General Situation as Sugar Grinding Season Approaches," G-2 Report, January 11, 1935, *ibid.*

11. Gimperling, "Public Order and Safety," G-2 Report, January 18, 1935, *ibid.*

12. Lieutenant Colonel T. N. Gimperling, military attaché, "Terrorist Activities," G-2 Report, March 5, 1935, File 2657-Q-81, RG 165.

13. Hartwell Johnson to Sumner Welles, August 19, 1933, File (1933) 800, American Consulate, Matanzas, Cuba, Correspondence, RG 84.

14. Horace J. Dickson, American consul, to F. T. F. Dumont, August 18, 1933, File (1933) 800, Consulate General, Havana, Cuba, Correspondence, RG 84.

15. See Riera Hernández, *Cuba politica, 1899–1955,* pp. 425–512.

16. William P. Blocker, American consul, Santiago de Cuba, to Jefferson Caffery, October 5, 1935, File (1935) 800, American Consulate, Santiago de Cuba, Miscellaneous Correspondence, RG 84.

17. Major E. W. Timberlake, military attaché, "Distribution of Troops, Permanent Military Posts and Stations," G-2 Report, June 17, 1938, File 2012-119(42), RG 165.

18. Blocker to American Embassy, November 29, 1935, File (1935) 800, American Consulate, Santiago de Cuba, Miscellaneous Correspondence, RG 84.

19. Sheridan Talbot to American Embassy, September 3, 1935, *ibid.*

20. Blocker to American Embassy, November 29, 1935, *ibid.*

21. Major E. W. Timberlake, military attaché, "Dissension Between Members of the Armed Forces," G-2 Report, December 1, 1937, File 2012-133(84), RG 165.

22. Major E. W. Timberlake, military attaché, "Attempted Graft in the Army," G-2 Report, February 16, 1938, File 2012-133(86), RG 165.

23. Major E. W. Timberlake, military attaché, "Restoration of Colonel Julio Velasco as Adjutant General of the Cuban Army," G-2 Report, May 5, 1938, File 2012-133(88), RG 165.

24. Raoul Acosta Rubio, *Batista ante la historia (relato de un civilista)* (Havana, 1938), p. 155. Riera Hernández, *Un presidente constructivo,* p. 17.

25. Captain L. V. H. Durfee, military attaché, "Resumé of Situation," G-2 Report, March 12, 1935, File 2657-Q-330(336), RG 165. Aureliano Sánchez Arango, "The Recent Strike in Cuba," *Three Americas* (Mexico), 1 (June 1935), pp. 14–15.

26. *New York Times,* May 24, 1936, sec. 5, p. 5.

27. Caffery to secretary of state, March 15, 1935, 837.00/6190, RG 59.

28. See Russell H. Fitzgibbon and H. Max Healy, "The Cuban Elections of 1936," *The American Political Science Review,* 30 (August 1936), pp. 724–35.

29. Colonel T. N. Gimperling, military attaché, "Rumors of Disaffection in the Army," G-2 Report, June 10, 1936, File 2012-133(29), RG 165.

30. Milton Patterson Thompson to H. Freeman Matthews, March 4, 1936, File (1936) 800, American Consulate, Matanzas, Cuba, Correspondence, RG 84.

31. Phillips, *Cuba: Island of Paradox,* p. 175.

32. Colonel T. N. Gimperling, military attaché, "Rumors," G-2 Report, December 17, 1936, File 2657-Q-330(375), RG 165.

33. Caffery to secretary of state, December 18, 1936, 837.00/7761, RG 59.

34. Caffery to secretary of state, December 19, 1936, 837.00/7765, RG 59.

35. Carlos Márquez Sterling, *Historia de Cuba, desde Colón hasta Castro* (New York, 1963), pp. 320–21. Cf. Embajada de Cuba to Franklin D. Roosevelt, n.d., President's Secretary's File, Cuba, 1933–1935, 1942–1944, Box 5, Roosevelt Papers.

36. Edward E. Benet, American vice consul, to American Embassy, December 22, 1936, File (1936) 800 American Consulate, Matanzas, Cuba, Correspondence, RG 84.

37. Caffery to secretary of state, December 18, 1936, 837.00/7761, RG 59.

38. Caffery to secretary of state, December 20, 1936, 837.00/7769, RG 59.

39. Embajada de Cuba to Franklin D. Roosevelt, n.d., President's Secretary's File, Cuba, 1933–1935, 1942–1944, Box 5, Roosevelt Papers.

40. Laurence Duggan, "Memorandum," December 21, 1936, 837.00/7787, RG 59.

41. *Ibid.*

42. Caffery to secretary of state, December 19, 1936, 837.99/7765, RG 59.

43. Caffery to secretary of state, December 10, 1936, 837.00/7764, RG 59.

44. Colonel T. N. Gimperling, military attaché, "Political Situation," G-2 Report, December 19, 1936, File 2657-Q-330, RG 165.

45. *Ibid.*

46. Caffery to secretary of state, December 18, 1936, 837.00/7763, RG 59. Pedro Luis Padrón, "Bajo la cúpula del Capitolio, cuartelazo a Miguel Mariano," *Granma,* April 7, 1969, p. 2.

47. Caffery to R. Walton Moore, December 29, 1936, President's Secretary's File, R. Walton Moore, Box 36, Roosevelt Papers.

48. Fulgencio Batista, "Texto íntegro de la alocución del 4 de septiembre, pronunciado por el Coronel Batista," in Arístides Sosa de Quesada, *Militarismo, anti-militarismo, seudo-militarismo* (Havana, 1939), p. 107.

49. Arístides Sosa de Quesada, "El militarismo, su contenido, pasado, presente y futuro," in Sosa de Quesada, *Militarismo, anti-militarismo, seudo-militarismo,* p. 18.

50. Major E. W. Timberlake, military attaché, "Rural Schools," G-2 Report, June 3, 1937, File 2277-Q-17(2), RG 165. Gerald Howard Read, "Civic Military Rural Education of Cuba: Eleven Eventful years (1936–1946)," (Ph.D. diss., Ohio State University, 1950).

51. Fulgencio Batista, *Revolución social o política reformista (once aniversarios)* (Havana, 1944), pp. 79–80.

52. Arístides Sosa de Quesada, *El Consejo Corporativo de Educación, Sanidad y Beneficencia y sus instituciones filiales* (Havana, 1937), p. 143.

53. *Ibid.,* pp. 115–116, 209–10.

54. *Plan Trienal de Cuba* (Havana, 1938), pp. 83–84.

55. Timberlake, "Rural Schools," G-2 Report, June 3, 1937, File 2277-Q-17(2), RG 165.

56. Milton Patterson Thompson to H. Freeman Matthews, September 18, 1936, File (1936) 800, American Consulate, Matanzas, Cuba, Correspondence, RG 84.

57. Major E. W. Timberlake, military attaché, "Mass Meeting in Favor of Three-Year Plan," G-2 Report, November 24, 1937, File 2271-Q-17(7), RG 165. Timberlake, "Schools: Rural Civic-Military and Technical," G-2 Report, May 24, 1938, RG 165.

58. Colonel F. H. Lincoln, assistant chief of staff, "Current Situation in Cuba," G-2 Report, December 21, 1936, File 2657-Q-330, RG 165.

59. Timberlake to assistant chief of staff, June 9, 1938, File 2657-Q-391, RG 165.

60. *Ibid.*

61. "Decreto-Ley Núm. 535," *Gaceta Oficial de la República,* January 29, 1936. Cf. E. W. Timberlake, military attaché, "Inspection of National Police (Central Division) on March 15, 1937," G-2 Report, File 2012-137(15), RG 165.

62. Edwin Foscue, "The Central Highway of Cuba," *Economic Geography,* 9 (October 1933), pp. 406–12.

63. Donald R. Dyer, "Urbanism in Cuba," *The Geographical Review,* 47 (April 1957), p. 224.

64. *Ibid.,* p. 226.

65. *Ibid.,* p. 228.

66. Lieutenant Colonel T. N. Gimperling, military attaché, "Nature and Objective of Training for Officers and Enlisted Men," G-2 Report, March 29, 1935, File 2012-159(2) RG 165. José A. Duarte Oropesa, *Historiología cubana* (5 vols., n.p., 1969–1970), IV, pp. 467–68.

67. Major E. W. Timberlake, military attaché, "Fortifications—General," G-2 Report, July 28, 1937, File 2667-Q-31(1), RG 165. "Beyond [the] capacity for keeping public order," one report maintained, "[the] Cuban army [is] considered [to be] inefficient and incapable of taking to the field against any well-trained force." "Monograph on Cuba," in counselor of embassy to secretary of state, January 19, 1944, 837.00/9542, RG 59.

68. See J. Martínez, captain, General Staff, "Relación numérica del personal de oficiales y alistados del Ejército, existentes en 31 de julio de 1933," File 2012-11(43), RG 165, and U. Matos Rodríguez, captain, General Staff, "Relación numérica del personal de oficiales alistados del Ejército, existentes en 31 de enero de 1941," File 2012-100(95), RG 165.

Chapter 10: The Civilian Interregnum, 1940–1952

1. J. Butler Wright to secretary of state, November 2, 1938, 837.00/8348, RG 59.
2. Wright to secretary of state, March 17, 1939, 837.00/8410, RG 59.
3. Wright to secretary of state, November 2, 1938, 837.00/8348, RG 59.
4. Major Henry A. Barber, Jr., military attaché, "Probability of Colonel Batista Becoming Candidate for President," G-2 Report, July 28, 1939, File 2056-250(9), RG 165.
5. Riera Hernández, *Cuba política, 1899–1955*, pp. 483–91.
6. "Relación de hechos cometidos principalmente por miembros de las Fuerzas Armadas de la República, contra el libre ejercicio del sufragio, presentada al Honorable Señor Presidente de la República por los Presidentes de los Partidos Revolucionario Cubano (Auténtico), Acción Republicana y A.B.C.," January 2, 1940, 837.00/18802, RG 59.
7. Edward P. Lawton, second secretary of the embassy, to secretary of state, March 2, 1939, 837.00/8401, RG 59.
8. Wright to secretary of state, August 25, 1938, 837.00/8299, RG 59.
9. Vega Cobiellas, *La personalidad y la obra del General Fulgencio Batista Zaldívar*, p. 112. León, *El origin del mal (Cuba, un ejemplo)*, p. 338.
10. Major Henry A. Barber, Jr., military attaché, "Internal Political Situation," G-2 Report, December 14, 1938, File 2056-250(1), RG 165.
11. Pedro Barrera Pérez, "Por que el ejército no derrotó a Castro," *Bohemia Libre*, 53 (July 16, 1961), pp. 7–8.
12. George S. Messersmith to secretary of state, February 3, 1941, 837.00/8939, RG 59. Cf. Fulgencio Batista, *Respuesta* (México, 1960), pp. 419–20.
13. Messersmith to secretary of state, February 3, 1941, 837.00/8939, RG 59. Cf. Ulpiano Vega Cobiellas, *Nuestra América y la evolución de Cuba* (Havana, 1944), pp. 328–20. Riera Hernández, *Un presidente constructivo*, pp. 27–28.
14. Messersmith to secretary of state, February 3, 1941, 837.00/8939, RG 59.
15. *Ibid.*
16. *Ibid.* The American ambassador promoted Batista's position to the State Department, noting:

> There is no doubt in my mind that President Batista has been influenced in his actions since he became President by two considerations. First, he has taken pride in being a Constitutional President of Cuba and he wishes to govern Constitutionally. To do this, he has realized that he must restrict gradually the powers of the Army. Secondly, he has not wished to be in the same position with respect to the Army that former President Laredo Bru was in with respect to him. President Batista realized that he could not do without the Army, but he wished it to be subordinate to him rather than to have it control him. For this reason he undoubtedly had in mind changes in the Army and Navy. [*Ibid.*]

17. Adam y Silva, *La gran mentira,* p. 416.

18. "La destitución de los coroneles," *Carteles,* 22 (February 9, 1941), p. 33.

19. Messersmith to secretary of state, February 5, 1941, 837.00 Revolutions/478, RG 59.

20. *Gaceta Oficial de la República,* February 3, 5, 10, 11, 14, and 26, 1941.

21. "Acuerdo-Ley Núm. 7," *Gaceta Oficial de la República,* January 27, 1942.

22. American vice consul, Nuevitas, to American Embassy, May 14, 1941, 837.00/9011, RG 59.

23. "Nada más que un hombre," *Carteles,* 22 (February 16, 1941), p. 21.

24. Coert de Bois, American consul general, "Confidential Memorandum for the Embassy," March 6, 1940, 837.00/8699, RG 59.

25. Spruille Braden to secretary of state, May 19, 1943, 837.00/9290, RG 59.

26. Chargé d' affaires ad interim to secretary of state, August 14, 1944, 837.00/9-1944, RG 59.

27. *Ibid.*

28. Barrera Pérez, "Por que el ejército no derrotó a Castro," p. 8. Barrera Pérez refers to this period as the "golden age of the Army."

29. Counsel of the embassy to secretary of state, November 27, 1944, 837.00/11-2744, RG 59.

30. *Havana Post,* March 6, 1945, pp. 1–2.

31. Chief of Staff Genovevo Pérez Dámera was a lieutenant in 1934. Colonel Manuel Pérez, the *grauísta* commander of Pinar del Río, Lieutenant Colonel José L. Chinea, chief of the Santa Clara regiment, Colonel Otalio Soca Llanes, military commander of Havana Province, and Lieutenant Colonels Juan Estévez Maymir and J. A. Rodríguez Corvo, inspectors general of the First and Fifth Military Districts, respectively, were all lieutenants in 1934. Colonel Basilio González Santana, the seond in command in Pinar del Río, Colonel José Velázquez, commander of Camp Columbia, Colonel Manuel Pérez Alvarez, later chief of Pinar del Río, Lieutenant Colonels Manual Alvarez Margolles, inspector general, and Pablo Cruz, quartermaster general, were all captains in 1934.

32. *Havana Post,* March 6, 1945, pp. 1–2.

33. *Ibid.,* January 10, 1945, p. 6.

34. Spruille Braden to secretary of state, December 19, 1944, RG 59. Cf. Ramón Grau San Martín, "Mi herencia," *Bohemia,* 41 (February 20, 1949), pp. 62–63.

35. *Tiempo en Cuba,* 1 (January 6, 1946), p. 8.

36. Herminio Portell Vilá, "Cuento y recuento," *Bohemia,* 44 (March 23, 1952), p. 56.

37. Mario Kuchilán Sol, "Curti," *Bohemia,* 32 (January 29, 1950), p. 68.

38. "The Cuban Army," *Havana Post,* July 4, 1949, n.p.

39. Kuchilán Sol, "Curti," p. 69.

40. See "¡Hasta cuando presidente!" *Bohemia,* 41 (September 25, 1949), p. 72.

41. On February 23, 1952, the eve of Batista's coup, the Havana daily *El Mundo* in an editorial cartoon depicted a newsboy selling an extra edition of the newspaper with the caption: "¡Extra! ¡Un cuarto de hora sin atentados! ¡Extra!" ("Extra! A quarter hour without assaults! Extra!"). For an excellent description of these groups, see Thomas, *Cuba: The Pursuit of Freedom,* pp. 741–43.

42. *Havana Post,* September 25, 1949, p. 1.

43. Manuel Romero Gómez, "Situación de Cuba," *Estudios Americanos* (Sevilla), 5 (May 1953), p. 564.

44. Luis Conte Agüero, *Eduardo Chibás, el adalid de Cuba* (Mexico, 1955).

45. *Tiempo en Cuba,* 2 (May 12, 1946), pp. 7–8.

46. *Ibid.*, 4 (December 5, 1948), p. 4.

47. *Hispanic World Report,* 2 (December 1948), p. 30.

48. Batista, *Respuesta,* pp. 448–49.

49. Javier Pazos, *Cambridge Opinion: Cuba* (Cambridge, England), 32 (February 1963), p. 19. Barrera Pérez, "Por que el ejército no derrotó a Castro," p. 78.

50. Pazos, *Cambridge Opinion: Cuba,* p. 18.

51. Edward Shils suggests that under conditions of disorders, such as prevailed in Auténtico Cuba, academy trained officers emerge as the "major representatives of modernity in technology and administration." "When the state flounders and civilian politicians make a mess of things," Shils concludes, "these officers feel that the standards given them by their training are affronted." Edward Shils, "The Military in the Political Development of New States," in John J. Johnson, ed., *The Role of the Military in Underdeveloped Countries* (Princeton, 1962), p. 23.

52. Barrera Pérez, "Por que el ejército no derrotó a Castro," p. 78.

53. *Ibid.,* (July 23, 1961), p. 9.

54. *Ibid.* (July 16, 1961), p. 78.

55. "If one recalls that the success of the coup is predicated on the formation of a decisive coalition to support it," Martin C. Needler suggests, "then it is clear that the last adherent or set of adherents to the movement provided the critical margin of support, not just in its size, but especially in its 'weight.' " Needler further indicates that the

> importance of this hypothetical 'swing man' in the situation, that is, may be due to any one of a series of factors—his personal influence within the armed forces; his prestige among the public; and/or his critical position in the command structure of the armed forces. It then becomes probable that because of his higher rank, greater prestige, and crucial importance for the coup, the 'swing man' is placed at the head of the provisional government that emerges after the revolt is successful—as provisional president, as chairman of the ruling military junta, or as minister of the armed forces behind the facade of a civilian provisional government. [Martin C. Needler, "Political Development and Military Intervention in Latin America," *The American Political Science Review,* 60 (September 1966), p. 621]

Chapter 11: The Restoration of Army Preeminence, 1952—1953

1. Francis L. Mc Carthy, "Historia de una revolucìon," *Bohemia*, 39 (March 30, 1952), p. 68.

2. "10 de marzo de 1952: una fecha negra en la historia," *Bohemia,* 51 (March 8, 1959), p. 69.

3. Luis G. Wanguemart, "Cómo cae un gobierno," *Carteles,* 33 (March 16, 1952), p. 41.

4. "10 de marzo de 1952: una fecha negra en la historia," p. 71.

5. Espinet Borges, "La radio tomada militarmente," *Carteles,* 33 (March 16, 1952), p. 66.

6. Javier Barahona, "El 10 de marzo en La Habana," *Carteles,* 33 (March 16, 1952), p. 52.

7. McCarthy, "Historia de una revolución," p. 68.

8. Wanguemart, "Cómo cae un gobierno," p. 41.

9. *El Mundo,* March 11, 1952, p. 16.

10. *Ibid.*, p. 5.

11. "10 de marzo de 1952: una fecha negra en la historia," p. 72.

12. *El Mundo,* March 11, 1952, p. 16.

13. *Ibid.*, p. 1.

14. Addressing himself generally to military seizures of power, David Rapoport suggests that the impulse to "support or resist any particular act on grounds of abstract principle will be minimized; most soldiers will want to retain their jobs which means that they will not commit themselves until it is safe to do so or dangerous not to." David C. Rapoport, "The Political Dimensions of Military Usurpation," *Political Science Quarterly,* 83 (December 1968), p. 563.

15. *El Mundo,* March 11, 1952, p. 16.

16. *Ibid.*, pp. 1, 16.

17. *Ibid.*, p. 4.

18. Enrique Serpa, "Los últimos instantes de Carlos Prío en el Palacio Presidencial," *Bohemia,* 44 (March 16, 1952), p. 82. Cf. Vicente León, "Lo que pasó realmente en Palacio el 10 de marzo," *Bohemia,* 48 (August 12, 1956), p. 59.

19. *El Mundo,* March 12, 1952, p. 8.

20. *Ibid.*, March 11, 1952, p. 1. William S. Stokes, "National and Local Violence in Cuba Politics," *The Southwestern Social Science Quarterly,* 34 (September 1953), p. 57.

21. "Ante el hecho consumado," *Bohemia,* 44 (March 16, 1952), p. 51.

22. Jorge Mañach, "El drama de Cuba," *Cuadernos,* 30 (May–June 1958), p. 65.

23. Carlos M. Lechuga, "Destilación de valores," *El Mundo,* March 13, 1952, p. 7.

24. Rafael Estenger, "La doble cara del golpe de estado," *Bohemia,* 44 (March 16, 1952), p. 49.

25. José Antonio Portuondo, "Cuba nación 'para si,'" *Cuadernos Americanos,* 119 (November–December 1961), p. 158.

26. *El Mundo,* March 11, 1952, p. 5.

27. Mario Lazo, *Dagger in the Heart: American Policy Failures in Cuba* (New York, 1968), p. 54. Cf. Wyatt MacGaffey and Clifford Barnett, *Twentieth Century Cuba* (Garden City, 1965), p. 158.

28. *El Mundo,* March 15, 1952, p. 1.

29. *Ibid.*, March 9, 1952, pp. 1, 8.

30. *Ibid.*

31. *Ibid.*, March 15, 1952, p. 8.

32. "Nacionalistas: un ingreso polémico," *Bohemia,* 48 (July 29, 1956), p. 70.

33. Pedro Barrera Pérez, "Por que el ejército no derrotó a Castro," (July 15, 1961), p. 78.

34. "Golpe de estado," *Bohemia,* XLV (16 de marzo de 1956), p. 64.

35. *El Mundo,* March 12, 1952, p. 10.

36. Antonio Ortega, "Todos seremos iguales ante la ley porque todos somos cubanos," *Bohemia,* 45 (March 23, 1952), p. 64.

37. *El Mundo,* June 6, 1952, p. 1.

38. *Ibid.*, November 7, 1952, p. A-1.

39. *Ibid.*, April 19, 1953, p. A-9.

40. Juan Amador Rodriguez, "Si el pueblo derrota a Batista aceteremos a su decisión," *Bohemia,* (April 27, 1952), p. 58.

41. Junior officers participating in the coup secured the greatest rewards: Captains Jorge García Tuñon and Juan Rojas González were raised to general; Captains Dámaso Sogo y Hernández, Alberto del Río Chaviano, Víctor Dueñas, and Leopoldo Coujil were promoted to colonel. Lieutenant Pedro Barrera Pérez secured the rank of

lieutenant colonel, while retired Captain José E. Rodríguez Calderón was promoted to rear admiral. See "Jefes de regimientos de las provincias," *Bohemia*, 34 (April 20, 1952), pp. 48–49. "La nueva oficialidad del Ejército," *Bohemia*, 34 (March 30, 1952), pp. 56–59, 69. Gonzalo Zorrilla, "Los nuevos jefes de la Marina," *Carteles*, 32 (April 13, 1952), pp. 42–44.

42. *El Mundo,* March 23, 1952, p. 10.

43. "Ley-Decreto Núm. 2 de 31 de marzo de 1952," *Gaceta Oficial de la Rep*ública, March 31, 1952. *El Mundo,* April 1, 1952, pp. 1, 8.

44. *El Mundo,* August 19, 1953, p. A-8.

45. *Diario de la Marina,* May 16, 1952, p. 32.

46. *Ibid.,* p. 26.

47. *El Mundo,* May 23, 1952, p. 8.

48. *Ibid.,* February 20, 1954, p. A-7.

49. *Ibid.,* October 30, 1954, p. A-11.

50. *Ibid.,* April 23, 1952, p. 5.

51. *Ibid.,* October 17, 1952, pp. A-1, A-8.

52. *Ibid.*

53. *Ibid.,* December 18, 1952, p. A-1.

54. Carlos M. Lechuga, "Tema prohibido," *El Mundo,* January 17, 1959, p. A-6.

55. See *El Mundo,* September 26, 1953, p. A-8.

56. *Ibid.,* March 17, 1956, p. A-10.

Chapter 12: Patterns of Resistance: The Armed Forces and Opposition, 1953–1958

1. *El Mundo,* August 2, 1952, p. A-1.

2. Aureliano Sánchez Arango, "Carta a la juventud," April 1954, in Organización Nacional de Bibliotecas Ambulantes y Populares, *13 documentos de la insurrecció*n (Havana, 1959), pp. 23–24.

3. *El Mundo,* November 7, 1953, p. A-1. Cf. Alberto Baeza Flores, *La cadenas vienen de lejos* (México, 1960), p. 31.

4. *El Mundo,* December 21, 1952, pp. A-1, A-10.

5. "El Movimiento Nacionalista Revolucionario (MNR): historia, doctrina, estrategia principios . . . abril de 1953," in Organización Nacional de Bibliotecas Ambulantes y Populares, *13 documentos de la insurrección,* pp. 9–10.

6. Mario Llerena, "Memoir" (4 vols., manuscript, Hoover Institution on Revolution and Peace, Stanford, California, 1966), I, p. 2. Cf. Martín Duarte y Enrique Vignier, "Moncada: método y ejemplo," *Teoría y Práctica* (Havana), 38 (July 1967), p. 78.

7. It is difficult to determine, in fact, if there was army complicity in the Moncada attack. After the abortive assault, government officials, in a manner soon to be characteristic of other antigovernment conspiracies in which the military participated, went to great lengths to assure the nation that the armed forces remained completely loyal to Havana. More interesting, Raúl Castro was reported to have suggested that the attackers expected the support of troops in Moncada who were disgusted with the administration. Curiously, a year later, in August 1954, a general amnesty specifically excluded "members of the armed forces" who participated in the Moncada assault. See *El Mundo,* July 31, 1953, p. 1–8, and August 11, 1954, p. A-4.

8. Marta Rojas R. "La cause 37," *Bohemia,* 51 (February 15, 1959), p. 114. Marta Rojas R., "El asalto al Moncada," *Bohemia,* 51 (1959), pp. 28–30, 166–67.

9. Raúl Castro, "VIII aniversario del 26 de julio," *Verde Olivo,* 2 (July 16, 1961), p. 4. Rojas R., "La causa 37," p. 114. Rafael Otero Echeverría, *Reportaje a una revolución. De Batista a Fidel Castro* (2nd ed., Santiago de Chile, 1959), p. 34.

10. Rubén Castillo Ramos, "En el cuartel de Bayamo se escribió otra página heroica," *Bohemia,* 53 (July 23, 1961), pp. 62–63. Marta Rojas, *La generación de centenario en el Moncada* (Havana, 1964), p. 9.

11. Vicente Cubillas, "Un 30 de noviembre en Santiago de Cuba," *Bohemia,* 52 (November 27, 1960), p. 46. Gabriel A. Gómez, *De la dictadura a la liberación (interpretación política y social de la revolución)* (Havana, 1959), p. 145.

12. *El Mundo,* November 22, 1964, pp. 1, 8.

13. Eduardo Yasells, "Bajo la consigna de 'libertad o muerte,'" *Verde Olivo,* 3 (December 16, 1962), pp. 40–41.

14. Pazos. *Cambridge Opinion; Cuba,* p. 21.

15. *El Mundo,* December 4, 1956, pp. A-1, A-8.

16. Barrera Pérez, "Por que el ejército no derrotó a Castro" (August 27, 1961), p. 24. Cf. Batista, *Respuesta,* pp. 47–48.

17. Ernesto "Che" Guevara, "Pasajes de la guerra revolucionaria," in Ernesto "Che" Guevara, *Obra Revolucionaria,* ed. Roberto Fernández Retamar (2nd ed., México, 1968), pp. 114–16.

18. Fidel Castro, "El 26 de Julio: fruto de la inagotable confianza en las fuerzas revolucionarias del pueblo," *Cuba Socialista,* 15 (August 1966), p. 7. See speech of Raúl Castro, *Obra Revolucionaria,* 23 (September 20, 1963), pp. 8–9.

19. *El Mundo,* December 14, 1956, p. A-1.

20. *Ibid.,* December 18, 1956, p. A-7.

21. Batista, *Respuesta,* p. 48.

22. Barrera Pérez, "Por que el ejército no derrotó a Castro," (Auguat 13, 1961), p. 25.

23. "El panorma: entre sombras," *Bohemia,* 49 (March 31, 1957), p. 78.

24. Rodolfo Rodríguez Zaldívar, "Sin despejar la incógnita de Fidel Castro," *Bohemia,* 49 (April 21, 1957), p. 68.

25. *El Mundo,* March 6, 1957, p. A-1.

26. *Ibid.,* March 1, 1957, p. A-11.

27. *Ibid.,* April 13, 1957, p. A-4.

28. *Times of Havana,* April 18, 1957, p. 1.

29. "Sierra Maestra: la guerra total," *Bohemia,* 49 (June 9, 1957), p. 83. *La Prensa* (New York), June 11, 1957, pp. 1–2.

30. "Oriente: el destino inmediato," *Bohemia,* 49 (June 30, 1957), p. 79. *La Prensa* (New York), June 18, 1957), p. 5.

31. *El Mundo,* June 1, 1957, p. A-1.

32. "Oriente: frente de batalla," *Bohemia,* 49 (June 16, 1957), p. 81.

33. *El Mundo,* June 1, 1957, p. A-7.

34. "Sierra Maestra: la guerra total," p. 83.

35. *La Prensa* (New York), July 11, 1957, p. 1.

36. *Times of Havana,* June 3, 1957, p. 1.

37. *El Mundo,* July 10, 1957, pp. A-1, A-10.

38. *Ibid.,* November 22, 1957, p. A-1.

39. Foreign Broadcast Information Service, *Daily Reports,* December 13, 1957, p. G-2.

40. Castro later recalled the peasants' "great terror of the army." See *Obra Revolucionaria,* 46 (December 11, 1961), p. 18. One farmer later related: "Everytime the

Rural Guards used to come by, it meant a neighbor was going to lose a pig or some vegetables. I remember I had a bunch of bananas saved up for Christmas once, and a soldier came by on a little horse, and there went my bananas! I had to give them to him, or he'd have struck me with his whip." In Tubal Pérez, "Why the Attack on Moncada? Nieves Cordero Tells His Story and That of 'The Cape,' " *Granma*, February 11, 1973, p. 9.

41. Guevara, "Pasajes de la guerra revolucionaria," p. 169.

42. *El Mundo*, September 15, 1957, p. A-8.

43. *Ibid.*, June 7, 1957, p. A-8.

44. Rafael Guas Inclán, "Todos erramos," *Cuba Libre* (Miami), 2 (October 28, 1960), p. 1.

45. In Harold Robert Aaron, "The Seizure of Political Power in Cuba, 1956–1959" (Ph.D. diss., Georgetown University, 1964), pp. 118–19. Cf. Harold R. Aaron, "Why Batista Lost," *Army*, 15 (September 1965), p. 66. The willingness of the field command to capture the guerrilla band, further, may have been less than enthusiastic. One observer accused the field officers of prolonging the campaign unnecessarily so as to continue receiving combat pay. Baeza Flores, *Las cadenas vienen de lejos*, p. 362.

46. Roland C. Brunet, "Así se cobró la dictadura la muerte de Fermí Cowley," *Bohemia*, 51 (February 1, 1959), pp. 84–85, 105–06.

47. Arnaldo Ramos Lechuga, "La verdad sobre el ataque al Giocuría," *Bohemia*, 51 (May 3, 1959), pp. 62–64.

48. Faure Chomón, "El ataque al Palacio Presidencial el 13 el marzo de 1957," *Bohemia*, 51 (March 15, 1959), pp. 80–82, 106; and (March 22, 1959), pp. 72–74, 96. Julio García Olivares, "La operación Radio Reloj," *Bohemia*, 51 (March 15, 1959), pp. 10–12, 152–53.

49. Regino Martín, "La causa de la libertad merece todos los sacrificios," *Bohemia*, 51 (February 1, 1959), pp. 142, 401. Max Lesnik Menéndez, "10 de noviembre: Escambray heroico," *Bohemia*, 51 (November 22, 1959), pp. 46–47, 99–100. Eloy Gutiérrez Menoyo, "El II Frente Nacional del Escambray," *Combate* (San José, Costa Rica), 2 (July–August, 1959), pp. 48–50.

50. *Sierra Maestra* (Miami), 1 (June 1958), p. 3.

51. Vicente Cubillas, Jr. "Los sucesos del 9 de abril en La Habana," *Revolución*, April 9, 1959, pp. 16–17. Cf. Rolando E. Bonachea and Nelson P. Valdés, eds., *Revolutionary Struggle, 1947–1958* (Cambridge, 1972), pp. 106–08.

52. See Carlos Manuel Rubiera, "Traían en las sayas desde Miami armas y balas las muchachas de resistencia cívica," *Bohemia*, 51 (February 15, 1959), p. 23.

53. "El 9 de abril de 1958," *Bohemia*, 51 (April 19, 1959), p. 112.

54. *Obra Revolucionaria*, 36 (December 2, 1960), p. 15.

55. Barrera Pérez, "Por que el ejército no derrotó a Castro," (July 23, 1961), p. 11.

56. "Nacionalistas: un ingreso polémico," p. 70.

57. To arrest sagging morale within the service academies, the army command reduced the program leading to a commission by one year. See Rodolfo Villamil, "Por que me uní a las fuerzas de Fidel Castro," *Bohemia*, 51 (March 8, 1959), pp. 40–41.

58. *El Mundo*, March 11, 1952, p. 5.

59. Barrera Pérez, "Por que el ejército no derrotó a Castro," (July 30, 19610, pp. 20–21.

60. "La conspiración del 3 de abril," *Bohemia*, 48 (April 15, 1956), p. 68.

61. *El Mundo*, April 10, 1956, p. A-10. *Hispanic American Report*, 9 (May 1956), pp. 172–73.

62. Batista, *Respuesta*, p. 41.

63. *El Mundo,* April 10, 1956, p. A-13.

64. *Ibid.,* April 20, 1956, p. A-10.

65. *Ibid.,* April 7, 1956, p. A-10. "La conspiración del 3 de abril," p. 70.

66. For an account of the changes in command see Barrera Pérez, "Por que el ejército no derrotó a Castro," (August 6, 1961), p. 80.

67. "La sublevación de Cienfuegos," *Bohemia,* 50 (February 2, 1958), p. 74. Cf. Julio Camacho, "El alzamiento de Cienfuegos," *Revolución.* September 5–10, 1962, p. 10. Robert Taber, *M-56: Biography of a Revolution* (New York, 1961), p. 175.

68. Vicente Cubillas, Jr. "Cienfuegos: la gesta heroica del 5 de septiembre de 1957," *Bohemia,* 51 (September 13, 1959), pp. 127–29. "La sublevacioón de Cienfuegos," p. 74.

69. Cubillas, "Cienfuegos: la gesta heroica del 5 de septiembre de 1957," *Bohemia,* 51 (September 20, 1959), p. 127.

70. Phillips, *Cuba: Island of Paradox,* pp. 328–29. Taber, *M-26: Biography of a Revolution,* p. 172. Cubillas, "Cienfuegos: la gesta heroica del 5 de septiembre de 1957," (September 13, 1959), p. 127.

71. Eduardo Yasells, "Habla un condenado a muerte por los hechos de Cienfuegos," *Verde Olivo,* 4 (September 8, 1963), p. 9.

72. "La sublevación de Cienfuegos," pp. 96–97.

73. *Ibid.,* p. 97.

74. Fernando González Lines, "Yo presencié el consejo de guerra sumarismo de mi hermano," *Bohemia,* 50 (March 16, 1958), pp. 70–71. "La sublevación de Cienfuegos," p. 97.

75. *New York Times,* September 15, 1957, sec. 4, p. 11.

76. Earl E. T. Smith, *The Fourth Floor* (New York, 1962), p. 31.

Chapter 13: The Final Confrontation: The Eclipse of the *Marcista* Order, 1958–1959

1. Smith, *The Fourth Floor,* p. 128.

2. Fidel Castro to Mario Llerena and Raúl Chibás, April 26, 1958, in Llerena, "Memoir," IV, Document no. 29.

3. Luis Conte Agüero, *Los dos rostros de Fidel Castro* (México, 1960), pp. 194–95.

4. Batista, *Respuesta,* p. 84.

5. *La Prensa* (New York), December 14, 1958, p. 3.

6. Ramón Calero, "Yo fuí un 'bocadito,' " *Bohemia,* 51 (March 15, 1959), p. 45.

7. During the offensive, rebel planes distributed to soldiers in the field photographs of the army command in houses of prostitution and wining and dining in fashionable Havana nightclubs. See Marta Rojas R., "El Segundo Frente Oriental 'Frank País': El reencuentro de los hermanos héroes," *Bohemia,* 51 (August 16, 1959), p. 104.

8. In Pedro Araneda Figueroa, "Con Fidel Castro en Sierra Maestra," *Revista de América,* 619 (November 2, 1957), pp. 34–35.

9. *Sierra Maestra* (Miami), 1 (June 1958), p. 4.

10. Fidel Castro, "Report on the Tyranny's Last Offensive," Radio Rebelde broadcast, August 19, 1958, in "Fidel Over Radio Rebelde," *Granma* (special supplement), March 18, 1973, p. 18.

11. In José Pardo Llada, *Memorias de la Sierra Maestra* (Havana, 1960), p. 43.

12. Fidel Castro, "Manifiesto político-social desde la Sierra Maestra," in Castro, *La revolución cubana,* ed. Gregorio Selser (Buenos Aires, 1960), p. 122.

13. There were, to be sure, some practical reasons for the prompt release of prisoners. In explaining the Twenty-Sixth of July policy, Castro indicated that to have kept prisoners, in the first place, would have placed an intolerable strain on insurgent

supplies. In addition, the rebel leader explained, the "dictator's men or arms are not important to us;" ultimately, victory depended "not so much on arms as it does on morale. Once we capture the heart of the soldier, he will find it hard to fight those who treated him so well. To kill a soldier or to imprison him would only serve to make defeated units resist. A free prisoner is the perfect answer to the tyranny's propaganda." In Jules Dubois, *Fidel Castro: Rebel-Liberator or Dictator?* (Indianapolis, 1959), pp. 295–96. Castro, "Report on the Tyranny's Last Offensive," pp. 16–17.

14. Pardo Llada, *Memorias de la Sierra Maestra*, p. 83.

15. Ricardo Adan y Silva, "El desplome militar del batistato," *Bohemia*, 51 (July 12, 1959), pp. 38, 115.

16. Calero, "Yo fuí un 'bocadito,' " p. 121.

17. General Silito Tabernilla to Fulgencio Batista, February 13, 1959, in Batista, *Respuesta*, p. 112.

18. Camilo Cienfuegos, "Informe de la invasión," October 9, 1958, *Verde Olivo*, 2 (October 29, 1961), p. 5.

19. Batista, *Respuesta*, pp. 36–37.

20. Villamil, "Por que me uní a las fuerzas de Fidel Castro," pp. 40–41, 114.

21. *New York Times*, April 4, 1958, pp. 2, 4 and April 7, 1958, p. 9.

22. *Revolución*, February 27, 1959, p. 14. "Aviadores: alas de la muerte," *Bohemia*, 51 (January 18–25, 1959), pp. 112–14.

23. Baeza Flores, *Las cadenas vienen de lejos*, p. 366.

24. Aaron, "The Seizure of Political Power in Cuba, 1956–1959," p. 176.

25. United States Congress, Senate, *Hearings Before the Subcommittee to Investigate the Administration of the Internal Security Laws of the Committee on the Judiciary: Communist Threat to the United States Through the Caribbean*, 86th Cong. 2d sess. (16 parts, Washington, 1959–1960), pt. 9, p. 666 (hereafter cited as *Hearings*).

26. In Aaron, "The Seizure of Political Power in Cuba, 1956–1959," p. 176.

27. *New York Times*, January 2, 1959, p. 7.

28. Enrique Meneses, "Mis diálogos con Fidel Castro, los hombres de Sierra Maestra: Camilo Cienfuegos, Raúl Castro, 'Che' Guevara," *Blanco y Negro* (Madrid), (March 17, 1962), n.p. Enrique Meneses, *Fidel Castro, siete aõs de poder* (Madrid, 1956), p. 54.

29. Ray Brennan, *Castro, Cuba and Justice* (Garden City, 1959), p. 229. Cf. Meneses, "Mis diálogos con Fidel Castro . . . ," n.p.

30. *El Mundo*, September 13, 1958, p. A-1.

31. *La Prensa* (New York), December 29, 1958, p. 2. A *New York Times* dispatch reported that "many soldiers are trigger-happy teenagers with a taste for brutality" (July 21, 1958, p. 14).

32. *La Prensa* (New York), December 1, 1957, p. 25.

33. Aaron, "The Seizure of Political Power in Cuba, 1956–1959," p. 176.

34. Barrera Pérez, "Por que el ejército no derrotó a Castro" (August 7, 19610, p. 71.

35. Pardo Llada, *Memorias de la Sierra Maestra*, p. 62.

36. Otero Echeverría, *Reportaje a una revolución. De Batista a Fidel Castro*, p. 187.

37. *New York Times*, January 2, 1959, p. 1. Batista, *Respuesta*, pp. 167–68.

38. Antonio Núñez Jiménez, *Geografía de Cuba* (2d ed., Havana, 1959), pp. 75–76. Lowry Nelson, *Rural Cuba* (Minneapolis, 1950), p. 53.

39. *La Prensa* (New York), June 7, 1958, p. 1.

40. *Ibid.*, June 9, 1958, p. 1. Ray Brennan gives a graphic description of the army's situation:

> And then came the rainy season. The rain pelted straight down from the sky for hours. The trees and other foliage dripped water night and day. The Batista soldiers learned the discomforts of sleeping in wet clothing on wet ground. The

nights were chilly in the mountains, after blazing hot days. Mud on the trails became ankle-deep or more, and so gummy that it could pull off a man's boots. Horses and mules balked at carrying burdens through the quagmire, and no amount of flogging by the cursing soldiers would make them budge. [Brennan, *Castro, Cuba and Justice*, pp. 235–36]

41. Florentino E. Rosell y Leyva, *La verdad* (Miami, 1960), pp. 15–21.

42. An estimated twelve thousand troops, including select members of aviation, artillery, and tank units were in Camp Columbia when Camilo Cienfuegos assumed command in January 1959. Abelardo Iglesias, *Revolución y dictadura en Cuba* (Buenos Aires, 1963), p. 23.

43. *New York Times,* February 24, 1957, p. 1.

44. *Ibid.,* February 3, 1958, p. 1.

45. Pedro Araneda Figueroa, "Llegó la hora 'o' para Batista," *Revista de América*, 622 (November 23, 1957), p. 18.

46. *Sierra Maestra* (New York), 1 (March 1958), p. 7.

47. From the standpoint of the Cuban experience, Régis Debray wrote that the government—because it is the government—must "protect everywhere the interests of property owners; the guerrilleros don't have to protect anything anywhere. They have no dead weight. Therefore the relation of forces cannot be measured in arithmetical terms. In Cuba, for example, Batista could never utilize more than 10,000 out of his 50,000 men against the guerrillas at any one time." Debray, *Revolution in the Revolution?* trans. Bobbye Ortiz (New York, 1967), pp. 75–76.

48. Smith, *The Fourth Floor,* p. 82.

49. *El Mundo,* April 13, 1957, p. A-4.

50. *Ibid.,* July 10, 1957, p. A-8.

51. *La Prensa* (New York), April 13, 1958, pp. 1, 2.

52. Francisco Tabernilla Dolz al General Batista, "Carta abierta," *Cuba Libre* (Miami), (September 30, 1960), p. 2. Cf. José Suárez Núñez, *El gran culpable* (Caracas, 1963), p. 96.

53. Marta Rojas R. "El Segundo Frente Oriental 'Frank País:' Ante de la retención de los americanos," *Bohemia,* 51 (June 28, 1959), p. 50.

54. Smith, *The Fourth Floor,* p. 145.

55. Marta Rojas R., "El Segundo Frente Oriental 'Frank País:' operación antiaérea," *Bohemia,* 51 (July 5, 1959), p. 101. Juan Carlos Santos, "Al marcha la II Frente 'Frank País:' operación antiaérea,"*El Mundo,* September 16, 1966, p. 5. Raúl Castro, "Operación antiaérea," *Verde Olivo,* 4 (September 22, 1963), pp. 32–38.

56. Batista no doubt shared Machado's dilemma when the latter complained to the American ambassador in 1931 that he could have ended "the unrest, but that he did not wish to vex the United States, the inference being that the killing of the opposition leaders would have been his natural inclination except for fear of the American reaction." Harry F. Guggenheim, "Memorandum of Conference with President Machado," December 4, 1931, 837.00 Revolutions/89, RG 59.

57. "Batista selected Núñez Portuondo because he was well regarded in the United States and at the United Nations." Smith, *The Fourth Floor,* p. 75.

58. Adolfo G. Merino, *Nacimiento de un estado vasallo* (México, 1966), pp. 84–85.

59. Smith, *The Fourth Floor,* pp. 116–18.

60. Brennan, *Castro, Cuba and Justice,* p. 66.

61. Smith, *The Fourth Floor,* pp. 48, 107.

62. Batista, *Respuesta,* p. 37.

63. Ernesto Che Guevara, "La guerra de guerrillas," in Guevara, *Obra Revolucionaria,* p. 27. See speech of Fidel Castro in *Obra Revolucionaria,* 36 (December 2, 1961), p. 15.

64. *New York Times,* May 20, 1957, p. 8.

65. *Revolución,* February 25, 1959, p. 14. Fidel Castro, "Ante los campesinos," February 24, 1959, in Castro, *La revolución cubana,* p. 275. Lee Lockwood, *Castro's Cuba, Cuba's Fidel* (New York, 1969), p. 168. Between the failure of the spring offensive and the flight of Batista, the Rebel Army increased to an estimated three thousand men.

66. José Rego Rubido, "No es cierto que haya habido rendición en Oriente," *Bohemia Libre,,* 53 (October 8, 1961), p. 29.

67. Rosell Leyva, *La verdad,* p. 23.

68. General Silito Tabernilla to Fulgencio Batista, February 13, 1959, in Batista, *Respuesta,* p. 11.

69. Rosell Leyva, *La verdad,* p. 26. Cf. William Gálvez, "Diario de la columna invasora 'Antonio Maceo,' " *Verde Olivo,* 4 (November 3, 1963), pp. 5–8.

70. Claude Julien, *La revolución cubana,* trans. Mario Trajtenberg (Montevideo, 1961), p. 93.

71. Fidel Castro, *Palabras para la historia* (Havana, 1960), p. 18.

72. *Hearings,* pt. 7, p. 421.

73. Batista, *Respuesta,* p. 75.

74. *New York Times,* September 15, 1957, sec. 4, p. 11.

75. Smith, *The Fourth Floor,* pp. 155–56.

76. *Excelsior* (México), November 7, 1958, p. 26. Gerardo Rodríguez Morejór, *Fidel Castro, biografía* (Havana, 1959), p. 192.

77. General Silito Tabernilla to Fulgencio Batista, February 13, 1959, in Batista, *Respuesta,* p. 112.

78. Smith, *The Fourth Floor,* p. 158. Cf. Paul D. Bethel, *The Losers* (New Rochelle, 1969), pp. 63–64.

79. *Hearings,* pt. 9, p. 687.

80. Batista, *Respuesta,* p. 83.

81. *Hearings,* pt. 9, pp. 696–97.

82. *Ibid.,* pt. 10, p. 739. The Pawley mission is further discussed in Lyman B. Kirkpatrick, Jr., *The Real CIA* (New York, 1968), pp. 178–79, and Dwight D. Eisenhower, *Waging Peace, 1956–1961* (Garden City, 1965), p. 521.

83. *Hearings,* pt. 10, p. 739.

84. *Ibid.,* pt. 9, p. 687.

85. *La Prensa* (New York), December 30, 1958, p. 1.

86. Smith, *The Fourth Floor,* p. 177. *Hearings,* pt. 9, pp. 709–10.

87. Rosell Leyva, *La verdad,* pp. 32–37. Cf. Carl John Regan, "The Armed Forces of Cuba: 1933–1959" (master's thesis, University of Florida, 1970), pp. 144.

88. Fidel Castro, "Pronunciamientos del Comandante en Jefe del moviemiento revolucionario 26 de Julio, en el mitín celebrado el 2 de enero, en el Parque Céspedes, de Santiago de Cuba, que fué declarada capital provisional de la República, y proclamado presidente de la República el Dr. Manuel Urrutia Lleó," in Fidel Castro, *Discursos del Dr. Fidel Castro Ruz, Comandante en Jefe del Ejército Rebelde 26 de Julio y Primer Ministro del Gobierno Provisional,* comp. Emilio Roig de Leuchsenring (Havana, 1959), pp. 77–79.

89. Fidel Castro, "Instrucciones de la Comandancia General a todos los comandantes del Ejército Rebelde y al pueblo," in Castro, *Discursos del Dr. Fidel Castro Ruz . . . ,* p. 73.

90. Smith, *The Fourth Floor,* p. 200.

91. Angel Valeri Busto, "Actuación en Columbia de los oficiales presos en Isla de Pinos en la gloriosa alborada del primero de enero," *Bohemia,* 51 (January 18–25, 1959), p. 108.

92. *Revolución,* January 2, 1959, pp. 1, 4. Cf. Andrés Suárez, "The Cuban Revolution: The Road to Power," *The Latin American Research Review,* 7 (Fall 1972), p. 22.

93. Cuba, Gobierno Provisional, *Proclamas y leyes del Gobierno Provisional de la Revolución* (25 vols., Havana, 1959–1960), I, pp. 42–43.

Chapter 14: The Cuban Army, 1898–1958: In Retrospect

1. Carlos Loviera, *Generales y doctores,* ed. Shasta M. Bryant and J. Riis Owre (New York, 1965), pp. 239–40.

2. Gino Germani and Kalman Silvert, "Politics, Social Structure and Military Intervention in Latin America," *Archives Européenes de Sociologie,* 2 (1961), p. 62.

3. John Steward Ambler, *The French Army in Politics, 1945–1962* (Columbus, 1966), pp. 365–66.

4. See Jorge Mañach, *El militarismo en Cuba* (Havana, 1939), p. 7.

5. MacGaffey and Barnett, *Twentieth Century Cuba,* pp. 128–29.

6. José Barbeito, *Realidad y masificación* (Caracas, 1964), pp. 118–23.

Bibliography

Unpublished Material

Archival Sources

National Archives of the United States. General Records of the Department of the Navy. Record Group 80.
_____. General Records of the Department of State. Record Group 59.
_____. Naval Records Collection of the Office of Naval Records and Library. Record Group 45.
_____. Records of the Adjutant General's Office. Record Group 94.
_____. Records of the Adjutant General's Office, 1917—. Record Group 407.
_____. Records of the Bureau of Insular Affairs. Record Group 350.
_____. Records of the Foreign Service Posts of the Department of State. Record Group 84.
_____. Records of the Military Government of Cuba. Record Group 140.
_____. Records of the Office of Naval Operations. Record Group 38.
_____. Records of the Provisional Government of Cuba. Record Group 199.
_____. Records of the United States Marine Corps. Record Group 127.
_____. Records of the War Department General and Special Staffs. Record Group 165.

Manuscript Collections

Enoch Crowder Papers. Western Historical Manuscript Collection. University of Missouri. Columbia, Missouri.
William Fullam Papers. Library of Congress. Manuscript Division. Washington, D.C.
Cordell Hull Papers. Library of Congress. Manuscript Division. Washington, D.C.
William McKinley Papers. Library of Congress. Manuscript Division. Washington, D.C.
Franklin D. Roosevelt Papers. Franklin D. Roosevelt Library. Hyde Park, New York.
Theodore Roosevelt Papers. Library of Congress. Manuscript Division. Washington, D.C.
William Howard Taft Papers. Library of Congress. Manuscript Division. Washington, D.C.

Charles W. Taussig Papers. Franklin D. Roosevelt Library. Hyde Park, New York.
Joseph Wheeler Papers. Alabama Department of Archives and History. Montgomery, Alabama.
Francis White Papers. General Records of the Department of State, Record Group 59. National Archives. Washington, D.C.
James Harrison Wilson Papers. Library of Congress. Manuscript Division. Washington, D.C.
Leonard Wood Papers. Library of Congress. Manuscript Division. Washington, D.C.

Theses and Manuscripts

Aaron, Harold Robert. "The Seizure of Political Power in Cuba, 1956–1959." Ph.D. dissertation, Georgetown University, 1964.
Bail, Hamilton V. "The Military Government of Cuba, 1898–1902." Manuscript, Hoover Institution on War and Peace, Stanford, California, 1943.
Llerena, Mario. "Memoir." 4 vols. Manuscript, Hoover Institution on War and Peace, 1966.
Meyer, Leo J. "Relations Between the United States and Cuba from 1895–1917." Ph.D. dissertation, Clark University, 1928.
Read, Gerald Howard. "Civic-Military Rural Education of Cuba: Eleven Eventful Years (1936–1946)," Ph.D. dissertation, Ohio State University, 1950.
Regan, Carl John. "The Armed Forces of Cuba, 1933–1959." Master's thesis, University of Florida, 1970.

Published Material

Public Documents

Archivo Nacional. *Boletín del Archivo Nacional*. 63 vols. Havana, 1901–1963.
Barry, Brigadier General Thomas H. *Annual Report . . . 1907–1908*. Marianao, Cuba, 1907–1908.
Camagüey. *Reglamento para el gobierno interior del Cuerpo de le Guardia Rural*. Camagüey, 1899.
Cuba. Comisión Consultiva. *Diario de Sesiones, 1907–1909*. 4 vols. Havana, 1907–1909.
Cuba. Congreso. Cámara de Representantes. *Mensajes presidenciales remitidos al congreso, transcurridos desde el veinte de mayo de mil novecientos dos, hasta el primero de abril de mil novecientos diez y siete*. Havana, n.d.
———. *Memoria de los trabajos realizados durante las cuatros legislaturas ordinarias . . . 1917–1923*. Havana, 1917–1923.
Cuba. Ejército Constitucional. Cuartel General. *Cultura Militar y Naval*. 1935–1943.
———. *Memoria contentiva de las obras, mejoras, leyes, órdenes y disposiciones que en algun sentido han beneficiado al ejército y sus miembros, desde el 4 de septiembre de 1936, asi como de la actuación cívico-militar desarrollada en el mismo periodo de tiempo*. Havana, 1936.
———. Estado Mayor. *Ejército. Organo Oficial de las Fuerzas Armadas*. 1958.
Cuba. Ejército. Cuartel General del Ejército Constitucional. *El Ejército Constitucional. Revista Oficial*. 1936–1945.
Cuba. Ejército Nacional. Estado Mayor. *Boletín del Ejército*. 1916–1933.
Cuba. Estado Mayor del Ejército. *Lista directorio y escalafones*. Havana, 1916.
Cuba. *Gaceta Oficial de la República de Cuba*. 1902–1959.
Cuba. Gobierno Provisional. *Proclamas y leyes del Gobierno Provisional de la Revolución*. 25 vols. Havana, 1959–1960.

Cuba. Guardia Rural. *Memoria explicativa de la fundación y reorganización del Cuerpo y de los trabajos realizados por el mismo durante el año fiscal 1904.* Havana, 1904.

———. *Memoria explicativa de los trabajos realizados . . . 1905–1912.* Havana, 1906–1913.

Cuba. Presidente. *Memoria de la administración del presidente de la República de Cuba Alfredo Zayas y Alfonso. . . .* 1921–1924. Havana, 1923–1925.

———. *Memoria de la administración del presidente de la República de Cuba Gerardo Machado y Morales. . . .* 1925–1931. Havana, 1927–1932.

———. *Memoria de la administración del presidente de la República Mario G. Menocal. . . .* 1913–1921. Havana, 1915–1923.

———. *Memoria de la administratión del presidente de la República de Cuba Mayor General José Miguel Gómez. . . .* 1909–1913. Havana, 1910–1913.

———. *Mensaje del presidente Alfredo Zayas y Alfonso al Congreso de la República de Cuba referente a los actos de la administración. . . .* 1921–1924. Havana, 1921–1924.

———. *Mensaje del presidente Gerardo Machado y Morales al Congreso de la República de Cuba referente a los actos de la administración. . . .* 1925–1931. Havana, 1925–1931.

Cuba. Provisional Government. *Project of Electoral Law Adopted by the Advisory Commission and Submitted to the Provisional Governor, December 30, 1907.* Havana, 1908.

Cuba. Secretaria de Defensa Nacional. Patronato Administrativo de las Escuelas Rurales-Cívico-Militares. *Memoria Annual.* 2 vols. Havana, 1938–1939.

Cuba. *Under the Provisional Government of the United States, Decrees, 1906–1909.* 9 vols. Havana, 1907–1909.

Lee, Brigadier General Fitzhugh. *Special Report of Brigadier General Fitzhugh Lee on the Industrial, Economic and Social Conditions Existing in the Province of Havana and Pinar del Rio.* Quemados, Cuba, 1899.

Llaverías, Joaquín, and Santovenia, Emeterio S., *Actas de las Asambleas de Representantes y del Consejo del Gobierno durante la Guerra de Independencia.* 5 vols. Havana, 1932.

Machado y Morales, Gerardo. *Declarations of General Gerardo Machado y Morales.* Havana, 1928.

Magoon, Charles E. *Report of the Provisional Administration. . . .* 1906–1908. Havana, 1908–1909.

———. *Supplemental Report, Provisional Governor of Cuba, For the Period December 1, 1908 to January 28, 1909.* United States Congress, Senate, 61st Cong. 1st sess., Document no. 80, ser. 5572, Washington, D.C., 1909.

Mueller y Tejeiro, José. *Battles and Capitulations of Santiago de Cuba.* Office of Naval Intelligence. War Notes No. 1, Information from Abroad. United States Congress, Senate, *Notes on the Spanish-American War.* 56th Cong. 1st sess., Document no. 388, ser. 3876, Washington, D.C., 1900.

Parker, Captain Frank. *Informe anual del instructor de la Guardia Rural sobre la instrucción militar durante el año académico que expiró en 30 de junio de 1912.* Havana, 1912.

Porter, R. *Report on the Commercial and Industrial Conditions of Cuba. Special Report on the Commissioner's Visit to General Gómez, and in Relation to the Payment and Disbandment of the Insurgent Army of Cuba.* Washington, D.C., 1899.

Taft, William Howard, and Bacon, Robert. "Cuban Pacification: Report of William H. Taft, Secretary of War, and Robert Bacon, Assistant Secretary of State, of What Was Done Under the Instructions of the President in Restoring Peace in Cuba." Department of War. *Report of the Secretary of War, 1906.* Appendix E. United States Congress, House, 59th Cong. 2d sess., Document no. 2, ser. 1505, Washington, D.C., 1906.

United States, Bureau of Insular Affairs, *The Establishment of Free Government in Cuba.* United States Congress, Senate, 58th Cong., 2d sess., Document no. 312, Washington, D.C. 1904.

United States, Congress. House. *Affairs in Cuba*. 54th Cong., 1st sess., Document no. 224, ser. 3425, Washington, D.C., 1896.

_____. Senate. *Hearings Before the Subcommittee to Investigate the Administration of the Internal Security Act and Other Internal Security Laws of the Committee on the Judiciary: Communist Threat to the United States Through the Caribbean*. 86th Cong., 2d sess., Washington, D.C., 1959–1960.

_____. Senate. *Report of the Commission Appointed by the President to Investigate the Conduct of the War with Spain*. 56th Cong., 1st sess., ser. 3859–3866, Washington, D.C., 1900.

_____. Senate. *Report of the Committee on Relations: Affairs in Cuba*. 55th Cong., 2d sess., Report no. 885, ser. 3654, Washington, D.C. 1898.

United States, Department of State. *Papers Relating to the Foreign Relations of the United States*. 1902–1944. Washington, D.C., 1902–1967.

United States, Department of War. *Annual Report of the War Department*. . . . 1898–1902. Washington, D.C.

_____. Office of the Chief of Staff. *Military Notes on Cuba, 1909*. Washington, D.C., 1909.

United States, Foreign Broadcast Information Service. *Daily Reports. Foreign Radio Broadcast*. 1954–1959.

Welles, Sumner. *Two Years of the "Good Neighbor" Policy*. Department of State, Latin American Series, no. 11, Washington, D.C., 1935.

_____. *Relations Between the United States and Cuba*. Department of State, Latin American Series, no. 7, Washington, D.C., 1934.

Wood, Leonard. *Civil Report of Brigadier General Leonard Wood, Military Governor of Cuba, January 1st to May 20th, 1902*. 6 vols., Washington, D.C., 1902.

Memoirs, Autobiographies, and Reminiscences

Atkins, Edwin F. *Sixty Years in Cuba*. Cambridge: Riverside Press, 1926.

Batista, Fulgencio. *Paradojas*. México: Ediciones Botas, 1963.

_____. *Respuesta*. . . . México: Imp. "Manuel León Sánchez," 1960.

Bayo, Alberto. *Mi aporte a la Revolución Cubana*. Havana: Imp. Ejército Rebelde, 1960.

Bethel, Paul D. *The Losers*. New Rochelle, N.Y.: Arlington House, 1969.

Cabrera, Raimundo. *Mis malos tiempos*. Havana: Imp. "El Siglo XX," 1920.

Consuegra, W. I. *Hechos y comentarios. La revolución de febrero de 1917 en Las Villas*. Havana: La Comercial, 1920.

Duque, Matías. *Ocios del presidio*. Havana: Imp. "Avisador Comercial," 1919.

Eisenhower, Dwight D. *Waging Peace, 1956–1961*. New York: Doubleday, 1965.

Ferrer, Horacio. *Con el rifle al hombro*. Havana: Imp. "El Siglo XX," 1950.

Foraker, Joseph Benson. *Notes of a Busy Life*. 3d ed. 2 vols. Cincinnati: Stewart & Kidd, 1917.

Funston, Frederick. *Memories of Two Wars: Cuban and Philippine Experiences*. New York: Scribner's, 1911.

Góngora Echenique, Manuel. *Lo que he visto en Cuba*. Madrid: Editorial Góngora, 1929.

Gonzales, N. G. *In Darkest Cuba*. Columbia, S.C.: The State Co., 1922.

Hull, Cordell. *The Memoirs of Cordell Hull*. 2 vols. New York: Macmillan, 1948.

Ickes, Harold L. *The Secret Diaries of Harold L. Ickes*. 3 vols. New York: Simon & Schuster, 1953–1954.

Kennan, George. *Campaigning in Cuba*. New York: Century Co., 1899.

Kirkpatrick, Lyman B. *The Real CIA*. New York: Macmillan, 1968.

Lamar Schweyer, Alberto. *Cómo cayó el presidente Machado*. Madrid: Espasa-Calpe, S.A., 1941.

Laurent, Emilio A. *De oficial a revolucionario*. Havana: Ucar, García y Cía, 1941.

Lazo, Mario. *Dagger in the Heart: American Policy Failures in Cuba*. New York, Funk & Wagnalls, 1968.

Lima, Alfredo. *La odisea de Río Verde*. Havana: Cultural, S.A., 1934.

López-Fresquet, Rufo. *My Fourteen Months with Castro*. Cleveland: World, 1966.

Miró Argenter, José. *Cuba: Crónicas de la guerra, las campañas de invasión y de occidente, 1895–1896*. 4th ed. 3 vols. Havana: Editorial Lex, 1945.

Pardo Llada, José. *Memorias de la Sierra Maestra*. Havana: Editorial Tierra Nueva, 1960.

Phillips, R. Hart. *Cuba: Island of Paradox*. New York: McDowell, Obolensky, 1959.

Porter, Robert P. *Industrial Cuba*. New York: G. P. Putnam, 1899.

Rosell Leyva, Florentino E. *La verdad*. Miami: n.p., 1960.

Smith, Earl E. T. *The Fourth Floor*. New York: Random House, 1962.

Solano Alvarez, Luis. *Mi actuación militar o apuntes para la historia de la revolución de febrero de 1917*. Havana: Imp. "El Siglo XX," 1920.

Torriente, Cosme de la. *Cuarenta años de mi vida, 1898–1938*. Havana: Imp. "El Siglo," 1939.

Ventura Novo, Esteben. *Memorias*. México: Imp. M. León Sanchez, 1961.

Welles, Sumner. *The Time for Decision*. New York: Harper & Bros., 1944.

Periodicals

Bohemia (Havana)
Bohemia Libre (Caracas/San Juan)
Bulletin of the Pan American Unión
Carteles (Havana)
The Cuba Review and Bulletin
Hispanic American Report
Magazine Político (Havana)
Obra Revolucionaria (Havana)
Tiempo en Cuba (Havana)
Verde Olivo (Havana)

Newspapers

Ahora (Havana)
Army and Navy Journal
El Avance (Miami)
La Calle (Havana)
La Crónica (Miami)
Cuba Libre (Miami)
Cuban Revolutionary Party (Auténtico) (Miami/Tampa)
Diario de la Marina (Havana)
Excelsior (México)
Granma (Havana)
Havana Post
El Liberal (New York)
La Lucha (Havana)
El Mundo (Havana)
New York Herald Tribune
New York Times
La Prensa (New York)

Revolución (Havana)
Sierra Maestra (New York/Miami)
Times of Havana

Books

ABC. *El ABC en la mediación.* Havana: Maza, Caso y Cía, 1934.

Acosta Rubio, Raoul. *Batista ante la historia (relato de un civilista).* Havana: Jesús Montero, 1938.

Adam y Silva, Ricardo. *La gran mentira. 4 de septiembre de 1933.* Havana: Editorial Lex, 1947.

_____. *Cuba: Raíces del desastre.* Jerez de la Frontera: Gráficas del Exportador, 1971.

Aguilar, Luis. *Cuba, 1933: Prologue to Revolution.* Ithaca, N.Y.: Cornell University Press, 1972.

_____. *Pasado y ambiente en el proceso cubano.* Havana: Ediciones Insula, 1957.

Alba, Víctor. *Historia del movimiento obrero en América Latina.* México: Libreros Mexicanos, 1964.

Alexander, Robert J. *Organized Labor in Latin America.* New York: Free Press, 1965.

Alloza, Fernando. *Noventa entrevistas políticas.* Havana: Imp. Cuba Intelectual, 1953.

Alvarez del Real, Evelio. *Patrias opacas y caudillos fulgurantes.* Havana: Imp. "La Verónica," 1942.

Alvarez Díaz, José et al. *Cuba: geopolítica y pensamiento económico.* Miami: Colegio de Economistas de Cuba en exilio, 1964.

_____. *Un estudio sobre Cuba.* Miami: University of Miami Press, 1963.

Amaral Agramonte, Raúl. *Al margen de la revolución.* Havana: Cultural, S.A., 1935.

Amaro, Nelson, and Mesa-Lago, Carmelo. "Inequality and Classes." In Carmelo Mesa-Lago, ed., *Revolutionary Change in Cuba,* pp. 341–74. Pittsburgh: University of Pittsburgh Press, 1971.

Ambler, John Steward. *The French Army in Politics, 1945–1962.* Columbus: Ohio State University Press, 1966.

Andreski, Stanislav. *Military Organization and Society.* 2d ed. Berkeley: University of California Press, 1968.

Arce, Luis A. de. *Emilio Núñez (1875–1922): historiografía.* Havana: Editorial "Niños," 1943.

Arredondo, Alberto. *Batista: un año de gobierno.* Havana: Editorial Ucacia, 1942.

_____. *Cuba: tierra indefensa.* Havana: Editorial Lex, 1945.

_____. *El negro en Cuba.* Havana: Editorial "Alfa," 1939.

Arvelo, Perina. *Revolución de los barbudos.* Caracas: Editorial Landi, 1961.

Azcuy y Cruz, Aracelio. *Cuba: campo de concentración.* México: Ediciones Humanismo, 1954.

Baeza Flores, Alberto. *Las cadenas vienen de lejos.* México: Ed. Letras, 1960.

Barbarrosa, Enrique. *El proceso de la república, análisis de la situación económica bajo el gobierno presidencial de Tomás Estrada Palma y José Miguel Gómez.* Havana: Imp. Militar, 1911.

Barbeito, José. *Realidad y masificación.* Caracas: Ediciones "Nuevo Orden," 1964.

Baroni, Aldo. *Cuba, país de poca memoria.* México: Ediciones Botas, 1944.

Batista, Fulgencio. *Alocución del 4 de septiembre de 1939.* Havana: Burgay y Cía, 1939.

_____. *Cuba. Su política interna y sus relaciones exteriores.* Havana: Prensa Indoamericana, 1939.

_____. *Ideario de Batista.* Edited by M. Franco Varona. Havana: Prensa Indoamericana, 1940.

_____. *Piedras y leyes.* México: Ediciones Botas, 1961.

_____. *Revolución social o política reformista (once aniversarios).* Havana: Prensa Indoamérica, 1944.

_____. *Sombras de América.* Mexico: Ediapsa, 1946.

Beals, Carleton. *The Crime of Cuba.* Philadelphia: Lippincott, 1933.

Benítez, Fernando. *La batalla de Cuba.* México: 1960.

Bonachea, Rolando E., and Valdés, Nelson P., eds. *Revolutionary Struggle, 1947–1958.* Cambridge, Mass.: MIT Press, 1972.

Bosch, Juan. *Cuba, la isla fascinante.* Santiago de Chile: Editorial Universitaria, 1955.

Braña Chansuolme, Manuel. *El aparato.* Coral Gables: Service Offset Printers, 1964.

Brennan, Ray. *Castro, Cuba and Justice.* Garden City: Doubleday, 1959.

Brown, Charles H. *The Correspondents' War: Journalists in the Spanish-American War.* New York: Scribner's, 1967.

Buell, Raymond Leslie et al. *Problems of the New Cuba.* New York: Foreign Policy Association, 1935.

Buttari y Gaunaurd, J. *Boceto crítico histórico.* Havana: Editorial Lex, 1954.

Camacho, Pánfilo D. *Estrada Palma, el gobernante honrado.* Havana: Editorial Tropical, 1938.

Campoamor, Fernando G. *La tragedia de Cuba.* Havana: Editorial Hermes, 1934.

Canelas O., Amado. *Cuba, socialismo en español.* La Paz: Empresa Industrial Gráfica E. Burillo, 1964.

Carballal, Rodolfo Z. *Estudio sobre la administración del general José M. Gómez (1909–1913).* Havana: Imp. Rambla, Bouza y Cía, 1915.

Cárdenas, Angel G. *Soga y sangre. Una página de horror del machadato y su acusación pública.* Havana: Ediciones Montero, 1945.

Castellanos G., Gerardo. *Hacia Gibara.* Havana: Seone y Fernández, 1933.

_____. *Panorama histórico.* Havana: Ucar, García y Cía, 1934.

Castro, Fidel. *Cartas del presidio.* Edited by Luis Conte Agüero. Havana: Editorial Lex, 1959.

_____. *Discursos del Dr. Fidel Castro Ruz, Comandante en Jefe del Ejército Rebelde 26 de Julio y Primer Ministro del Gobierno Provisional.* Edited by Emilio Roig de Leuchsenring. Havana: Oficina del Historiador de la Ciudad, 1959.

_____. *Guía del pensamiento económico de Fidel.* Havana: Editorial Lex, 1959.

_____. *Palabras para la historia.* Havana: Cooperativa Obrera de Publicidad, 1960.

_____. *La revolución cubana.* Edited by Gregorio Selser. Buenos Aires: Editorial Palestra, 1960.

Catá, Alvaro. *De guerra a guerra.* Havana: Imp. "La Razón," 1906.

Chapelle, Dickey, "How Castro Won." In Franklin Mark Osanka, ed., *Modern Guerrilla Warfare,* pp. 325–35. New York:, 1962.

Chapman, Charles E. *A History of the Cuban Republic: A Study in Hispanic American Politics.* New York: Macmillan, 1927.

Chester, Edmund A. *A Sergeant Named Batista.* New York: Henry Holt, 1954.

Chorley, Katherine. *Armies and the Art of Revolution.* London: Faber and Faber, 1943.

Collazo, Enrique. *Los americanos en Cuba.* Havana: Imp. C. Martínez y Cía, 1905.

_____. *Cuba intervenida.* Havana: Imp. C. Martínez y Cía, 1910.

_____. *La revolución de agosto de 1906.* Havana: Imp. C. Martínez y Cía, 1907.

Conte Agüero, Luis. *Los dos rostros de Fidel Castro.* México: Editorial Jus, 1960.

_____. *Eduardo Chibás, el adalid de Cuba.* México: Editorial Jus, 1955.

_____. *Fidel Castro: vida y obra.* Havana: Editorial Lex, 1959.

Contoño, Miguel. *Tesis política. Primera reunión nacional del Ala Izquierdo Estudiantil (Octubre de 1933).* Havana: n.p., 1934.

Cox, George Howland. "Machado, Welles and the Cuban Crisis." In A. Curtis Wilgus, ed., *The Caribbean Area*, pp. 195–209. Washington, D.C.:, 1934.

Cruz, Carlos Manuel de la. *Proceso histórico del machadato*. Havana: Imp. "La Milagrosa," 1935.

Cuba bajo la administración presidencial del Mayor General José Miguel Gómez. Havana: Imp. Rambla y Bouza, 1911.

Cuba: ejemplo revolucionario de Latinoamérica. Lima: Editorial Libertad, 1961.

Debray, Régis. *Revolution in the Revolution?* Translated by Bobbye Ortiz. New York: Grove Press, 1967.

Defensa Institucional Cubana. *Tres años*. México: Ediciones Botas, 1962.

Díaz, Emilio. *Essay of the Cuban History*. Coral Gables: Service Offset Printers, 1964.

Díaz-Versón, Salvador. *Cuando la razón se vuelve inútil*. México: Ediciones Botas, 1962.

Draper, Theodore. *Castroism: Theory and Practice*. New York: Praeger, 1962.

———. *Castro's Revolution: Myth and Realities*. New York: Praeger, 1962.

Duarte Oropesa, José A. *Historiología cubana*. 5 vols. n.p.: 1969–1970.

Dubois, Jules. *Fidel Castro: Rebel-Liberator or Dictator?* Indianapolis: Bobbs-Merrill, 1959.

Duque, Matías. *Nuestra patria*. Havana: Imp. y Librería Nueva, 1928.

Fergusson, Erna, *Cuba*. New York: Knopf, 1946.

Fernández, Julio César. *Yo acuso a Batista*. Havana: n.p., 1940.

Finer, S. E. *The Man on Horseback: The Role of the Military in Politics*. New York: Praeger, 1962.

Fitzgibbon, Russell H. *Cuba and the United States, 1900–1935*. Menasha, Wis. George Banta, 1935.

Ford, Worthington Chauncey, ed. *Letters of Henry Adams*. 2 vols. Boston: Houghton Mifflin, 1930–1938.

Franco Varona, M. *La revolución del 4 de septiembre*. Havana: Editorial Varona-Cruz, 1934.

Frank, Waldo. *Cuba: Prophetic Island*. New York: Marzan & Munsell, 1961.

Frondizi, Silvio. *La revolución cubana, su significación histórica*. Montevideo: Editorial Ciencias Políticas, 1960.

Gantenbein, James W. *The Evolution of Our Latin-American Policy: A Documentary Record*. New York: Columbia University Press, 1950.

García Kohly, Mario. *El problema constitucional de Cuba y de nuestra América*. Paris: Imprimerie Labor, 1930.

Giménez, Armando. *Sierra Maestra. La revolución de Fidel Castro*. Translated by Carmen Alfaya. Buenos Aires: Editorial Lautaro, 1959.

Goldenberg, Boris. *The Cuban Revolution and Latin America*. New York: Praeger, 1965.

Gómez, Gabriel A. *De la dictadura a la liberación (interpretación política y social de la revolución cubana)*. Havana: Publicaciones G. A. Gómez, 1959.

González, Edelmira. *Batista. Septiembre 4, 1933. Junio 1, 1940. Marzo 10, 1952*. Havana: n.p., 1952.

———. *La revolución en Cuba. Memorias del coronel Rosendo Collazo*. Havana: Editorial "Hermes," 1934.

González Múñoz, Rafael. *Doctrina Grau*. Havana: Publicaciones del Ministerio de Estado, 1948.

González Palacios, Alberto. *El alzamiento del Ocujal*. Santiago de Cuba: n.p., 1934.

González Palacios, Carlos. *Revolución y seudo-revolución en Cuba*. Havana: n.p., 1948.

Grau San Martín, Ramón. *La revolución cubana ante América*. México: Ediciónes del Partido Revolución Cubano (Auténtico), 1936.

Guas Inclán, Rafael. *El general Gerardo Machado y Morales*. Havana: n.p., 1956.

Guerra y Sánchez, Ramiro et al. *Historia de la nación cubana.* 10 vols. Havana: Editorial Historia de la Nación Cubana, S.A., 1952.

Guevara, Ernesto Che. *Obra Revolucionaria.* Edited by Roberto Fernández Retamar. 2d ed. México: Ediciones Era, 1968.

Guggenheim, Harry F. *The United States and Cuba.* New York: Macmillan, 1934.

Hagedorn, Hermann. *Leonard Wood, a Biography.* 2 vols. New York: Harper & Bros., 1931.

Healy, David F. *The United States in Cuba, 1898–1902: Generals, Politicians and the Search for Policy.* Madison: University of Wisconsin Press, 1963.

Hernández-Cata, Alfonso. *Un cementerio en las Antillas,* Madrid: Imp. de Galo Sáez, 1933.

Horowitz, Irving Louis. "Electoral Politics, Urbanization, and Social Development in Latin America." In Glen H. Beyer, ed., *The Urban Explosion in Latin America,* pp. 215–54. Ithaca: Cornell University Press, 1967.

Horstmann, Jorge A. *Aguacero.* Havana: Empresa Editorial de Publicaciones, S.A., 1956.

Huntington, Samuel P. *The Soldier and the State: The Theory and Politics of Civil-Military Relations.* Cambridge, Mass.: Belknap Press, 1957.

Iglesias, Abelardo. *Revolución y dictadura en Cuba.* Buenos Aires: Editorial Reconstruir, 1963.

Infiesta, Ramón. *Máximo Gómez.* Havana: Imp. "El Siglo XX," 1937.

International Bank for Reconstruction and Development. *Report on Cuba.* Baltimore: Johns Hopkins University Press, 1951.

International Commission of Jurists. *Cuba and the Rule of Law.* Geneva: H. Studer, S.A., 1962.

Iznaga, J. M. *Por Cuba.* Havana: Imp. Rambla y Bouza, 1907.

Iznaga, R. *Tres años de República.* Havana: Imp. Rambla y Bouza, 1905.

Jenks, Leland Hamilton. "Cuba Faces a New Deal." In A. Curtis Wilgus, ed., *The Caribbean Area,* pp. 158–74. Washington, D.C.: 1934.

————. *Our Cuban Colony: A Study in Sugar.* New York: Vanguard Press, 1928.

Johnson, John J. *The Military and Society in Latin America.* Stanford: Stanford University Press, 1964.

Johnson, Willis Fletcher. *The History of Cuba.* 5 vols. New York: B. F. Buck, 1920.

Julien, Claude. *La revolución cubana.* Translated by Mario Trajtenberg. Montevideo: Ediciones Marcha, 1961.

Langley, Lester D. *The Cuban Policy of the United States.* New York: Wiley, 1968.

León, Rubén de. *El origen del mal (Cuba, un ejemplo).* Miami: Service Offset Printers, 1964.

Lequerica Velez, Fulgencio. *600 días con Fidel. Tres misiones en La Habana.* Bogotá: Ediciones Mito, 1961.

Lieuwen, Edwin. *Arms and Politics in Latin America.* New York: Praeger, 1960.

Lizaso, Félix. *Panorama de la cultura cubana.* México: Fondo de Cultura Económica, 1949.

Lockmiller, David A. *Magoon in Cuba: A History of the Second Intervention, 1906–1909.* Chapel Hill: University of North Carolina Press, 1938.

Lockwood, Lee. *Castro's Cuba, Cuba's Fidel.* New York: Vintage, 1969.

Loveira, Carlos. *Generales y doctores.* Edited by Shasta M. Bryant and J. Riis Owre. New York: Oxford University Press, 1965.

Lumen, Enrique. *La revolución cubana. 1902–1934.* México: Ediciones Botas, 1934.

MacGaffey, Wyatt, and Barnett, Clifford R. *Twentieth Century Cuba.* Garden City: Anchor Books, 1965.

Mañach, Jorge. *El militarismo en Cuba.* Havana: Seone, Fernández y Cía, 1939.

Márquez Sterling, Carlos. *Don Tomás (Biografía de una época).* Havana: Editorial Lex, 1953.

_____. *Historia de Cuba, desde Colón hasta Castro.* New York: Las Américas, 1963.

Márquez Sterling, M. *Proceso histórico de la Enmienda Platt (1897–1934).* Havana: Imp. "El Siglo XX," 1941.

Martí, Carlos. *Forjando patria.* Havana: Maza y Cía, 1917.

Martínez, Marcial. *Cuba, la verdad de su tragedia.* México: Talleres Gráficos "Galeza," 1958.

Martínez, Fraga, Pedro. *El general Menocal. Apuntes para su biografía.* Havana: Talleres de Editorial "Tiempo," 1941.

Martínez Ortiz, Rafael. *Cuba, los primeros años de independencia.* 3d. ed. 2 vols. Paris: Editorial "Le Livre Libre," 1929.

_____. *General Leonard Wood's Government in Cuba.* Paris: Imprimerie Dubois et Bauer, 1920.

Masetti, Jorge Ricardo. *Los que luchan y los que lloran (El Fidel Castro que yo vi).* Havana: Editorial Adiedo, 1959.

Masó y Vázquez, Calixto. *Consideraciones en torno a las revoluciones.* Havana: Editorial Lex, 1959.

Matthews, Franklin. *The New-Born Cuba.* New York: Harper & Bros., 1899.

Matthews, Herbert L. *The Cuban Story.* New York: George Braziller, 1961.

Meneses, Enrique. *Fidel Castro. Siete años de poder.* Madrid: Afrodiso Afuado, S.A., 1966.

Merino, Adolfo G. *Nacimiento de un estado vasallo.* México: B. Costa-Amic, 1966.

Merino, Bernardo y Ibarzabal, F. de. *La revolución de febrero. Datos para la historia.* 2d ed. Havana: Libraría "Cervantes," 1918.

Mestre y Amabile, Vicente. *Cuba, un año de república. Hechos y notas.* Paris: n.p., 1903.

Millett, Allan Reed. *The Politics of Intervention: The Military Occupation of Cuba, 1906–1909.* Columbus: Ohio State University Press, 1968.

Millis, Walter. *The Martial Spirit: A Study of Our War with Spain.* Boston: Houghton Mifflin, 1931.

Navas, José. *La convulsión de febrero.* Matanzas, Imp. y Monotypo "El Escritorio," 1917.

Nelson, Lowry. *Rural Cuba.* Minneapolis: University of Minnesota Press, 1950.

Núñez Jiménez, Antonio. *Cuba, con la mochila al hombro.* Havana: Ediciones Union, 1963.

_____. *Geografía de Cuba.* 2d ed. Havana: Editorial Lex, 1959.

Organización Nacional de Bibliotecas Ambulantes y Populares. *13 documentos de la insurrección.* Havana: ONBAP, 1959.

Ortiz, Fernando. *La decadencia cubana.* Havana: Imp. y Papelería Universitaria, 1924.

_____. *Discurso sobre el proyecto de ley acerca del servicio militar obligatorio (sus aspectos político y diplomático).* Havana: Imp. de Ruiz y Cia, 1918.

Otero Echeverría, Rafael. *Reportaje a una revolución. De Batista a Fidel Castro.* 2d ed. Santiago de Chile: Editorial del Pacífico, S.A., 1959.

Palacios, Alfredo L. *Una revolución auténtica en Nuestra América.* México: Editorial Cultura, 1960.

Pazos, Javier. *Cambridge Opinion: Cuba.* Cambridge: At the University Press, 1963.

Peralta, Víctor M. de. *Conmonitorio de intervención á intervención.* Havana: Imp. la Prueba, 1907.

Peraza, Carlos G. *Machado, crímenes y horrores de un régimen.* Havana: Cultural, 1933.

Pinto-Santos, Oscar. *Historia de Cuba. Aspectos fundamentales.* Havana: Editorial Nacional de Cuba, 1964.

Pío Elizalde, Leopoldo. *Defamation.* México: Defensa Institucional Cubana, 1961.

Plan Trienal de Cuba. Havana: Cultural, 1938.

Poblete Troncoso, Moisés, and Burnett, Ben. G. *The Rise of the Latin American Labor Movement.* New York: Bookman Associates, 1960.

Portell Vilá, Herminio. "Cuba Past and Present." In A. Curtis Wilgus, ed., *The Caribbean Area,* pp. 175–94. Washington, D.C. 1934.

_____. *Historia de Cuba en sus relaciones con los Estados Unidos y España.* 4 vols. Havana: Jesús Montero, 1938–1941.

Portuondo, Jose Antonio. *Crítica de la época.* Havana: Universidad Central de Las Villas, 1965.

Portuondo Linares, Serafín. *Los independientes de color. Historia del Partido Independiente de Color.* 2d ed. Havana: Editorial Libreria Selecta, 1950.

Primelles, León. *Crónica cubana, 1915–1918.* Havana: Editorial Lex, 1955.

_____. *Crónica cubana, 1919–1922.* Havana: Editorial Lex, 1957.

Quesada, Gonzalo de. *Archivo de Gonzalo de Quesada. Documentos históricos.* Compiled by Gonzalo de Quesada y Miranda. Havana: Editorial de la Universidad de La Habana, 1965.

Quesada y Miranda, Gonzalo de ¡*En Cuba Libre! Historia documentada y anecdóctica del machadato.* 2 vols. Havana: Seone, Fernández y Cia, 1938.

Raggi Ageo, Carlos M. *Condiciones económicas y sociales de la República de Cuba.* Havana: Editorial Lex, 1944.

Riera Hernández, Mario. *Cuba politica, 1899–1955.* Havana: Impresora Modelo, 1955.

_____. *Historial obrero cubano, 1574–1965.* Miami: Rema Press, 1965.

_____. *Un presidente constructivo.* Miami: Colonial Press, 1965.

Rivero, Nicolás. *Castro's Cuba: An American Dilemma.* Washington, D.C.: Luce, 1962.

Rivero Múñiz, José. *El movimiento laboral cubano durante el período 1906–1911.* Havana: Empresa Consolida de Artes Gráficas, 1962.

_____. *El movimiento obrero durante la primera intervención (1899–1902).* Havana: Impresores Ugar, García, 1961.

Roa, Raúl. *Retorno a la alborada.* 2 vols. Havana: Universidad de Las Villas, 1964.

Robinson, Albert G. *Cuba and the Intervention.* New York: Longman's, Green & CO., 1905.

Roca, Blas. *The Cuban Revolution: Report to the Eighth National Congress of the Popular Socialist Party of Cuba.* New York: New Century, 1961.

Rodríguez Morejón, Gerardo. *Fidel Castro, biografía.* Havana: P. Fernández, 1959.

_____. *Grau San Martín.* 2d ed. Havana: Ediciones Mirador, 1944.

_____. *Menocal.* Havana: Cárdenas y Cía, 1941.

Roig, Enrique. *El servicio militar obligatorio.* Havana: Compañía Impresora y Papelria "La Universal," 1918.

Roig de Leuchsenring, Emilio. *Juan Gualberto Gómez, paladín de la independencia y la libertad de Cuba.* Havana: Oficina del Historiador de la Ciudad, 1954.

_____. *La lucha cubana por la república, contra la anexión y la Enmienda Platt, 1899–1902.* Havana: Oficina del Historiador de la ciudad, 1952.

Rojas R., Marta. *La generación del centenario en el Moncada.* Havana: Ediciones R., 1964.

Root, Elihu. *The Military and Colonial Policy of the United States.* Edited by Robert Bacon and James Brown Scott. Cambridge, Mass.: Harvard University Press, 1916.

Rubens, Horatio S. *Liberty, the Story of Cuba.* New York: Warren & Putnam, 1932.

Ruiz, Leovigildo. *Diario de una traición.* Miami: Florida Typesetting of Miami, 1965.

Ruiz, Ramón Eduardo. *Cuba: The Making of a Revolution.* Amherst: University of Massachusetts Press, 1968.

Sainz de la Peña, Arturo. *La revolución de agosto.* Havana: Imp. "La Prueba," 1909.

Sánchez Amaya, Fernando. *Diario del Granma.* Havana: Editorial Tierra Nueva, 1959.

Sanjenís, A. *Tiburón.* Havana: Librería Hispanoamericana, 1915.

San Martín, Rafael. *El grito de la Sierra Maestra.* Buenos Aires: Ediciones Gure, 1960.

Santovenia, Emeterio S. *Armonía y conflictos en torno a Cuba.* México: Fondo de Cultura, 1956.

Shils, Edward. "The Military in the Political Development of the New States." In John J. Johnson, ed., *The Role of the Military in Underdeveloped Countries,* pp. 7–67. Princeton: Princeton University Press, 1962.

Smith, Robert F. *The United States and Cuba: Business and Diplomacy, 1917–1960.* New Haven: College and University Press, 1960.

―――. *What Happened in Cuba? A Documentary History.* New York: Twayne, 1963.

Sosa de Quesada, Arístides. *El Consejo Corporativo de Educación, Sanidad y Beneficencia y sus instituciones filiales.* Havana: Instituted Civico-Militar, 1937.

―――. *Militarismo, anti-militarismo, seudo-militarismo.* Havana: Instituto Civico-Military, 1939.

―――. *Por la democracia . . . y por la libertad.* Havana: P. Fernández y Cía, 1943.

Souchy, Agustin. *Testimonios sobre la revolución cubana.* Buenos Aires: Editorial Reconstruir, 1960.

Souza, B. *Máximo Gómez, el Generalismo.* Havana: Editorial Trópico, 1936.

Special Operations Research Office. *Casebook on Insurgency and Revolutionary Warfare: 23 Summary Accounts.* Washington, D.C.: The American University, 1963.

―――. *Case Study in Insurgency and Revolutionary Warfare: Cuba, 1953–1959.* Washington, D.C.: The American University, 1963.

―――. *Special Warfare Area Handbook for Cuba.* Washington, D.C.: The American University, 1961.

Strode, Hudson. *The Pageant of Cuba.* New York: Random House, 1934.

Suárez, Andrés. *Cuba: Castroism and Communism, 1959–1966.* Translated by Joel Carmichael and Ernst Halperin. Cambridge: MIT Press, 1967.

Suárez Núñez, Jose. *El gran culpable.* Caracas: n.p., 1963.

Tabares del Real, José A. *Ensayo de interpretación de la revolución cubana.* La Paz: Talleres Gráficos "Gutenberg," 1960.

Taber, Robert. *M-26: Biography of a Revolution.* New York:Lyle Stuart, 1961.

―――. *The War of the Flea: A Study of Guerrilla Warfare: Theory and Practice.* New York: Lyle Stuart, 1965.

Thomas, Hugh. *Cuba: The Pursuit of Freedom, 1762–1969.* New York: Harper & Row, 1971.

―――. "Middle-Class Politics and the Cuban Revolution." In Claudio Veliz, ed., *The Politics of Conformity in Latin America,* pp. 249–77. London: Oxford, 1967.

Torriente, Cosme de la. *Fin de la dominación de España en Cuba (12 de agosto de 1898).* Havana: Imp. "El Siglo XX," 1948.

―――. *Libertad y democracia.* Havana: Imp. "El Siglo XX," 1941.

Torriente Brau, Pablo de la. *Realengo 18 y Mella, Rubén y Machado.* Havana: Ediciones Nuevo Mundo, 1962.

Trelles, Carlos M. *El progreso (1902 a 1905) y el retroceso (1906 a 1922) de la república de Cuba.* Matanzas: Imp. de Tomás González, 1923.

Tres años de Cuba libre. Paz, prosperidad y progreso. Havana: Imp. de Solana y Cía, 1905.

Valdés-Miranda, Jorge. *Cuba revolucionaria.* Havana: n.p., n.d.

Varela Zequeira, Eduardo. *La política en 1905. Espisodios de una lucha electoral.* Havana: Imp. Rambla y Bouza, 1905.

Varona, Enrique. *De la colonia a la República.* Havana: Editorial Cuba Cóntemporánea, 1919.

Varona, Manuel A. de. *El drama de Cuba o la revolución traicionada.* Buenos Aires: Editorial Marymar, 1960.

Vázquez, Eduardo I. *Cuba independiente. Primer período presidencial. 1902–1906.* Havana: Editorial Acosta, 1906.

Vega Cobiellas, Ulpiano. *Los doctores Ramón Grau San Martín y Carlos Saladrigas Zayas.* Havana: Editorial Lex, 1944.

_____. *El General Fulgencio Batista y la sucesión presidencial.* Havana: Editorial Colegial, S.A., 1957.

_____. *Nuestra América y la evolución de Cuba.* Havana: Cultural, S.A., 1944.

_____. *La personalidad y la obra del General Fulgencio Batista Zaldivar.* Havana: Cultural, S.A., 1943.

Velasco, Carlos de. *Estrada Palma, contribución histórica.* Havana: Imp. "La Universal," 1911.

Vilches de la Maza, Bartolomé. *La tiranía de Machado.* Havana: Impresos "Martín," 1933.

Winocur, Marcos. *Cuba a la hora de América.* Buenos Aires: Ediciones Proyon, 1963.

Wood, Bryce. *The Making of the Good Neighbor Policy.* New York: Columbia University Press, 1961.

Articles

Aaron, Harold R. "Why Batista Lost." *Army,* 15 (September 1965): 64–71.

Acosta, Agustín. "Carlos Mendieta (1934–1935)." *Bohemia,* 30 (June 5, 1938): 65, 87, 95–96.

Adams, Frederick Upham. "Cuba, Its Condition and Outlook." *The World's Work,* 12 (November 1906): 8237–42.

Adan y Silva, Ricardo. "Las conspiraciones durante la tiranía en el ejército." *Bohemia,* 26 (October 14, 1934): 14–15, 51–53.

_____. "El desplome militar del batistato." *Bohemia,* 51 (June 12, 1959): 36–38, 115.

Aguilera, Estrella. "Frank País." *Verde Olivo,* 3 (August 5, 1962): 6–7.

Aguirre, Sergio. "La desaparición del Ejército Libertador." *Cuba Socialista,* 3 (December 1963): 51–68.

Alba, Víctor. "Cuba: A Peasant Revolution." *The World Today,* 15 (May 1959): 183–95.

Alexander, Robert J. "El desmoronamiento de la tiranía de Batista." *Combate* (San Jose), 1 (January–February 1959): 76–80.

Alles Soberón, Agustín. "Los primeros periodistas cubanos en la Sierra Maestra." *Bohemia,* 51 (February 22, 1959): 24–27, 134–37, 146.

Almeida, Juan. "Habla el comandante Almeida." *Bohemia,* 51 (March 1, 1959): 46–49, 124.

Amador Rodríguez, Juan. "Si el pueblo derrota a Batista acateremos su decisión." *Bohemia,* 45 (April 27, 1952): 56–58, 81–82.

Ameijeiras, Efigenio. "El Uvero fué la respuesta de la hombria del Ejército Rebelde." *Verde Olivo,* 4 (June 2, 1963): 19–26.

Andreski, Stanislav. "Conservatism and Radicalism of the Military." *Archives Européenes de Sociologie,* 2 (1961): 53–61.

Araneda Figueroa, Pedro. "Con Fidel Castro en Sierra Maestra." *Revista de América,* 619 (November 2, 1957): 33–38.

————. "Llegó la hora 'o' para Batista." *Revista de América.* 622 (November 23, 1957): 18–20.

Baeza Flores, Alberto. "El silencio pavorosa que precede a un ciclón." *Bohemia.* 48 (August 12, 1956): 46–47.

Barahona, Javier. "El 10 de marzo en La Habana." *Carteles,* 33 (March 16, 1952): 52–53.

Barrera Pérez, Pedro A. "Por que el ejército no derrotó a Castro." *Bohemia Libre* (Caracas), 53 (July 9, 1961–September 3, 1961).

Barry, Richard. "Batista—Ruler of Cuba." *Review of Reviews,* 91 (January 1935): 48–51, 73.

Benítez y Valdés, Manuel. "Mi conducta militar y política." *Bohemia,* 36 (November 12, 1944): 28–29, 44.

Blackburn, Robin. "Prologue to the Cuban Revolution." *New Left Review* (London), 21 (October 1963): 52–91.

Boan Acosta, Angel. "El fraude histórica de la 'generación del 30.' " *Bohemia,* 48 (June 2, 1956): 48–50, 76.

Borges, Espinet. "La radio tomada militarmente." *Carteles,* 33 (March 16, 1952): 66–67.

Brunet, Rolando C. "Así se cobró la dictadura la muerte de Fermín Cowley." *Bohemia,* 51 (February 1, 1959): 84–85, 105–06.

————. "Tenían que ser siete." *Bohemia,* 51 (March 29, 1959): 8–10, 157.

Bryce, James. "Some Reflections on the State of Cuba." *North American Review,* 174 (April 1902): 445–65.

Buell, Raymond Leslie. "The Caribbean Situation: Cuba and Haiti." *Foreign Policy Reports,* 9 (June 21, 1933): 82–92.

————. "Cuba Ousts Machado." *Foreign Policy Bulletin,* 12 (August 18, 1933): 1–2.

————. "The Cuban Revolt." *Foreign Policy Bulletin,* 14 (March 15, 1935): 1–2.

Cabrera, Luis Rolando. "Sagua de Tánamo, la ciudad mártir." *Bohemia,* 51 (February 1, 1959): 70–73, 120–21.

Calero, Ramón. "Yo fuí un 'bocadito.' " *Bohemia,* 51 (March 15, 1959): 44–45, 121.

Camacho, Julio. "El alzamiento de Cienfuegos." *Revolución,* September 5–10, 1962.

Caparros, Rogelio. "Todo está preparado para las elecciones." *Bohemia,* 46 (October 31, 1954): 68–69.

Carbó, Sergio. "Cómo y por culpa de quien cayó Grau San Martín." *Bohemia,* 26 (March 25, 1934): 28–29, 40–42.

Cárdenas, Raúl de. "Los gobiernos de Cuba: Estrada Palma (1902–1906)." *Bohemia,* 30 (June 5, 1938): 26–27, 122–23, 126–27.

Carrera Justiz, Francisco. "Los gobiernos de Cuba: Charles E. Magoon." *Bohemia,* 30 (June 5, 1938): 20–21, 106, 118.

Casero, Luis. "Las provincias derrocaron a Batista." *Bohemia,* 51 (March 8, 1959): 30, 137.

Castillo Ramos, Rubén. "¡Buenos, señores periodistas, aquí estoy!" *Bohemia,* 49 (July 14, 1957): 74–75, 92.

————. "En el cuartel de Bayamo se escribió otra página heroica." *Bohemia,* 53 (July 23, 1961): 62–63, 82.

Castro, Fidel. "Carta de Fidel Castro." *Bohemia,* 50 (February 2, 1958), sup. 48, 83–85.

————. "Fidel Over Radio Rebelde." *Granma* (March 18, 1973) (special supplement).

————. "¡Frente a todos!" *Bohemia,* 48 (January 8, 1956): 81–82, 89.

————. "El 26 de Julio: fruto de la inagotable confianza en las fuerzas revolucionarias del pueblo." *Cuba Socialista,* 15 (August 1966): 2–37.

Castro, Raúl. "Operación antiaérea." *Verde Olivo,* 4 (September 15, 1963): 32–38.

———. "VIII aniversario del 26 de Julio." *Verde Olivo* (July 16, 1961): 3–11.

———. "Raúl le habla al pueblo." *Obra Revolucionaria,* 2 (May 17, 1960): 7–31.

Chibás, Eddy. "Los gobiernos de Cuba: Grau San Martín (1933–1934)." *Bohemia,* 30 (June 5, 1938): 62–63, 94–95.

Chibás, Raúl; Pazos, Felipe; and Castro, Fidel. "Al pueblo de Cuba." *Bohemia,* 49 (July 28, 1957): 69, 96–97.

Chomón, Faure. "El ataque al Palacio Presidencial el 13 de marzo de 1957." *Bohemia,* 51 (March 15–22, 1959).

Cienfuegos, Camilo. "Informe de la invasión." *Verde Olivo,* 2 (October 29, 1961): 4–7.

Conte Agüero, Luis. "Cosas de la Sierra." *Bohemia,* 50 (February 9, 1958): sup. 14, 84–85.

———. "Estamos en un tranque." *Bohemia,* 49 (July 14, 1957): 51, 100.

———. "La línea del deber." *Bohemia,* 49 (June 23, 1957): 69, 88.

———. "La verdad sobre la Sierra Maestra." *Bohemia,* 49 (July 7, 1957): 76, 95.

Cortina, José Manuel. "Los gobiernos de Cuba: Alfredo Zayas (1921–1925)." *Bohemia,* 30 (June 5, 1938): 46–49, 116–17, 121, 124–25, 128–29.

Costales Latatu, Manuel. "Una revolución efímera en el tiempo y gloriosa en los hechos." *Bohemia,* 46 (September 12, 1954): 62–63, 80–81.

Coyula, Miguel. "Los gobiernos de Cuba: Mario G. Menocal (1913–1921)." *Bohemia,* 30 (June 5, 1938): 44–45, 110–14.

Cronon, E. David. "Interpreting the New Good Neighbor Policy: The Cuban Crisis of 1933." *The Hispanic American Historical Review,* 39 (November 1959): 538–67.

Cubillas, Vicente. "La carga heroica del 'Granma.' " *Bohemia,* 52 (December 4, 1960): 32–35, 98–99.

———. "Cienfuegos: la gesta heroica del 5 de septiembre de 1957." *Bohemia,* 51 (September 13–20, 1959).

———. "Los sucesos del 9 de abril en La Habana." *Revolución* (April 9, 1959): 16–17.

———. "Un 30 de noviembre en Santiago de Cuba." *Bohemia,* 52 (November 27, 1960): 44–47, 72.

Cuervo Navarro, Pelayo. "La república convertida en un cuartel." *Bohemia,* 44 (August 10, 1952): 80–82.

Díaz-Balart, Rafael L. "Militarismo y revolución." *Bohemia,* 46 (April 4, 1954): 60.

Dorta-Duque, Manuel. "La mediación." *Bohemia,* 30 (June 5, 1938): 56–57, 86.

Dyer, Donald. "Urbanism in Cuba." *The Geographical Review,* 47 (April 1957): 224–33.

Emiro Valencia, Luis. "Realidades y perspectivas de la revolución cubana." *Casa de las Américas,* 1 (March–April 1961): 2–7.

Estenger, Rafael. "La doble cara del golpe de estado." *Bohemia,* 44 (March 16, 1952): 49.

Fe, Gonzalo de la. "La conspiración en la Policía Nacional." *Bohemia,* 51 (February 8, 1959): 110–12.

Ferrera, Orestes. "Fidel Castro y el caos." *Bohemia Libre,* 54 (May 13, 1962): 4–6, 113–15.

———. "Los últimos días del régimen de Machado." *Bohemia,* 49 (August 10, 1952): 4–6, 113–15.

Ferrer, Horacio. "Cuba por encima de todo." *Bohemia,* 25 (August 20, 1933): 42.

———. "El golpe de estado." *Bohemia,* 42 (August 13, 1950): 4–6, 8–9, 123.

Fiallo, René. "Hay que ganar la otra batalla." *Bohemia,* 41 (September 4, 1949): 62–63, 81.

———. "No los enseñe a leer, general." *Bohemia,* 48 (April 15, 1956): 54, 76–77.

Fitzgibbon, Russell H., and Healey, Max H. "The Cuban Elections of 1936." *The American Political Science Review,* 30 (August 1936): 724–35.

Foscue, Edwin J. "The Central Highway of Cuba." *Economic Geography*, 9 (October 1933): 406–12.

Fundora Núñez, Gerardo. "Ya está bueno de sangre derramada intutilmente." *Bohemia*, 49 (January 13, 1957): 37, 82–83.

Gálvez, William. "Diario de la columna invasora 'Antonio Maceo.'" *Verde Olivo*, 4 (November 3, 1963): 5–8.

García, Calixto. "Combate de La Plata." *Bohemia*, 56 (November 27, 1964): 102–03.

García Bárcena, Rafael. "Razón y sinrazón del 4 de septiembre." *Bohemia*, 44 (September 7, 1952): 60–61.

García-Olivares, Julio. "La operación Radio-Reloj." *Bohemia*, 51 (March 15, 1959): 10–12, 152–53.

García y Azcuy, Angel A. "La Guardia Rural, su función, sus obligaciones y su espíritu." *Boletín del Ejército*, 1 (September–October 1950): 56–57.

Germani, Gino, and Silvert, Kalman. "Politics, Social Structure and Military Intervention in Latin America." *Archives Européenes de Sociologie*, 2 (1961): 62–81.

Gil, Federico. "Antecedents of the Cuban Revolution." *The Centennial Review of Arts and Science*, 6 (Summer 1961): 373–93.

González, Manuel Pedro. "Cuba, una revolución en marcha." *Cuadernos Americanos*, 153 (July–August 1967): 7–24.

González del Campo, L. "Con el Capitán Mario Torres Menier." *Bohemia*, 26 (January 28, 1934): 28, 41–42.

González Lines, Fernando. "Yo presencié el consejo de guerra sumarismo de mi hermano." *Bohemia*, 50 (March 16, 1958): 70–71, 94–95.

González Pedrero, Enrique. "La caída de otra dictadura." *Cuadernos Americanos*, 103 (March–April 1959): 25–35.

González Valdés, José. "La Guardia Rural." *Boletín del Ejército*, 6 (February 1919): 783–85.

———. "Los oficiales y los conscriptos." *Boletín del Ejército*, 6 (October 1918): 205–10.

———. "El sargento." *Boletín del Ejército*, 5 (June 1918): 353–57.

"La gran tragedia de la verdadera oficialidad cubano." *Bohemia*, 26 (January 7, 1934): 36, 40–41.

Grau San Martín, Ramón. "The Cuban Terror." *The Nation*, 140 (April 3, 1935): 381–82.

———. "Mi herencia." *Bohemia*, 41 (February 20, 1949): 62–63.

Guas Inclán, Rafael. "Los gobiernos de Cuba: Gerardo Machado (1925–1933)." *Bohemia*, 30 (June 5, 1938): 54–55, 100–01, 105.

———. "Todos erramos." *Cuba Libre* (Miami), 2 (October 28, 1960): 1, 3.

Guerra Puente, Faustino. "Causes of the Cuban Insurrection." *The North American Review*, 183 (September 21, 1906): 538–40.

Guiral Moreno, Mario. "Nuestros problemas políticos, económicos y sociales." *Cuba Contemporánea*, 5 (August 1914): 401–24.

———. "El problema de la burocracia en Cuba." *Cuba Contemporánea*, 2 (August 1913): 257–67.

Gutiérrez, Enrique. "La conspiración para la rebelión militar." *Carteles*, 37 (April 15, 1956): 38–40.

Gutiérrez Menoyo, Eloy. "El II Frente Nacional del Escambray." *Combate* (San José), 2 (July–August 1959): 48–50.

Hanna, Matthew Elting. "The Necessity of Increasing the Efficiency of the Cuban Army." *Journal of the Military Service Institution of the United States*, 35 (July–August 1904): 28–36.

Hernández y Hernández, Heriberto. "Origen del ejército cubano." *Boletín del Ejército,* 27 (June 1929): 459–60.

Herrero, Gustavo. "De José Miguel a Laredo Bru." *Bohemia,* 30 (June 5, 1938): 80, 96–97.

Hevia, Carlos. "El golpe reaccionario del 10 de marzo." *Bohemia,* 44 (April 6, 1952): 55.

Hitchman, J. H. "The American Touch in Imperial Administration: Leonard Wood in Cuba, 1898–1902." *The Americas,* 24 (April 1968): 394–403.

Ichaso, Francisco. "El caso de Genovevo dentro del ciclo de la impunidad." *Bohemia,* 41 (September 1949): 41, 96–97.

———. "La hipótesis revolucionaria." *Bohemia,* 48 (March 11, 1956): 35, 96.

Inglis, William. "The Future in Cuba." *The North American Review,* 183 (November 16, 1906), 1037–140.

"Intrigas y secretos del machadato: La casa militar del dictador Machado." *Bohemia,* 26 (February 11, 1934): 16–17, 50.

"Jefes de regimientos de las provincias." *Bohemia,* 44 (April 20, 1952), 48–49, 103.

Kling, Merle. "Cuba: A Case Study of a Successful Attempt to Seize Political Power by the Application of Unconventional Warfare." *The Annals of the American Academy of Political and Social Science,* 341 (May 1962): 43–52.

Kuchilán Sol, Mario. "Curti." *Bohemia,* 42 (January 29, 1950): 68–69.

———. "12 de agosto de 1933." *Bohemia,* 62 (August 7, 1962).

Laurent y Dubet, Julio. "Datos esenciales de la expedición de Gibara." *Bohemia,* 25 (August 20, 1933): 24–25, 72, 74–77.

Lechuga, Carlos M. "Panorama política de Cuba." *Humanismo* (México), (October 1954): 155–64.

León, Rubén de. "La verdad de lo ocurrido desde el cuatro de septiembre." *Bohemia,* 26 (February 4, 1934): 28–30, 39–40.

———. "La verdad de lo ocurrido desde el cuatro de septiembre: la crisis del gobierno del Dr. Grau San Martín." *Bohemia,* 26 (February 25, 1934): 30–31, 38, 42.

———. "La verdad de lo ocurrido desde el cuatro de septiembre: Grau, sus leyes y la oposición." *Bohemia,* 26 (February 11, 1934): 30–31, 44–45, 48.

———. "El cuartelazo del 15 de enero: la renuncia de Grau." *Bohemia,* 27 (March 18, 1935): 22–23, 46.

León, Vicente. "Lo que pasó realmente en Palacio el 10 de marzo." *Bohemia,* 48 (August 12, 1956): 59, 86–87.

León, Waldemar. "Como fueron capturados Menocal, Mendieta y su Estado Mayor en Río Verde." *Bohemia,* 59 (January 13, 1967): 105–06, 109.

Lesnick, Max. "Cuba pierde sin solución nacional pero Batista perderá también." *Bohemia,* 49 (July 21, 1957): 48, 100–01.

———. "10 de noviembre: Escambray heroico." *Bohemia,* 51 (November 22, 1959): 46–47, 99–100.

Llerena, Mario. "El manifiesto ideológico del 'Movimiento 26 de Julio.'" *Humanismo* (México), 4 (July–August 1957): 88–103.

Losada, Jorge. "Batista: Master of the Coup d'Etat." *United Nations World,* 7 (April 1953): 31–35.

McCarthy, Francis L. "Historia de una revolución." *Bohemia,* 49 (March 30, 1952): 66–68.

MacGaffey, Wyatt. "Social Structure and Mobility in Cuba." *Anthropological Quarterly,* 34 (January 1961): 94–110.

Maldonado-Denis, Manuel. "La revolución cubana en perspectiva histórica." *Cuadernos Americanos,* 161 (November–December 1968): 48–62.

Mañach, Jorge. "El drama de Cuba." *Cuadernos,* 30 (May–June 1958): 63–76.

———. "El proceso cubano y su perspectiva." *Humanismo* (México), 3 (October 1954): 97–106.

———. "Revolution in Cuba." *Foreign Affairs,* 2 (October 1933): 46–56.

Márquez Sterling, Carlos. "Alfredo Zayas, el abogado de la revolución de 1906." *Bohemia,* 42 (March 19, 1950): 60–61, 92–93.

———. "Estrada Palma y la revolución de 1906." *Bohemia,* 42 (March 12, 1950): 62–63, 92–93.

Martínez, Felipe. "Por qué se frustró nuestra atentado contra Ainciart." *Bohemia,* 26 (February 4, 1934): 29, 41, 48.

Martínez Márquez, Guillermo. "La huelga de marzo." *Bohemia,* 30 (June 5, 1938): 64, 104.

———. "Proyección civil del cuatro de septiembre." *Bohemia,* 29 (September 5, 1937): 36–37, 56–57.

Martínez Ortiz, Rafael. "Juicio acerca de los sucesos políticos de Cuba en 1906." *Cuba Contemporánea,* 15 (October 1917): 118–30.

Martínez Sáenz, Joaquín. "El ABC y Machado." *Bohemia,* 30 (June 5, 1938): 58, 103, 107.

Martínez Villena Rubén. "The Rise of the Revolutionary Movement in Cuba." *The Communist,* 12 (June 1933): 559–69.

Masiques Landeta, Francisco. "Puntos sobresalientes del septembrismo." *Bohemia,* 41 (September 11, 1949): 54–57, 83.

Masó y Vázquez, Calixto. "Cuba: una isla singular." *Aportes* (Paris), 11 (January 1969): 10–39.

———. "La revolución cubana." *Combate* (San José), 1 (May–June, July–August 1959).

Meeker, Oden. "Cuba Under Batista: More Apathy than Disaffection." *The Reporter,* 11 (September 14, 1954): 21–23.

Menéndez, Manolo. "La revolución se va." *Bohemia,* 26 (April 15, 1934): 26.

Meneses, Enrique. "Mis diálogos con Fidel Castro, los hombres de Sierra Maestra: Camilo Cienfuegos, Raúl Castro, 'Che' Guevara." *Blanco y negro* (Madrid), (March 17, 1962), n.p.

———. "Misión: Sierra Maestra." *Bohemia,* 50 (March 9, 1958): 52–58, 96–99.

Meruela, Otto. "Figuras y cosas del '10 de marzo' (un aporte verídico para la historia)." *Bohemia,* 48 (August 26, 1956): 58–60, 86.

Mignone, A. Frederick. "Whither Cuba?" *The South Atlantic Quarterly,* 51 (April 1952): 199–210.

Millett, Allan R. "The General Staff and the Cuban Intervention of 1906." *Military Affairs,* 31 (Fall 1967): 113–19.

———. "The Rise and Fall of the Cuban Rural Guard, 1898–1912." *The Americas,* 29 (October 1972): 191–213.

Meyer, Leo J. "The United States and the Cuban Revolution of 1917." *The Hispanic American Historical Review,* 10 (May 1930): 138–66.

Minger, Ralph Eldin. "William H. Taft and the United States Intervention in Cuba in 1906." *The Hispanic American Historical Review,* 41 (February 1961): 75–89.

Molina y Alfonso, Simón R. "Importancia de la infantería como núcleo estratégico de nuestro ejército." *Boletín del Ejército,* 1 (September–October 1950): 77–82.

Needler, Martin C. "Political Development and Military Intervention in Latin America." *The American Political Science Review,* 60 (September 1966):616–26.

Novas, Benito. "En realidad esto no es un gobierno sino una ocupación." *Bohemia,* 44 (October 26, 1952): 70–71, 94.

"La nueva oficialidad del ejército." *Bohemia,* 44 (March 30, 1952): 56–59, 69.

"El nueve del abril de 1958." *Bohemia,* 51 (April 19, 1959): 58–61, 111–12.

Núñez, Jiménez, Antonio. "Así es la Sierra Maestra." *Bohemia,* 38 (December 30, 1956): 48–50, 96–97.

⸻. "La Sierra Maestra en la historia de Cuba." *Verde Olivo,* 1 (April 17, 1960): 34–38.

O'Connor, James. "The Foundations of Cuban Socialism." *Studies on the Left,* 10 (February 1964): 97–117.

Officer of the Army Occupation. "The Logic of Our Position in Cuba." *North American Review,* 169 (July 1899): 109–15.

"Orígenes de nuestro ejército." *Boletín del Ejército,* 3 (July–August 1952), 11–50.

Ortega, Antonio. "Todos seremos iguales ante la ley porque todos somos cubanos." *Bohemia,* 44 (March 23, 1952): 62–64, 82.

Ortiz, Fernando. "La crisis política cubana. Sus causas y remedios." *Revista Bimestre Cubana,* 14 (January–February 1919), 5–22.

Padrón, Pedro Luis. "Bajo la cúpula del Capitolio, cuartelazo a Miguel Mariano." *Granma* (April 7, 1969), 2.

Pardo Llada, José. "Ante la situación nacional." *Bohemia,* 49 (July 7, 1957): 68–69, 91.

Parker, John H. "How the Cuban Problem Might Be Solved." *The American Review of Reviews,* 37 (January 1908): 65–70.

Pasalodos, Dámaso. "El gobierno del General Gómez." *Bohemia,* 30 (June 12, 1938): 8–9, 57.

Perdomo y Granela, Bernardo. "La Guardia Rural en la conservación del orden público." *Boletín del Ejército,* 7 (May–June 1956): 40–44.

Pérez, Tubal. "Why the Attack on Moncada? Nieves Cordero Tells His Story and That of 'The Cape.' " *Granma* (February 11, 1973): 9.

Pérez Vega, Oscar. "El frente interior y la Guardia Rural." *Boletín del Ejército,* 6 (May–June 1955): 83–91.

Pérez y Figueiras, Wilfredo J. V. "La caballería como fuerza militar en paises poco poblados," *Boletín del Ejército,* 1 (September–October 1950): 82–88.

Pío Elizalde, Leopoldo. "Oriente: principal escenario de dos modos de vida." *Bohemia,* 49 (July 14, 1957): sup. 1, 112.

Platt, Orville H. "Cuba's Claim Upon the United States." *North American Review,* 170 (August 1902): 145–51.

⸻. "The Solution of the Cuban Problem." *The World's Work,* 2 (May 1901): 729–35.

Portell Vilá, Herminio. "Aclarando un punto." *Bohemia,* 44 (April 13, 1952): 47–48, 85.

⸻. "Civilismo y militarismo." *Bohemia,* 48 (April 15, 1956): 27, 92–93.

⸻. "Cuento y recuento." *Bohemia,* 44 (March 23, 1952): 56–57, 82.

⸻. "Datos para la historia." *Bohemia,* 47 (March 6, 1955): 41, 93.

⸻. "El ejército y la política." *Bohemia Libre,* 53 (February 26, 1961): 24–25, 73.

⸻. "La Escuela Superior de Guerra de Cuba." *Bohemia,* 42 (November 19, 1950): 44–46, 107.

⸻. "La intervención militar norteamericana, 1899–1902." *El Mundo* (May 20, 1952): 34–36.

⸻. "El juicio histórico." *Bohemia,* 42 (November 26, 1950): 60–61, 106–07.

Portuondo, José Antonio. "Cuba nación 'para sí.' " *Cuadernos Americanos,* 119 (November–December 1961): 147–72.

"Posición correcta de las fuerzas armadas." *Bohemia,* 41 (February 13, 1949): 57.

Prieto, Enrique. "The Organization of the Cuban Army." *The Military Engineer,* 20 (September–October 1928): 386–89.

Querejeta Valdés, Gregorio. "Querejeta no fomenta revoluciones." *Bohemia,* 41 (October 30, 1949): 60–61, 113.

Quevado, Jose. "Por que se rindió el comandante José Quevado." *Bohemia,* 51 (January 18–25, 1959): 52–54, 120.

Quintana, Jorge. "Fué el 12 de agosto de 1933." *Bohemia,* 41 (August 12, 1949): 36–39, 98–100.

Ramos, Rubén. "Las panteras de Merob Sosa no puedieron llegar a la Sierra." *Bohemia,* 51 (March 1, 1959): 76–77, 97.

Ramos Lechuga, Arnaldo. "La verdad sobre el ataque al Goicuría." *Bohemia,* 51 (May 3, 1959): 62–64.

Rapoport, David C. "The Political Dimensions of Military Usurpation." *Political Science Quarterly,* 83 (December 1968): 551–72.

Rego Rubido, José M. "No es cierto que haya habido rendición en Oriente." *Bohemia Libre,* 53 (October 8, 1961): 29, 80.

Remos, Juan J. "La gestión personal del Coronel Batista." *Bohemia,* 30 (June 5, 1938): 84–85, 97.

Reyes Trejo, Alfredo. "Los días que precedieron al desembarco del Granma." *Verde Olivo,* 7 (December 4, 1966): 10–14, 60–63.

———. "El ejército de la tiranía." *Verde Olivo,* 7 (November 27–December 4, 1966).

Roa, Raúl. "Rafael Trejo y el 30 de septiembre." *Granma* (September 30, 1968), 2.

Robinson, Albert G. "Our Legacy to the Cuban Republic." *The Forum,* 33 (June 1902): 450–58.

Rodríguez, C. R. "The Cuban Revolution and the Peasantry." *World Marxist Review,* 8 (October 1965): 62–71.

Rodríguez Zaldívar, Rodolfo. "Hora cero: 2:40 A.M." *Bohemia,* 34 (April 20, 1952): 76–83.

———. "Sin despejar la incógnita de Fidel Castro." *Bohemia,* 49 (April 21, 1957): 68–70, 94–95.

Rojas R., Marta. "El asalto al Moncada." *Bohemia,* 51 (February 1, 1959): 28–30, 166–67.

———. "La causa 37." *Bohemia,* 51 (February 15, 1959): 36–39, 112–18.

———. "El Segundo Frente Oriental 'Frank País': Ante de la retención de los americanos." *Bohemia,* 51 (June 28, 1959): 50–53, 98–99.

———. "El Segundo Frente Oriental 'Frank País': Un estado rebelde modelo." *Bohemia,* 51 (July 19, 1959): 42–46, 114–15.

———. "El Segundo Frente Oriental 'Frank País': Exitos y reveses." *Bohemia,* 51 (June 21, 1959): 36–38, 40, 110–12.

———. "El Segundo Frente Oriental 'Frank País': La fundación." *Bohemia,* 51 (June 14, 1959): 8–10, 143, 155.

———. "El Segundo Frente Oriental 'Frank País': Operación antiaérea." *Bohemia,* 51 (July 5, 1959): 50–53, 101.

———. "El Segundo Frente Oriental 'Frank País': El reencuentro de los hermanos heroes." *Bohemia,* 51 (August 16, 1959): 36–38, 39, 104–05.

Romero Gómez, Manuel. "Situación política en Cuba." *Estuadios Americanos* (Sevilla), 5 (May 1953): 563–79.

Rosell Leyva, Florentino E. "Confirme el acuerdo Batista-Cantillo." *La Crónica* (Miami) (August 16, 1968): 19.

———. "El tren blindado." *La Crónica* (Miami) (July–August 1968).

Rosello, Arturo Alfonso. "El coronel Batista discurre en torno a la crisis cubana. Origen y desarrollo del brote sedicioso frustado." *Carteles,* 22 (February 16, 1941): 28–29.

Rubens, Horatio S. "The Insurgent Government in Cuba." *The North American Review,* 166 (May 1898): 560–69.

Rubiera, Carlos Manuel. "Orlando Lara y sus muchachos." *Bohemia,* 51 (April 19, 1959): 8–10, 135–37.

———. "Traían en las sayas desde Miami armas y balas las muchachas de resistencia cívica." *Bohemia,* 51 (February 15, 1959): 20–23, 131.

Rubio y Padilla, Juan Antonio. "Como nació y como fué asesinada la Comisión Ejecutiva." *Bohemia,* 26 (September 30, 1934): 8–9, 58, 61.

Sánchez Arango, Aureliano. "Carta a la juventud." *Humanismo,* 3 (January 1955): 28–40.

———. "The Recent Strike in Cuba." *Three Americas* (Mexico), 1 (June 1935): 10–15.

Sandino Rodríguez, José Q. "Operación captura de 29 infantes de marina de la base naval norteamericana." *Verde Olivo,* 4 (September 15, 1963): 10–15, 45.

Serpa, Enrique. "Los últimos instantes de Carlos Prío en la Palacio Presidencial." *Bohemia,* 44 (March 16, 1952): 58–59, 81–82.

Shaw, Paul V. " 'Good Neighbor'—and Cuba." *The North American Review,* 240 (September 1935): 325–41.

Sosa de Quesada, Arístides. "El militarismo." *Ultra* (Havana), 7 (September 1939): 276–78.

Soto Barroso, Israel. "La verdad se abre paso: no fué derrotado sino traicionado el Ejército Constitucional de Cuba." *La Crónica* (Miami) (August 16, 1968): 5.

Spinden, Herbert T. "Elecciones espurias en Cuba." *Reforma Social* (New York/Havana), 19 (April 1921): 353–67.

Sténger, Rafael. "Política . . . que no es política." *Bohemia,* 47 (June 12, 1955): 51, 78.

Stokes, William S. "The 'Cuban Revolution' and the Presidential Elections of 1948." *The Hispanic American Historical Review,* 31 (February 1951): 37–79.

———. "National and Local Violence in Cuban Politics." *The Southwestern Social Science Quarterly,* 34 (September 1953): 57–63.

———. "The Welles Mission to Cuba." *Central America and Mexico,* 1 (December 1953): 3–21.

• Suárez, Andrés. "The Cuban Revolution: The Road to Power." *Latin American Research Review,* 7 (Fall 1972): 5–29.

Suárez Blanco, Pepe. "Relato del combatiente del Moncada Pepe Suárez." *Verde Olivo,* 3 (July 29, 1962): 83–85.

Suchlicki, Jaime. "El estudiantil de la Universidad de La Habana en la política cubana, 1956–1957." *Journal of Inter-American Studies,* 9 (January 1967): 145–67.

———. "Stirrings of Cuban Nationalism: The Student Generation of 1930." *Journal of Inter-American Studies,* 10 (July 1968): 350–68.

Tabares, José A. "Guiteras y el alzamiento de abril de 1933." *Bohemia,* 61 (May 3, 1974): 88–96.

Tabernilla, Dolz, Francisco. "Carta abierta." *Cuba Libre* (Miami) (October 1960): 2.

Tamargo, Agustín. "Los chipojos." *Bohemia,* 51 (February 1, 1959): 62–64, 121.

———. "Cuba: república de billeteros y soldados." *Bohemia,* 48 (April 15, 1956): 52–54, 78.

———. "Jóvenes que avanzan y viejos que retroceden." *Bohemia,* 49 (January 13, 1957): 50, 82.

Thomas, Hugh. "The Origins of the Cuban Revolution." *The World Today,* 19 (October 1963): 448–60.

Thomson, Charles A. "Cuba Changes President." *Foreign Policy Policy Bulletin.* 13 (January 19, 1934): 1–2.

———. "Cuba Battles Labor Unrest." *Foreign Policy Bulletin,* 13 (March 16, 1934): 1–2.

———. "The Cuban Revolution: Fall of Machado." *Foreign Policy Reports,* 11 (December 18, 1935): 251–60.

_____. "The Cuban Revolution: Reform and Reaction." *Foreign Policy Reports,* 11 January 1, 1936): 262–76.

_____. "Reaction in Cuba." *Foreign Policy Bulletin,* 14 (May 24, 1935): 2.

Torres Menier, Mario. "Mi diario: la conversación con el tirano." *Bohemia,* 26 (February 11, 1934): 12–13, 46–47.

_____. "Mi diario." *Bohemia,* 26 (February 4, 1934): 34–35, 40–41.

_____. "Mi diario: Batista, Belisario y yo." *Bohemia,* 26 (February 25, 1934): 12–13, 57, 59, 62–63.

_____. "Mi diario: la toma del Hotel Nacional." *Bohemia,* 26 (March 4, 1934): 28–29, 37, 39.

Torriente, Cosme de la. "La renuncia de Sumner Welles." *Revista de La Habana,* 3 (October 1943) 198–203.

Torriente, Loló de la. "Realidad y esperanza en la política cubana." *Cuadernos Americanos,* 107 (November–December 1959): 36–65.

_____. "La revolución y la cultura cubana." *Cuadernos Americanos,* 111 (July–August 1960): 13–26.

Torriente-Brau, Pablo de la. "Posthumous Elegy of Colonel Batista." *Three Americas* (Mexico), 1 (January–February 1936): 17–23.

"Los tragicos acontecimientos del Hotel Nacional." *Bohemia,* 25 (October 15, 1933): 34–36, 42, 48.

"Training Cuba's Rural Guard." *The Cuba Review,* 9 (December 1910): 11.

"El último día del presidente Grau en Palacio." *Bohemia,* 26 (January 21, 1934): 36–37, 44–45, 49.

Valdespino, Andrés. "¿Culpables de que?" *Bohemia,* 68 (April 22, 1956): 55, 92–93.

_____. "La provocación no es el camino." *Bohemia,* 49 (June 30, 1957): 53, 101–02.

Valeri Busto, Angel. "Actuación en Columbia de los oficiales presos en Isla de Pinos en la gloriosa alborada del primero de enero." *Bohemia,* 51 (January 18–25, 1959): 108–09, 114.

Velasco, Carlos de. "Estrada Palma y la formación de ciudadanos." *Cuba Contemporánea,* 18 (November 1918): 261–73.

_____. "La obra de la revolución cubana." *Cuba Contemporánea,* 5 (July 1914): 273–83.

Velis, Florencio. "Los gobiernos de Cuba: Federico Laredo Bru." *Bohemia,* 30 (June 5, 1938): 74–77, 88–89, 93, 96.

Viera Trejo, Bernardo. "La fuga del tirano." *Bohemia,* 51 (March 8, 1959): 4–7, 131.

_____. "Salvaguarda de la sobernía no macula de la nacionalidad sera nuestra ejército." *Bohemia,* 51 (March 8, 1959): 21–23.

_____. "7 preguntas fundamentales al comandante Camilo Cienfuegos." *Bohemia,* 51 (February 22, 1959): 52–54.

Villamil, Rodolfo. "Por que me uní a las fuerzas de Fidel Castro." *Bohemia,* 51 (March 8, 1959): 40–41, 114.

Wanguemert, Luis. "Cómo cae un gobierno." *Carteles,* 33 (March 16, 1952): 41–44.

Wood, Leonard. "The Existing Conditions and Needs in Cuba." *North American Review,* 168 (May 1898): 593–601.

_____. "The Military Government of Cuba." *The Annals of the American Academy of Political and Social Science,* 21 (March 1903): 153–82.

Woodward, Ralph Lee, Jr. "Union Labor and Communism: Cuba." *Caribbean Studies,* 3 (October 1963): 17–50.

Wright, Hamilton M. "Modern Road Building in Cuba, Argentina and Colombia." *Bulletin of the Pan American Union,* 63 (February 1929): 143–48.

Yasells, Eduardo. "Bajo la consigna de 'libertad o muerte.'" *Verde Olivo,* 3 (December 1962): 39–41.

_____. "Hable un condenado a muerte por los hechos de Cienfuegos." *Verde Olivo*, 4 (September 8, 1963): 9–10.

Yeste y Cabrera, Adolfo. "Génesis y transformaciones del ejército de Cuba." *El Ejército Constitucional. Revista Oficial*, (September–October 1941): 284–85.

Zaydín, Ramón. "Los gobiernos de Cuba: Miguel Mariano Gómez (Mayo a Diciembre 1936)." *Bohemia*, 30 (June 5, 1938): 70–71, 90, 92, 98.

Zorrilla, Gonzalo. "Los nuevos jefes de la Marina." *Carteles*, 33 (April 13, 1952): 42–44.

Index